AF352724

Engaging Appalachia

ENGAGING APPALACHIA

A Guidebook for Building Capacity and Sustainability

Edited by Rebecca Adkins Fletcher,
Rebecca-Eli Long,
and William Schumann

UNIVERSITY PRESS OF KENTUCKY

Scholarly publisher for the Commonwealth, serving Bellarmine University, Berea College, Centre College of Kentucky, Eastern Kentucky University, The Filson Historical Society, Georgetown College, Kentucky Historical Society, Kentucky State University, Morehead State University, Murray State University, Northern Kentucky University, Spalding University, Transylvania University, University of Kentucky, University of Louisville, University of Pikeville, and Western Kentucky University.

Editorial and Sales Offices: The University Press of Kentucky
663 South Limestone Street, Lexington, Kentucky 40508-4008
www.kentuckypress.com

Library of Congress Cataloging-in-Publication Data

Names: Fletcher, Rebecca Adkins, editor. | Long, Rebecca-Eli, editor.
  | Schumann, William R., editor.
Title: Engaging Appalachia : a guidebook for building capacity and
  sustainability / edited by Rebecca Adkins Fletcher, Rebecca-Eli Long,
  and William R. Schumann.
Description: Lexington, Kentucky: The University Press of Kentucky, [2023]
  | Series: Place matters: New directions in Appalachian studies | Includes index.
Identifiers: LCCN 2022043914 | ISBN 9780813196947 (hardcover) |
  ISBN 9780813196961 (pdf) | ISBN 9780813196954 (epub)
Subjects: LCSH: Community development—Appalachia. | Sustainable
  development—Appalachia. | Social change—Appalachia.
Classification: LCC HN49.C6 E5465 2023 | DDC 307.1/40974—dc23/eng/20220923
LC record available at https://lccn.loc.gov/2022043914

This book is dedicated to Louis Gaunch (1969–2021) and to all others we have lost too soon.

We also thank all of our contributors for their patience and dedication in seeing this book to publication during a global pandemic.

Contents

Introduction
Collaborating toward sustainability

Rebecca Adkins Fletcher, Rebecca-Eli Long, and William Schumann

In Medias Res

At the time of this writing, we find ourselves immersed in a moment of unprecedented changes. The COVID-19 pandemic that began at the end of 2019 is changing the ways we live, work, and interact in the most basic ways. America is deeply divided politically and financially. The Black Lives Matter movement is gaining recognition and support, pushing and requiring reevaluations of social structures and representation. LGBTQ rights gained in the past few years are, once again, legally threatened. War in Ukraine has upended global energy policies and, indirectly, punctuated public debate about climate change. In this very moment, perspectives and ways of living are transforming, and we are all prompted to examine resources, deficits, risks, and networks to inform our next actions. What will tomorrow bring? How does social justice inform our actions and our next steps?

Engaging Appalachia: A Guidebook for Building Capacity and Sustainability represents diverse disciplinary approaches to regional community engagement, offering important lessons in place-based approaches toward sustainable development in Appalachian communities. Appalachians are reinventing the region, rethinking community spaces and workplaces, and rewriting narratives of identity in new ways. Applied and activist scholarships are the backbone of a segment of Appalachian studies that seeks to engage in partnership with communities to effect positive and just change. Reid and Taylor describe this in terms of the "civic professional," defined as "professional identity and training that include the experiences, ethics, and skills to be accountable to a regional public and capable of collaboration, communication, and identification with local communities." Puckett offers that this may result in "a different type of community of practice," one that recognizes how to create and exercise power that is embodied in personal action coarticulated with others to achieve a common good. In so doing, this volume offers transferrable lessons in community engagement, sustainable development, and capacity-building by utilizing campus–community partnerships.[1]

This volume picks up in the middle of things and examines how regional colleges and universities serve as vital institutions for supporting solutions to challenges in

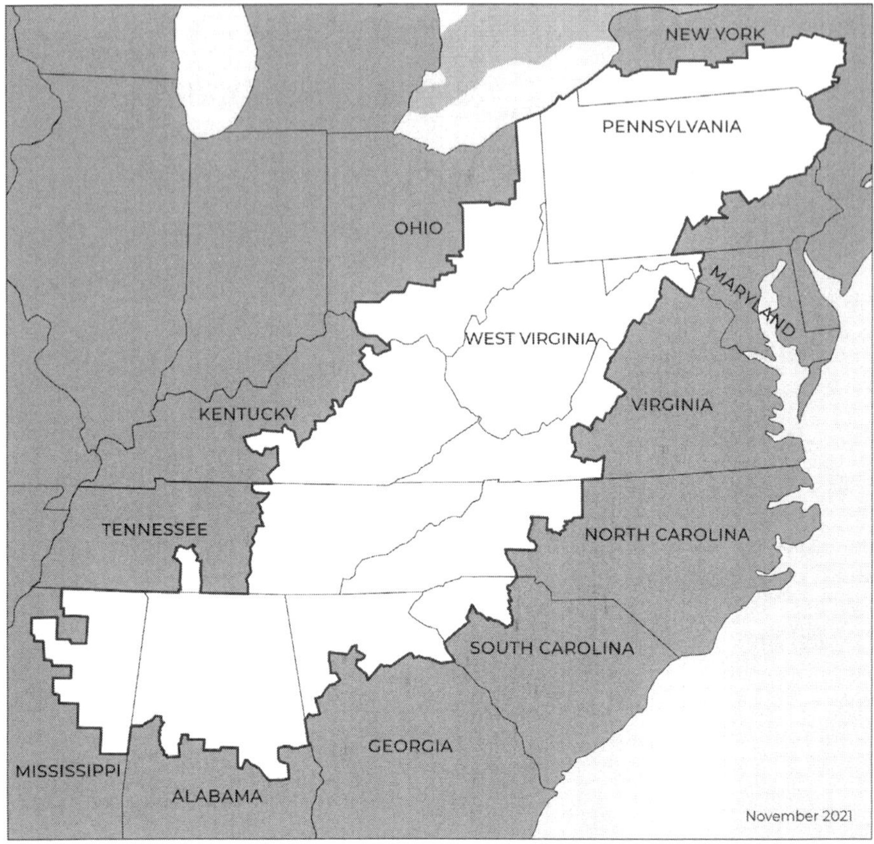

Figure 0.1. The Appalachian Region (Appalachian Regional Commission, December 1, 2021; http://www.arc.gov).

the contexts of place-based research and local collaborations involving faculty, students, and community organizations. Herein are practical strategies for sustainable community development in Appalachia that build on two areas of scholarship in Appalachian studies: critical pedagogies of place and participatory, community-based research. As editors, we understand this volume's moment as situated within multiple levels of change and challenge. We also know this is not a new position for Appalachian residents or Appalachian studies. Concern and uncertainty about access to basic resources, job security, and environmental and public health have long been determining factors across Appalachia. In response to change and to the recognized need to effect change in Appalachia, residents, organizations, activists, academics, and students have long engaged in multilevel activities throughout the region and within communities.

The contributors in this volume approach these partnerships, their challenges, as well as their potentials from various perspectives, but a common thread throughout these case studies is sustainability. As editors, we take the perspective that true sustainability must build local capacity and support inclusive community-based development. We also recognize the importance of applying these principles and acknowledge that such work is inherently messy and imperfect. Yet it is still important to try. The contributors emphasize transferrable points and lessons, as well as on-the-ground challenges, to serve as guideposts for future community engagement projects. Our intention is to showcase the processual lessons and tensions of university–community engagement in Appalachian communities and their applicability to other communities in need.

Faculty authors in these chapters represent diverse disciplines, rural and urban colleges and universities, and are at a variety of career points. Faculty face multiple challenges as they engage in multistep processes required for these projects. For example, in addition to the time required to create a course, the courses represented here are successful because they are built upon the relationships established within communities, among organizations, and with participants. Within this volume are hot spots of university–community engagement that highlight the importance of university-level support for place-based work. In representing diverse areas, environments, and issues across all three subregions of Appalachia, from Georgia to Pennsylvania, three relatable themes emerge within a practice viewpoint that is scalable to communities beyond Appalachia: fostering student leadership, asset building, and needs fulfillment within community engagement.

The first theme is *fostering student leadership*. We hold this as a priority for sustainable development, as training student leaders in culturally competent, broadly informed, and respectful community engagement stands as essential to capacity-building and asset transfer across generations. Following Hatcher, this also affords students opportunities to connect interdisciplinary theories and methodologies, learn critical analysis, and pay forward acquired skills in their home or other communities.[2] Throughout the chapters, students engage in guided community engagement and benefit from diverse forms of experience-as-knowledge while learning from faculty, community partners and participants, and their peers. For students, such experiences in nonhierarchical participation are often a frustrating but realistic undertaking of real-world projects that vastly differ from the predictable didactic coursework of which they are accustomed.

The second theme is *place-based development*. Chapters describe community-informed projects that encompass a variety of engagement strategies, including service learning, participatory research, citizen science, and asset-based community development. Each chapter represents a holistic project that works from an asset rather than a deficit (needs) perspective. In this way, community support and fruitful partnerships are more sustainable in that they inspire creativity, community buy-in, and positive change. Conventional development strategies have historically posed challenges to regional sustainability, whether in terms of (outside) capital concentration, limitations on employment, health and service disparities, or environmental mis-management.[3] Many Appalachian communities—here defined in a geographic sense, but also as cultures of belonging—are denied the same rights of representation and participation in development that are faced by other communities and world regions.[4] Vitally for Appalachian studies, asset-building approaches respect the place-based environmental and cultural resources of a community and honor what is valued by the local residents.

A third theme is *collaborative tensions in needs fulfillment*. Throughout the chapters, tensions in university–community partnerships are found in many forms: communications among collaborators; coordinating schedules; orienting students to nontraditional, real-world projects; simultaneously meeting needs and time-lines of community partners and university semester timelines and class require-ments; navigating interdisciplinary and political entanglements across and within universities and communities; university expectations for faculty teaching, service, and research; and university administrative priorities versus community or grant requirements.

Sustainability, Capacity, and Inclusion

Sustainable development (sustainability) is a concept widely used across disciplines and international policy circles with the intent to link concerns of environmental degradation, economics, and social inequalities. As a concept, sustainable develop-ment originated in a 1980 report by the International Union for the Conservation of Nature. However, sustainable development is often defined through the 1987 Brundtland Report as "development that meets the needs of the present without compromising the ability of future generations to meet their own needs."[5] Following this definition, sustainable development moves beyond narrow visions of economic development or community development and acknowledges the importance of the environment, cautions against resource overconsumption, and brings a more holistic perspective to development processes. A full critical evaluation of the varied applica-tions of sustainable development over the previous four decades is beyond the scope of this volume. Herein we invoke some of the most relevant issues informing this body of work.

While the Brundtland Report broadened the concept of development beyond simple economic considerations, sustainable development retains the implication that economic growth is "absolutely essential" to address poverty. Missing from early applications of sustainable development are questionings of the necessity of or harm in development, development as a series of processes, ideas of deep ecology, discus-sions of whose values are acknowledged in development, and true inclusion of minority and disability perspectives.[6] Tensions between global and local economic needs, values, and perspectives remain in sustainability initiatives. This signals the importance and need for deeper place-based considerations that account for chang-ing local needs, local assets, and multigenerational and inclusive involvement in change initiatives. Collins and Kearins argue that sustainability is a "dynamic state that has the capacity to endure . . . . It is simultaneously global and local in orientation." The dynamics of sustainability across spaces reflect the perspectives offered in these chapters and the connection of Appalachian places to global spaces. It too underscores the importance of localized, place-based sustainable development approaches that respond to economic and cultural dynamics. Importantly, place-based development must include inclusive, capacity-building approaches that offer avenues to address spatial inequalities, seen as local stratifications, that are rooted in biases (region, race, class, gender/sexuality, and disability).[7]

The goal of building capacity permeates many discussions of sustainability, including those that narrowly focus on "sustaining" organizations or systems, such as in business or education. Others examine "capacity" in the context of expanding our technical means to assess and plan for sustaining natural resources.[8] Our focus in this text is on building capacity for a broader, more holistic sustainability: we maintain that there is no meaningful distinction between sustainability and social justice.[9] However, an important lesson emerges from the breadth of use of "capacity" in the literature: sustainability is achievable when people—all people—are prepared for the moment. Simply put, capacity is the ability of individuals, groups, and institutions to jointly respond to challenges and opportunities in human and natural environments.

Sustainability, in turn, is an indicator of the extent to which different actors and organizations share the capacity to achieve social, economic, and ecological justice over time. In 2022, we face the opposite situation: broad-based sustainability requires everyone's participation, yet broad segments of society are marginalized from participating.[10] The United States has moved progressively (if unevenly) toward an inclusive, ecologically grounded union over its history. The Emancipation Proclamation, the New Deal, the Voting Rights Act, the Clean Air and Water Acts, and numerous constitutional amendments mark crucial weigh points along this arc. Yet none of these and other feats were inevitable. The foundations of common purpose and heightened capacity for change have always undergirded progressive outcomes. The women's suffrage movement, the Montgomery bus boycotts, the Stonewall riots, the American Indian Movement, the AIDS quilt project, landmark disability rights legislation, and the environmental movement were moments of purpose that collectively led us closer to becoming a more sustainable union in the last century. Black Lives Matter, opposition to the Dakota Access Pipeline and Atlantic Coast Pipeline, and the #MeToo movement are among many efforts that have carried this forward into the twenty-first century.

In spite of these gains, the market-first orientation of American politics still generally fails to serve poor people, people of color, and LGBTQ and disabled communities with regard to political representation and participation in economic planning and development; they are often the same groups that are disproportionately impacted by the worst effects of American capitalism. The impacts include glaring inequalities in services, public health, and environmental safety—and, to a growing extent, political disenfranchisement—all of which undercuts America's capacity to achieve sustainability. Conversely, inclusive approaches to development reveal mutually reinforcing outcomes of building capacity—for example, between environment and mental/public health, disability rights and local economic stability, or social justice and education.[11]

If inclusion is essential to sustainability (as we argue), then the social and human capital of communities that have too often been the objects of development must be respected and nurtured in order to meet current and future socioecological challenges.[12] Technical and bureaucratic expertise is vital to understanding and mitigating many of our barriers to sustainable development, but real sustainability will necessarily incorporate multiple forms of knowledge and encourage democratic participation.[13] Like elsewhere, the capacity of many Appalachian communities to participate has been diminished by the very economic processes that demand renewed civic engagement.[14] The good news is that Appalachia's marginalized communities have experience identifying and utilizing local assets in pursuit of social, economic, and environmental justice, and the region's higher education network is a considerable resource for supporting these goals.[15]

Sustainable Communities through Campus–Community Partnerships

We advocate for a re-envisioned connection between Appalachia's communities and campuses as a crucial support for sustaining the region. For example, Kingma proposes that "[c]ampus–community partnerships create value for the community by providing students, faculty and resources to make a difference in economic development, venture creation, or assistance to nonprofit organizations or local residents."[16] Effectively, we argue that higher education is an underutilized asset for achieving sustainability in the Appalachian region. Campus–community partnerships have a demonstrated ability to address problems that might fall through the cracks of top-down or asymmetrical development initiatives. In Appalachia, these types of civic–academic collaborations are already confronting ecological crises that are the unintended consequences of narrowly defined economic development.[17] We seek to contribute to this discussion through a wider look at sustainability and the many ways that campus–community partnerships can support sustainable Appalachian communities culturally, economically, and environmentally.

The literature describing the accomplishments of campus–community partnerships around the nation and world offers inspiration and guidance. Projects have taken on the issue of health care disparities and racial underrepresentation.[18] Innovative educational partnerships simultaneously train students in real world settings and address labor gaps in community-based organizations.[19] Alliances built on the skills of academic researchers and social workers can address the invisibility of queer communities.[20] Projects may bring to light and validate the perspective of youth who are often underrepresented/undervalued in research and engagement.[21] Citizen science and environmental awareness can be bolstered by academic supports.[22] Learning and working in cross-cultural or nontraditional educational settings can foster greater understanding and appreciation of diversity.[23] Validating local input into complex issues can inspire civic participation.[24]

There are also positive examples of "vertical" (i.e., multileveled/multi-institutional) university engagement in community-based projects, such as partnerships with nongovernmental organizations (NGOs) to address food insecurity.[25] When higher education emphasizes and rewards community-based research, it is possible to develop a range of engagement strategies (short-/longer-term, multileveled administrative support, cross-disciplinary participation, etc.) that can sustain partnerships over time.[26] Indeed, it is critical that partnerships do not rely on one or only a few individuals representing universities or communities. Community-based research incorporates local cultural values and knowledge, thus potentially strengthening the value and accuracy of data, particularly among underrepresented groups.[27] Community-based engagement can also encourage not only more student awareness but also better student learners in the classroom.[28]

Despite the potential for multidimensional positive change resulting from these projects, campus–community partnerships do not offer guaranteed outcomes for sustainability, inclusion, and justice. In no small part, this is because communities are not static, bounded entities but rather heterogenous entities with their own sets of power imbalances. Collaborating with the "community" may enable some views to stand in for diversity and social justice. At an extreme, the appearance of project cohesion can come at the expense of overlooking the racism, sexism, xenophobia, and/or homophobia that enables inequality. Moreover, there is an implicit "settler colonialism" mentality in any collaboration that strives to better society through projects taking place on former Indigenous lands.[29] Communities are not always respected or supported within the hierarchical structures of higher education, and collaborations can reinforce existing divisions based on access to knowledge and resources. Not only reinforcing the community as separate from the campus, built-in hierarchies can "delimit the possibilities for (more) ethical encounters across difference."[30] Yet, especially at Appalachian colleges where many students might come from the region, students may identify with the "community." In such cases, it is especially important to resist presenting the community as underprivileged and lacking, thus further marginalizing students, as well as faculty, who do not come from backgrounds of privilege.[31] When the value of partnerships to communities is taken for granted or assumed, the attendant power imbalances can derail and undermine community-based research and engagement.[32]

Additionally, owing to the embedded positionality of Appalachia and other regions within the neoliberal state, projects may mask the failings of the state to meet needs and address social inequalities. For example, community engagement potentially fills gaps in services hollowed out by the neoliberal state through volunteerism and service, thus supporting a market-oriented individualism that is at odds with sustainability.[33] Faculty and students may also lack the training necessary for effective collaboration and project leadership.[34] Without sustained engagement and careful reflection, students may come to view community engagement through a tourist mindset; faculty risk perpetuating these views by failing to educate about solidarity, mutuality, and interdependence as a pathway to substantive material change.[35] In light of these serious problems oftentimes inherent in collaboration, *Engaging Appalachia* offers thoughtful examples from experienced faculty and community collaborators that move us forward on pathways toward sustainability through campus–community partnerships. Crucially, we asked authors to address both the successes and short-comings of their projects to draw attention to the challenges of truly effective collaboration.

Our Contributions

Our text explores strategies for creating more inclusive and sustainable partnerships in the present and future but does not take for granted the value of campus–community collaborations to transform unsustainable practices. "Communities" take a wide variety of forms in the context of university–community engagement but are generally defined as "nonacademic" entities. As in this volume, many communities are place based and geographically nearby their higher education partners. Ideally, communities have "a full say in the identification of service needs and development challenges" related to collaborating with colleges and universities.[36] The chapters that follow offer many perspectives on the dynamics of campus–community relationships developed through the arts, humanities, social sciences, and natural sciences. *Engaging Appalachia* demonstrates that positive campus–community collaborations are not only possible but are sites of regional and community practice toward more sustainable and just communities. Collectively, these discussions reveal that successful project outcomes owe to many actors participating as *project equals*, while also acknowledging the inherent power imbalances implicit in collaboration *as cocreators of academic knowledge* about community-based sustainability. In soliciting chapters, we asked that all chapters be coauthored by a combination of faculty and students or community representatives (or both).[37] We have also taken the additional step of listing authors alphabetically, instead of by the order of their writing contributions, in acknowledgement that many individuals and groups ultimately contribute to the academy's capacity to observe and assess sustainability.

The chapters in this volume offer tangible end products that go beyond market-based expressions of development or colonial logic, or are divested from equity and inclusion within communities. Rather, contributions in this volume offer examples of fostering new and continued programs in seed-saving and tree planting, advancing citizen-science initiatives, intergenerational collaboration on oral history preservation, promotion of local arts, bolstering a drug treatment program, monitoring of abandoned gas and oil wells for health, safety, and environmental risks, and capacity-building student-citizen training across the Appalachian region. Through these examples, this volume offers a unique contribution and important cases of campus–community engagement for moving beyond simply neoliberal positionings and toward more inclusive engagements. The examples offered here do not fully reflect our goals for inclusivity within communities and across projects. We take responsibility for not recruiting specific examples of campus–community projects that directly address racial and gender-based injustices, while acknowledging that some such projects in development are in-process and not ready for publication.

Chapter 1, by Dockery, Fadroski, and Kent, describes the process of linking cultural memory, public health, and food security through arts-based programming at the University of North Georgia. The authors discuss how a multiyear project of collecting and visualizing local foodways through the arts encouraged the development of a nationally recognized seed saving program. In Chapter 2, Angel, Barton, Bell, Burriss, and Hall discuss the complexities of implementing a multistate tree-planting project involving community partnerships with Berea College, Radford University, the University of Kentucky, and the University of North Carolina. While grounded in technical expertise, the authors highlight how project successes—including the planting of 2.8 million trees—was most effective when stakeholder communication was strong and students were engaged as key collaborators. In contrast, Frank, Marvel, Terman, and Winnenberg, in Chapter 3, reflect on the long-term work at one institution, Ohio University, to engage with several communities comprising the Little Cities of Black Diamonds Region of southern Ohio. Tracing the origins of collaboration back to the local resonance of Lyndon Johnson's War on Poverty in the 1960s, the chapter reveals how campus–community collaborations have been invigorated more recently through coordination with community leaders, strategic use of service learning as a capacity "scaffold" and making "permeable" connections between the university's educational and outreach missions.

In Chapter 4, Heck, Kier, Johnson, and Piechnik from the University of Pittsburgh at Bradford speak to the impact that new projects and partnerships can make in response to local needs and opportunities. Their review of a student-led survey of invasive species monitoring in the Allegheny National Forest is an example of how coordination between academics and community organizations can enrich the efforts of citizen scientists and concerned citizens to protect the social and economic resources of the Pennsylvania wilds. Fletcher, Lynch, and Roach (Chapter 5) explore the parallel developments of long-term campus–community networks at East Tennessee State University and the Appalachian Teaching Project, a federally supported program designed to build Appalachia's capacity for regional sustainability through student leadership in applied learning. The authors present several case studies exploring how local community history and knowledge was utilized to create economic development assets in Unicoi County, Tennessee. In Chapter 6, Dickerson, Hollandsworth, Ingoldsby, Myers, Pauley, and Wagner discuss the (re)development of multigenerational community networks through Roots with Wings, a multistakeholder oral history collaboration involving Radford University faculty, area high schools and nonprofits, and students. Their analysis of fostering cross-institutional "buy-in" indicates how student leadership development was integral to meeting larger organizational goals, as well as to successfully preserving cultural knowledge in a digital age.

In Chapter 7, Gaunch and Laws examine the role of campus–community partnerships to bolster a holistic drug treatment and community reintegration program in South Charleston, West Virginia. Building on the work of nonprofit Pollen8 to provide educational support, skills training, and food security to local residents, the authors describe how a leadership development program at the nearby University of Charleston has incorporated a capacity-building partnership with Pollen8 into its curriculum. In Chapter 8, Burns, Friesen, Maples, McSpirit, and Scott extend this focus in reviewing the development and outcomes of student training at Eastern Kentucky University and the University of Kentucky to promote natural assets and sustainable economic development in two eastern Kentucky communities. They explain the difficulties (and rewards) of trying to empower students as project collaborators in a democratic action structure that is at odds with student expectations of college classroom learning.

In Chapter 9, Burriss, Campbell, and Leggett draw a critical distinction between project development and course development in discussing Radford University's participation in an economic regeneration project in southwest Virginia. The authors' rich description of engagement strategies with the Clinch River Valley Initiative— networking with community organizations, identifying needs, codeveloping project goals, designing course objectives, and implementing plans—reveals the commitments required in aligning "town" and "gown" to build local capacity. Chapter 10, by Kropf and Weis, revisits an abandoned well-monitoring project at the University of Pittsburgh at Bradford that grew to benefit state and federal agencies. The authors focus on meeting the technical and logistical challenges of effectively identifying unaccounted-for gas and oil wells and integrating their data with other records to enhance public awareness about the health, safety, and environmental risks of abandoned wells in Appalachian Pennsylvania. In Chapter 11, Roberts, Schumann, and Stewart question how to measure the capacity-building and sustainability of a fifteen-year study abroad partnership between Appalachian State University and former mining communities in southern Wales. While pointing out the steep challenges of creating and maintaining a program of community-based research across international spaces, they also reflect on the intangible and/or unforeseen gains that have accompanied the work of training students for leadership in sustainability and building the infrastructure of Welsh communities.

Through these varied settings, the chapters in this volume highlight student leadership, show the importance of place-based development, as well as highlight tensions and challenges in campus–community partnerships. We certainly do not claim that these projects are easy. However, campus–community partnerships do provide an opportunity to build strengths while addressing local challenges. Not only is this a model of education with an important history in Appalachia, but it is a model that has the potential to address issues of national concern in moving toward holistic sustainability.

The conclusion is collectively authored by the editors and each of the contributors. Each contributing author was asked to respond to an anonymous survey, which contained two writing prompts: "What advice would you offer others about lessons learned from your project?" and "Please give an example or examples of problems you encountered and how you addressed them." The responses have been combined, edited, and expanded to offer guidance to readers who are interested in building or expanding campus–community partnerships in their own places. Appalachia's problems are globally interconnected, but so too might our region's responses to them illuminate a path for others to respond. The Epilogue, finally, surveys the historical context of engaged pedagogy in Appalachia, including a case study of Just Connections, a now-defunct campus–community organizer in Appalachia, along with the ongoing case of the Appalachian Teaching Project. *Engaging Appalachia*'s case studies are thereby situated in a broader context of engagement that takes into account past, present, and future pathways to sustainability and social justice in Appalachia. While rooted in the region's history, the lessons presented here represent ongoing connections between places and movements for sustainability and justice.

Notes

1. Barbara Ellen Smith and Steve Fisher, "Reinventing the Region: Defining, Theorizing, Organizing Appalachia," *Journal of Appalachian Studies* 22, no. 1 (2016): 76–79; Silas House, "The Road Back: Appalachia as Internal Colony," *Journal of Appalachian Studies* 22, no. 1 (2016): 63–68; David D. Hart, Kathleen P. Bell, Laura A. Lindenfeld, Shaleen Jain, Teresa R. Johnson, Darren Ranco, and Brian McGill, "Strengthening the Role of Universities in Addressing Sustainability Challenges: The Mitchell Center for Sustainability Solutions as an Institutional Experiment," *Ecology and Society* 20, no. 2 (2015): n.p.; Herbert Reid and Betsy Taylor, "Appalachia as a Global Region: Toward Critical Regionalism and Civic Professionalism," *Journal of Appalachian Studies* 8, no. 1 (2002): 9–32; Anita Puckett, "Appalachia and 'the Commons:' An Introduction," *Practicing Anthropology* 36 no. 4 (2014): 3–7. Throughout this volume, we use the term "campus–community partnerships," as our chapters represent a range of higher education institutions. Elsewhere in the literature, such collaborations are categorized as "university-community partnerships," "service learning," "participatory action research," and "community engagement."

2. William Hatcher, "Using the Asset-Building Model of Development in Teaching the Politics of Community Development in Appalachia," *Journal of Appalachian Studies* 22, no. 1 (2016): 113–120.

3. For a broad-ranging survey of this history, see Ronald D Eller, *Uneven Ground: Appalachia since 1945* (Lexington: University Press of Kentucky, 2008).

4. See Dorothy Holland, Catherine Lutz, Donald M. Nonini, Lesley Bartlett, Maria Frederick-McGlathery, Thaddeus C. Guldbandsend, and Enrique G. Murillo, Jr., *Local Democracy Under Siege: Activism, Public Interests, and Private Politics* (New York: NYU Press, 2007); Neil Smith and David Harvey, *Uneven Development: Nature, Capital, and the Production of Space* (Athens: University of Georgia Press, 2008); Tania Murray Li, *The Will to Improve: Governmentality, Development, and the Practice of Politics* (Durham, NC: Duke University Press, 2007); Arturo Escobar, *Encountering Development: The Making and Unmaking of the Third World* (Princeton, NJ: Princeton University Press, 2011); Robert Chambers, *Rural Development: Putting the Last First* (New York: Routledge, 1983).

5. Brundtland Commission, *Our Common Future: Report of The World Commission on Environment and Development* (Oxford: Oxford University Press, 1987).

6. Alan Holland, "Sustainability," in *Environment and Society*, eds. Christopher Schlottmann, Dale Jamieson, Colin Jerolmack, Anne Rademacher, and Maria Damon (New York: NYU Press, 2017): 295–308; Amanda L. Fickey and Michael Samers, "Developing Appalachia: The Impact of Limited Economic Imagination," in *Studying Appalachian Studies: Making the Path While Walking*, eds. Chad Berry, Phillip J. Obermiller, and Shaunna L. Scott (Urbana: University of Illinois Press, 2015): 119–140; Michael J. Lorr, "Defining Urban Sustainability in the Context of North American Cities," *Nature and Culture* 7, no. 1 (2012): 16–30; Kim Q. Hall, "Cripping Sustainability, Realizing Food Justice," in *Disability Studies and the Environmental Humanities: Toward an Eco-Crip Theory*, eds. Sarah Jaquette Ray and Jay Sibara (Lincoln: University of Nebraska Press, 2017): 422–446; June Manning Thomas, "The Role of Ethnicity and Race in Supporting Sustainable Urban Environments," in *Urban Sustainability: A Global Perspective*, ed. Igor Vojnovic (East Lansing: Michigan State University Press, 2013): 475–508.

7. Pierce Greenberg, "Spatial Inequality and Uneven Development: The Local Stratification of Poverty in Appalachia," *Journal of Appalachian Studies* 22, no. 2 (2016): 187–209.

8. Examples of these approaches include Mary Murray, Mary Heather Munger, W. Bradley Colwell, and Alex J. Claussen, "Building Capacity in Special Education: A Statewide Initiative to Improve Student Outcomes through Parent-Teacher Partnerships," *School Community Journal* 28, no. 1 (2018): 91–105; Emerald Group Publishing, "Capacity Building for Sustained Competitive Advantage: A Conceptual Framework," *Marketing Intelligence & Planning* 34, no. 5 (2016): 671–691; Yang Hong, Yu Zhang, and Sadiq Ibrahim Khan, eds, *Hydrologic Remote Sensing: Capacity Building for Sustainability and Resilience* (New York: CRC Press, 2016).

9. A growing body of scholarship directly integrates social justice into analyses of sustainability. For example, see Andrew Dobson, *Fairness and Futurity: Essays on Environmental Sustainability and Social Justice* (Oxford, UK: Oxford University Press, 1999); Theodor Ketschau, "Social Justice as a Link between Sustainability and Educational Sciences," *Sustainability* 7, no. 11 (2015): 15754–15771; Moustapha Kamal, "Promoting Decent Work, Advancing Social Justice in the Ecological Transition," *Global Social Policy* 21, no. 2 (2021): 339–343. For a history of how "social sustainability" has been defined and utilized, see Iris Boroway, "The Social Dimension of Sustainable Development at the UN: From Brundtland to the SDGs," in *Moral Conflicts in Global Social Policy*, ed. Christopher Deeming (Bristol, UK: Bristol University Press, 2021), 89–108.

10. Isabel B. Franco and James Tracey, "Community Capacity-Building for Sustainable Development: Effectively Striving towards Achieving Local Community Sustainability Targets," *International Journal of Sustainability in Higher Education* 20, no. 4 (2019): 691–725.

11. Sabine O'Hara, "The Urban Food Hubs Solution: Building Capacity in Urban Communities," *Metropolitan Universities* 28, no. 1 (2017): 69–93; Hsin-Yi Hsiao, Chiu-Tien Hsu, Lei Chen, Jinli Wu, Pao-Sheng Chang, Chin-Lon Lin, Ming-Nan Lin, and Tin-Kwang Lin, "Environmental Volunteerism for Social Good: A Longitudinal Study of Older Adults' Health," *Research on Social Work Practice* 30, no. 2 (2020): 233–245; Jennifer Harrison and Timothy Palmer, "Interprofessional Study Abroad: Enhancing Social Justice and Sustainability through Shared Experiential Learning," *Journal of Teaching in International Business* 30, no. 2 (2019): 125–146; Mirfa Manzoor, Christina Keller, Sofie Wass, Owe Jansson, and Vivian Vimarlund, "From Prototype to Societal Inclusion: Identified Challenges for Sustainable Implementation of E-services for Individuals with Disabilities," *Technology & Disability* 30, no. 3 (2018): 97–103.

12. Adriane Macdonald, Amelia Clarke, and Lei Huang, "Multi-Stakeholder Partnership for Sustainability: Designing Decision-Making Processes for Partnership Capacity," *Journal of*

Business Ethics 160 (2018): 409–426; Glen Toner, ed., *Sustainable Production: Building Canadian Capacity* (Vancouver: UBC Press, 2006).

13. This point has been made repeatedly. In regards to race, see Stephen Pearson, "'The Last Bastion of Colonialism': Appalachian Settler Colonialism and Self-Indigenization," *American Indian Culture and Research Journal* 37, no. 2 (May 22, 2013): 165–84, https://doi.org/10.17953/aicr.37.2.g4522v766231r3xg; Barbara Ellen Smith, "De-Gradations of Whiteness: Appalachia and the Complexities of Race," *Journal of Appalachian Studies* 10, no. 1/2 (2004): 38–57. The importance of queer experience and theory in Appalachian studies has been made in recent years; see Z. Zane McNeill, *Y'all Means All: The Emerging Voices Queering Appalachia* (Oakland, CA: PM Press, 2022); Hillery Glasby, Sherrie Gradin, and Rachael Ryerson, eds., *Storytelling in Queer Appalachia: Imagining and Writing the Unspeakable Other* (Morgantown, West Virginia University Press, 2020); stef m. shuster, "Quaring the Queer in Appalachia," *Appalachian Journal* 46, no. 1/2 (2018): 72–84.

14. See Shannon Elizabeth Bell, "'There Ain't No Bond in Town Like There Used to Be:' The Destruction of Social Capital in the West Virginia Coalfields," *Sociological Forum* 24, no. 3 (2009): 631–657.

15. See Mary Ann Hinsdale, Helen Lewis, and Maxine Waller, *It Comes from the People: Community Development and Local Theology* (Philadelphia, PA: Temple University Press, 1995); Si Kahn, *Creative Community Organizing: A Guide for Rabble-Rousers, Activists, and Quiet Lovers of Justice* (New York: Berrett-Koehler Publishers, 2010).

16. Bruce Kingma, "Preface," in *Academic Entrepreneurship and Community Engagement: Scholarship in Action and the Syracuse Miracle*, ed. Bruce Kingma (Northhampton, MA: Edward Elgar Publishing, 2011), ix–xiii.

17. Stephanie McSpirit, Lynn Faltraco, and Conner Bailey, eds., *Confronting Ecological Crisis in Appalachia and the South: University and Community Partnerships* (Lexington: University Press of Kentucky, 2012).

18. Tina Volz, "Academic-Practice Collaboration: Extending Research into the Community," *Kentucky Nurse* 65, no. 2 (2017): 18–19.

19. R. W. C. Tourse, J. F. Mooney, J. Shindul-Rothschild, J. Prince, J. A. Pulcini, S. Platt, and H. Savransky, "The University/Community Partnership: Transdisciplinary Course Development," *Journal of Interprofessional Care* 22, no. 5 (2008): 461–474.

20. Michael Dentato, Shelley Craig, and Mark Smith, "The Vital Role of Social Workers in Community Partnerships: The Alliance for Gay, Lesbian, Bisexual, Transgender and Questioning Youth," *Child & Adolescent Social Work Journal* 27, no. 5 (2010): 323–334.

21. Ben Kirshner, "Supporting Youth Participation in School Reform: Preliminary Notes from a University-Community Partnership," *Children Youth and Environments* 17, no. 2 (2007): 354–363; Dentato et al., "The Vital Role of Social Workers in Community Partnerships."

22. Joy K. Wood, Warren G. Gold, James L. Fridley, Kern Ewing, and Dev K. Niyogi, "An Analysis of Factors Driving Success in Ecological Restoration Projects by a University-Community Partnership," *Ecological Restoration* 35, no. 1 (2017): 60–69.

23. Amanda C. Soto, Chee-Hoo Lum, and Patricia Shehan Campbell, "A University-School Music Partnership for Music Education Majors in a Culturally Distinctive Community," *Journal of Research in Music Education* 56, no. 4 (2009): 338–356.

24. Erin N. Haynes, Caroline Beidler, Richard Wittberg, Lisa Meloncon, Megan Parin, Elizabeth J. Kopras, Paul Succop, and Kim M. Deitrich, "Developing a Bidirectional Academic-Community Partnership with an Appalachian-American Community for Environmental

Health Research and Risk Communication," *Environmental Health Perspectives* 119, no. 10 (2011): 1364–1372.

25. Kim Buch, Sean Langley, Tamara Johnston, and Nakiel Coleman, "A University-Community Partnership to Combat Food Insecurity among College Students," *Partnerships* 7, no. 1 (2016): 16.

26. Beth Savan, "Community–University Partnerships: Linking Research and Action for Sustainable Community Development," *Community Development Journal* 39, no. 4 (2004): 372–384.

27. John Lowe, Huigang Liang, Cheryl Riggs, Jim Henson, and Tribal Elder, "Community Partnership to Affect Substance Abuse among Native American Adolescents," *American Journal of Drug & Alcohol Abuse* 38, no. 5 (2012): 450–455.

28. Lane Perry, Robert J. Lahm Jr., Annika Schauer, and Zachary Rumble, "The Crossroads of Social Entrepreneurship, Community Engagement, and Learning Communities," *American Journal of Entrepreneurship* 9, no. 2 (2016): 1–22.

29. Paul Bélanger, "Beyond the Campus: Building a Sustainable University-Community Partnership," Book Review, *International Review of Education* 63, no. 4 (2017): 609–610; Nicholas Buys and Samantha Bursnall, "Establishing University-Community Partnerships: Processes and Benefits," *Journal of Higher Education Policy and Management* 29, no. 1 (2007): 73–86; Amber Dean, "Colonialism, Neoliberalism, and University–Community Engagement: What Sorts of Encounters with Difference Are Our Institutions Prioritizing?" in *Unravelling Encounters: Ethics, Knowledge, and Resistance Under Neoliberalism*, eds. Cailin Janzen, Kristin Smith, and Donna Jeffery (Waterloo, ON: Wilfrid Laurier University Press, 2015): 184; Susan B. Hyatt, "Black Lives Matter and the Public Rediscovery of Structural Racism," *Anthropology News* (November 24, 2021), https://www.anthropology-news.org/articles/black-lives-matter-and-the-public-rediscovery-of-structural-racism/.

30. Amber Dean, "Colonialism, Neoliberalism, and University–Community Engagement," 176.

31. Roni Strier, "The Construction of University-Community Partnerships: Entangled Perspectives," *Higher Education* 62, no. 1 (2011): 81–97.

32. Roni Strier, "Fields of Paradox: University–Community Partnerships," *Higher Education* 68 (2014): 155–165; Jeannette Kindred and Claudia Petrescu, "Expectations Versus Reality in a University-Community Partnership: A Case Study," *Voluntas: International Journal of Voluntary & Nonprofit Organizations* 26, no. 3 (2015): 823–845.

33. Amber Dean, "Colonialism, Neoliberalism, and University–Community Engagement," 175–194; Susan B. Hyatt, "Black Lives Matter and the Public Rediscovery of Structural Racism."; Aurora Santiago-Ortiz, "From Critical to Decolonizing Service-Learning: Limits and Possibilities of Social Justice–Based Approaches to Community Service-Learning," *Michigan Journal of Community Service Learning* 25, no. 1 (2019): 43–54.

34. Valerie Bryan, Willette Brye, Kenneth Hudson, Leevones Dubose, Shantisha Hansberry, and Martha Arrieta, "Investigating Health Disparities through Community-Based Participatory Research: Lessons Learned from a Process Evaluation," *Social Work in Public Health* 29, no. 4 (2004): 318–334; Paul Bélanger, "Beyond the Campus"; Marilyn J. Amey and Dennis F. Brown, "Interdisciplinary Collaboration and Academic Work: A Case Study of a University-Community Partnership," *New Directions for Teaching & Learning* 102 (2005): 23–35.

35. Michelle Madsen Camacho, "Power and Privilege: Community Service Learning in Tijuana," *Michigan Journal of Community Service Learning* 10, no. 3 (2004): 31–42; Aurora Santiago-Ortiz, "From Critical to Decolonizing Service-Learning," 50.

36. Anouk Koekkoek, Maarten Van Ham, and Reinout Kleinhans, "Unraveling University–Community Engagement: A Literature Review," *Journal of Higher Education Outreach and Engagement* 25, no. 1 (2021): 3–12.

37. Coauthorship is one recognized strategy in academic subfields such as collaborative anthropology that seek to credit research participants, blunt the hierarchies inherent to academic fieldwork, and refocus the objectives of research. See Luke Eric Lassiter, *The Chicago Guide to Collaborative Ethnography* (Chicago: University of Chicago Press, 2005); Luke Eric Lassiter, Brian A. Hoey, and Elizabeth Campbell, eds. *I'm Afraid of That Water: A Collaborative Ethnography of a West Virginia Water Crisis* (Morgantown: West Virginia University Press, 2020).

1

Saving Appalachian Gardens and Stories

Growing community and sustainability through seeds and art

Chris Dockery, Karrie Ann Fadroski, and Rosann Kent

A Disappearing Resource

We are three gardeners—a biologist, a storyteller, and an art educator—who live and work in the disrupted landscape of north Georgia. Here, as in much of Southern Appalachia, regional economic disparities and environmental crises contradict rich biotic and cultural ecologies. Our project site is a case in point. About seventy miles north of Atlanta, Lumpkin and the surrounding Appalachian counties are among the nation's top 100 fastest growing.[1] In the thirty-year period from 1960 to 1990, Lumpkin's population doubled to 14,573; it doubled again to 30,319 during the next twenty-year period.[2] Such unmitigated development results in a drastic loss of rural spaces and accompanying agricultural practices. Foodways, such as canning, drying, and freezing, give way to meal delivery services. The ability to garden can be lost in one generation. This deep cultural knowledge of the "been here's" (those whose families arrived three or more generations ago) are often ignored by the "come here's" (those who arrived during their own lifetimes). On our campus, the University of North Georgia (UNG) in Dahlonega, students rarely interact with either group. In 2012 at the Appalachian Studies Center, we sought to create intentional opportunities for students and newcomers to participate in the local food system by privileging voices of those cultural tradition bearers who still save locally adapted seeds. Seeds are resources, both literally and, as anyone who has planted one knows, metaphorically because of their potential to cultivate hope. Someone with fewer economic resources may have a great wealth of family heirloom seeds, knowledge, and memories. There is a pride and power in that, renewed each season and harvest. But seeds lose their potential, both biologically and culturally, if there is no one or no place to plant them. Both threats, biological and cultural, are pressing where we live—generational differences and interlopers have isolated many of our elders.

This chapter discusses a five-year period of a project called Saving Appalachian Gardens and Stories (SAGAS) that featured cultural tradition bearers and their knowledge of saving and sharing locally adapted seeds. It had several interdependent features. First, we relied on mutual acquaintances, or gatekeepers, to identify "been here's" who save "old timey" seeds—open-pollinated seeds that have never been bought or sold but passed down among mountain families. We turned to colleagues at UNG in materials management who were from Lumpkin or surrounding counties. Custodians, machine operators, carpenters, electricians, and locksmiths donated seeds, offered their expertise, time, labor, and, most of all, their connections. These local men and women quickly became the backbone of the project. After the gatekeepers took the students to meet the seed keepers, the students documented gardening traditions and Southern Appalachian foodways through interviews and photographs. By the end of 2014, students and gatekeepers identified tradition bearers in seven of the fourteen voting districts of the county, conducted twelve interviews with community members, and collected and banked approximately thirty-five varieties of seeds. The expectation was that students would grow out the seeds in the center's demonstration garden and share them at farmers markets and festivals. Students also created visual and performance art that expressed local seed-keeping practices and shared that art with the community. Finally, students held potlucks, music jams, and harvest days that intentionally fostered connections among those like and unlike themselves. Collectively, our collaborations drew from existing connections to place and added new layers of meaning and action in northeastern Georgia. This chapter analyzes the project's successes, challenges, and future as well as considers institutional and interpersonal factors that shape the possibilities for long-term collaborations that seek to strengthen Appalachia's rich cultural and natural resources.

Seeds of Survival

Aunt Cora's Sunburst Tomato, Robert Lovell's Wintergreens, and Papa Holbrook's Longhorn Okra: for generations, north Georgia families have built a rich heritage of agricultural diversity, a bulwark against today's climate change and genetic erosion. Because this hyperlocal knowledge resides with individuals, not institutions, inviting them into conversations about our food supply is essential. Globally, about 75 percent of plant genetic diversity has disappeared since 1900, and three-quarters of the food consumed today come from twelve plant species. The UN Food and Agriculture Organization estimates that small farmers, not agribusinesses, hold up to 75 percent of the world's seed diversity, which represents humanity's best protection against environmental risks to our food supply.[3] Appalachia holds a vital place in this story. The region's southern mountains are among North America's most diverse food sheds, with nearly 1,500 of documented folk and indigenous crops varieties of fruits and vegetables.[4] This biodiversity is at risk as gentrification commodifies small towns into tourist destinations. Seed banks, however, don't go far enough in mitigating the loss, cautions anthropologist Virginia Nazarea, who coined the term "cultural memory banking" to describe the parallel collection and documentation of indigenous knowledge "about those crops and methods of farming held by the people who have long raised them."[5] Rather than sequestering this information in an archive, we wanted to use arts-based research to help students interpret these ethnocultural memories through visual and performance art that would be shared publicly and without pretension. Art making is an act of preservation and communication, a way to reinsert narrative into culture. J. H. Rolling Jr., for instance, describes art making as a system that fosters production, communication, and critical reflection.[6] It is a practice of understanding knowledge, process, and story that prioritizes accessibility to a wider population. Art-based inquiry is rooted in the idea that the researcher/ artist is "a writer rather than an author."[7] These inquiries require one who is willing to be educated and transformed in the process of discovery. This arts-based research component is what distinguishes our project from other regional seed collections or seed-saving exchanges.

Finding Our Place in This Place

Our research question was simple: *What is the state of heirloom seed saving in Lumpkin County?* The research process, however, was not. First, we needed a framework to help students become aware of their role in the dynamic of residents and interlopers and to challenge their misperceptions about this place. Appalachia—both the region and the construct—is complicated. To help students negotiate this complexity, we began each course by examining the implications of our county's original settlement patterns (i.e., militia districts) as well demographic trends. We examined treaties, federal and state Indian removal policies, and surveyor maps to see how the nation's first major gold rush was the catalyst for legislation that carved north Georgia into counties eight years before Cherokee were forcefully dislocated in 1838 as part of the Trail of Tears. After our gatekeepers explained that local people still identify "home" as one of the settlements in the former fourteen militia districts (roughly equivalent to today's voting districts), we projected a blank outline of the districts on the wall and students traced them, noting the boundaries, rivers, and other prominent landscape features. Then, we spent time riding through each district. We noted how the cultural and geographic landscape changed after we left Dahlonega, the only town in our 282-square mile county of 32,955, almost 95 percent of which is white.[8] Although a state-recognized Cherokee tribe is headquartered here, and many families have Cherokee ancestry, less than 1 percent identify as Cherokee today.[9] Almost 45 percent of our county is located within the Chattahoochee National Forest.

Without an introduction to Dahlonega's demographics, students may not be able to see past the manicured lawns and grand buildings of the university and the quaint historic square that attracts a multitude of tourists. In 2017, direct tourists spent $42 million, which corresponds to a local tax revenue of $1 million.[10] The industry also supported 344 jobs in wineries, restaurants, retail, and tourist attractions such as gold mining. This tourism infrastructure can cause students to miss the hidden pockets of poverty. Despite the presence of UNG as a major employer, per capita income for 2018 was $24,790 and nearly 15 percent of residents lived in poverty.[11]

To help students become comfortable with these incongruences, we used the model for studying "place" developed by Helen Lewis, the grandmother of Appalachian studies. She advocates for students, faculty, and community members to become *participants and partners* in the research; academics do not act as observers or leaders. Helen emailed:

> [Appalachia is] weekend cabins and homes in the holler. Yesterday's and tomorrow's people. Hillbillies and folks. Bluegrass and hip hop. Poets and politicians. Professors and protesters, preachers and prophets.
>
> Real and mythical, beautiful and devastated, geological and political, rich in resources and a poverty pocket, a place to exploit, a watershed for the eastern seaboard, and destroyed, polluted headwaters . . . A model and a warning signal for the nation.

So if you want to study Appalachia, here is what you do:

> Start where you live: Interview your elders, map your community, and write your local history. Who lives where and why? Who owns the land, minerals, and the resources? Who is rich and who is poor? Who has power and who is powerless? Who are the story tellers, the poets, the singers? Who is in jail, who is sick, who is angry, and who is throwing the bodies in the river and who is pretending it is not happening? Who is speaking truth to power, who is feeding the hungry, who is healing the sick? Who is writing the poetry, saving the stories, saving the land, singing the songs?"
>
> Find out who you are. What is your place in this place?[12]

Grow, Make, Listen

To create a community of meaning through arts-based research, we had to help students challenge their assumptions about Appalachian culture. Throughout the project, we invited students to not only analyze the initial quantitative data but also internalize qualitative data through art-based research. During their fieldwork and in their conversations with seed keepers, students learned about many varieties of heirloom seeds—how they were grown, cultivated, and saved—along with histories of families who have passed the tradition of gardening from one generation to the next. Students gained new skill sets, both practical ones related to foodways as well as transformative, intangible skills related to listening and learning from others. By taking and sorting through hundreds of photographs, telling and retelling elder stories to their classmates, and distilling the salient messages to incorporate into an art piece, students became aware of and able to address the qualitative nuances of a situation. By addressing what is subtle but significant, the arts can develop dispositions and habits of mind that reveal to an individual a world he or she may not have noticed or understood. This contributes to an empathic knowledge, which in turn has the capacity to bridge academia and communities.[13] This arts-based research approach yielded an interpretation of the data that combined the narratives of the seed keepers and the students' experiences. The process of story listening and art making, and the analytical reflection required in its development, allowed the students access to lessons beyond the scope of the syllabus.

During the next five years, they created artistic representations of their research and interactions with our seed keeper community through various public art installations. The first year, they created a communograph, a mapping concept developed by artist and activist Ashley Hunt that would serve as a reservoir of community knowledge and a mechanism for community conversation.[14] This nine-by-six-foot oilcloth resembled a tablecloth from a rustic farm kitchen and traced the routes seeds had traveled among local families. Quotes and photographic transparencies of the seeds and seed keepers were juxtaposed over an embroidered image of the voting districts. The next year, students captured seed keeper voices and images through a series of smaller garden flags; each flag was dedicated to an individual or a couple. We also introduced performance art by working with Appalachian artist-in-residence Sandra Van Pelt Hogue, who guided students in writing a reader's theater, a script based on the lives of seed keepers designed to be read on stage without the need for props. Finally, students created a moving panoramic shadowbox theater to explore a topic that kept surfacing in their interviews with seed keepers: "planting by the signs," a traditional practice of sowing, cultivating, and harvesting by the phases of the moon and its position in the zodiac.

Students exhibited and presented their art in academic and community venues, including public libraries, local music festivals, and schools. In this post-research phase, the relationships and mentorships formed between community elders and university students solidified. Sinding, Gray, and Nisker describe that "when research reports are presented as art, and public access to the work is both enabled and deliberately arranged, our recontextualization of research participants' stories and lives become audible, visible, felt by them, in visceral and potentially lasting ways."[15] The contributions of the seed keepers provided the opportunity for students to participate in a regional tradition that would otherwise have been beyond their reach as "come here's," and, in turn, students' artistic works became an invitation for the larger community, including newcomers, to engage in dialogue about local food systems. Students possessed their learning in a personal way. The relationships they developed through the research process uprooted and weeded out stereotypes about Appalachian elders that popular culture had implanted. For the seed keepers as well as newer members of the community, the project helped to conceptualize and celebrate the relevance of seed saving, validating the wisdom of the elders and their rich capacity in solving modern problems. The project became a holistic realization of the mission of the center to interrupt stereotypes and recognize the region's diversity. More importantly, the project became a bridge between the university and the community, resulting in additional, unanticipated outcomes. Library programming, for example, brought awareness of the heirloom gardening practices to a new generation of young children, and a number of conference workshops expanded the reach of the project from popular to scholarly circles and created a model for replication in other communities throughout the region.

Challenges

Such informal community collaborations do not conform to conventional pedagogies and present a unique set of obstacles for students, faculty, and community members. At first, students were skeptical of the nontraditional format of their class; they had to dispel their inherent hegemonies and stereotypes. They needed to balance individual demands of school, work, and family in addition to learning how to interact with our community members. Faculty constantly had to dispel the perception that a community engagement project is a soft, nonacademic learning method that lacks rigor or one that should function as a supplement instead of an integral aspect of coursework. Community members, who were exceptionally generous with donations of time, materials, and seeds, grew frustrated as the project was never officially funded or recognized by the institution.

Many of the collaboration's very assets—its interdisciplinary nature, community-based programming, and placed-based pedagogy—presented atypical institutional challenges. For example, we report to three different college deans. Academic units provide a structural framework that foster shared philosophies, cohesive training, collaborative research, and a functional authority. Funding processes reinforce these boundaries.[16] Although we overcame the difficulties of bridging philosophies and research techniques, the project was never formally adopted by any department. Without traditional disciplinary affiliation, funding became a barrier to our continued collaboration after five years, and the visual and performance aspect of the project was discontinued.

New Directions in Food Democracy

Despite the challenges, our project galvanized the community. While we do not make art, the project continues, albeit differently. We still save, grow, and share heirloom seeds. The garden still provides a physical space to connect with our seed keepers and hear their stories. But conversations and connections revealed a need to combat food insecurity and promote food access, especially for those in kindergarten through college. Although no food deserts officially exist in Lumpkin County according to the United States Department of Agriculture (USDA), there is only one grocery store in Dahlonega. Sidewalks exist only in the immediate downtown area. The farmers market, which is also located in town, does not accept Supplemental Nutrition Assistance Program (SNAP) benefits. About 46 percent of public school students in K–12 grades in Lumpkin County qualify for free or reduced-price lunches.[17] Several churches and nonprofits have food pantries that are serviced by Georgia Mountain Food Bank. About 25 percent of UNG students self-report as food insecure.[18]

While the seed keepers' support allowed the center to address the global problem of genetic erosion on a hyperlocal level, we realized we needed to collaborate with groups to grow the project.[19] Partners now include the local master gardeners, local extension agents, and a 4-H group, as well the nutrition program at our county's school system. These additional partnerships have resulted in more funding. For example, a civic group made substantial financial contributions and funded a seasonal high tunnel (a sixteen-by-twenty-foot unheated greenhouse) to enable us to extend the growing season. A campus club started a food pantry at our center, and community donations of food, supplies, and money continue to fund it. Biology faculty secured an internal grant that provided raised beds and installed technology for irrigation and soil moisture monitoring. Middle schools work alongside university students to grow food and save seeds. Institutional partnerships with the University of Georgia Extension Service and the College of Education have created webinars and curriculum on seed saving in school gardens. The demonstration garden, which once focused only on producing seeds, now grows produce for taste tests in lunchrooms and supplies our campus food pantry. We call this phase of our project Hometown Harvest, and it has been endorsed by two new college deans.

In this time of reflection, we realize that while SAGAS was never directly funded, it laid the groundwork for a larger initiative to bolster our food system. As we addressed the global problem of genetic erosion on a local level, we also began to apprehend and affect the status of sustainable food production within the community. We discovered that communities don't need expensive facilities to start a vegetable seed bank. Our collection is a simple refrigerator, and seeds are stored in recycled glass containers with desiccant. We also discovered that while seed banks are essential to preserving germplasm, they may not be accessible to the public; a demonstration garden, however, can showcase varieties and serve as an outdoor classroom. In this environment, local seed keepers can connect to novice student gardeners and newcomers. Such in situ conservation showcases local traditions, connects generations, and keeps the seeds circulating in the community. Moreover, as students listen to seed keeper stories of displacement, survival, and self-sufficiency, they come to find their own voice in these stories as well. In their reader's theater, they wrote:

> We are building bridges in the mountains of north Georgia. They cannot be named bean or truss, cantilever or suspension, covered or cable stayed. No. These bridges are forged with hearty heirloom seeds and powerful recounted stories. We built these bridges with the help and guidance of our professors, community volunteers and our seed keepers. Tell me and I will forget. Show me, and I will remember. Involve me, and I will understand.[20]

Notes

1. David Pendered, "Eleven Georgia Counties Make Census List of Nation's Fastest Growing Counties," *SaportaReport*.com, April 2, 2018, https://saportareport.com/eleven-georgia-counties-make-census-list-of-nations-fastest-growing-counties/ (accessed September 10, 2018).

2. "Lumpkin County Population," http://worldpopulationreview.com/georgia-counties/lumpkin-county/ (accessed September 27, 2018).

3. Chris Arsenault, "Small Farmers Hold the Key to Seed Diversity," *Reuters,* February 16, 2015.

4. J. R. Veteto, G. P. Nabhan, R. Fitzsimmons, K. Rouston, and D. Walker, eds., *Place-Based Foods of Appalachia: From Rarity to Community Restoration and Market Recovery* (Tucson: University of Arizona Southwest Center, 2011).

5. Virginia Nazarea, *Cultural Memory and Biodiversity* (Tucson: University of Arizona Press, 1998).

6. J. H. Rolling Jr., *Arts-Based Research* (New York: Peter Lang Publishing, 2013).

7. Wicomb, quoted in Tom Barone and Elliott W. Eisner, *Arts Based Research* (Thousand Oaks, CA: Sage Publishing, 2012), 134.

8. U.S. Census Bureau, "Quick Facts: Lumpkin County, Georgia," census.gov.

9. U.S. Census Bureau, "Quick Facts."

10. John Bynum, "McDuffie Steps up as New Tourism Director," *The Dahlonega Nugget,* July 19, 2019, https://www.thedahloneganugget.com/news/mcduffie-steps-new-tourism-director.

11. U.S. Census Bureau, "Quick Facts."

12. Kathryn Engle, "Why Study Appalachia: Wisdom from Helen Lewis," August 31, 2015, https://kathrynengle.wordpress.com/2015/08/31/why-study-appalachia-wisdom-from-helen-lewis/ (accessed September 27, 2018).

13. J. G. Knowles and A. L. Cole, "Arts-Informed Research," in *Handbook of the Arts in Qualitative Research,* ed. G. J. Knowles and A. L. Cole (Thousand Oaks, CA: Sage Publishing, 2008), 55–70.

14. "Communograph: Mapping Community for Community Action," http://www.communograph.com/.

15. C. Sinding, R. Gray, and J. Nisker, "Ethical Issues and Issues of Ethics," in *Handbook of the Arts in Qualitative Research,* ed. G. J. Knowles and A. L. Cole (Thousand Oaks, CA: Sage Publishing, 2008), 459–468: 465.

16. T. C. Pellmar and L. Eisenberg, eds., *Barriers to Interdisciplinary Research and Training. From Institute of Medicine (US) Committee on Building Bridges in the Brain, Behavioral, and Clinical Sciences* (Washington DC: National Academies Press, 2000).

17. Georgia Department of Education, *Lumpkin County Free and Reduced Lunch (FRL)–Fiscal Year 2020 Data Report.*

18. Sherry Parker, UNG Food Pantry Manager, personal communication, 2020.

19. J. Winskie and J. Murray, "Heirloom Seed and Story Keepers: Growing Community and Sustainability through Arts-Based Research," *Papers & Publications: Interdisciplinary Journal of Undergraduate Research* 2 (2013). https://digitalcommons.northgeorgia.edu/papersandpubs/vol2/iss1/10/

20. Avery Alexander, Kaitlin Brackett, Elizabeth Guzman, Rosann Kent, and Mary Lipold, "Seeds and Snakes and Bears Oh My," *Digest: A Journal of Foodways and Culture* 3, no. 2 (2013).

2

Bringing Back the Forest

University outreach, community engagement, and partnerships for the reforestation of coal mines in Appalachia

Patrick N. Angel, Christopher D. Barton, Geoffrey W. Bell, Theresa L. Burriss, and Sarah L. Hall

Introduction

Appalachian forests support some of the greatest biological diversity in the world's temperate region, but extraction of abundant coal reserves has negatively impacted the landscape. Since 1977, over 1.7 million acres of Appalachian forest have been destroyed by surface mining, producing significant economic, environmental, and ecological challenges. While the Appalachian economy has traditionally been based in the coal industry, this industry has declined severely over recent decades and regional economic diversification is a priority.[1] Degraded ecosystems, such as mined land, represent an immediate opportunity for the creation of a "restoration economy" by providing both jobs in the restoration industry and by improving long-term ecosystem productivity and associated goods and services.[2] The University of Kentucky (UK) participated in a broad-based collaboration that included other educational organizations, state and federal agencies, coal companies, environmental and conservation groups, landowners, and citizens to restore forests on surface-mined lands. Through research and discovery, we produced improved techniques for restoring ecosystems impacted by surface mining, while outreach and engagement have advanced knowledge by demonstrating these techniques with our partners. The Appalachian Regional Reforestation Initiative (ARRI) resulted from these partnerships and has paved the way for development of important federal and state regulatory documents providing guidance to property owners and coal companies for establishing productive forests after mining has been completed. The program's success has been mutually beneficial, producing increased university and stakeholder readiness to collaborate. Colleges and universities across the United States have participated in collaborative research, service-learning, and volunteer efforts to greatly enhance the visibility of the program. Ultimately, scholarly engagement has produced sustainable land solutions, developed a new generation of leaders who are carrying the work forward, and brought about a "reforestation renaissance" across Appalachia. Against a backdrop of project successes, this chapter examines the cultural, technical, and regulatory barriers that had historically hindered reforestation efforts. It further reflects on the opportunities and challenges to building and sustaining large-scale, cross-institutional partnerships that can benefit the Appalachian region.

Growing Support for New Reclamation Strategies

After the implementation of the federal Surface Mining Control and Reclamation Act of 1977 (SMCRA), reforestation of surface mines was generally avoided. SMCRA required mined sites to be stabilized, but reclaimed mined sites most often amounted to pastoral grasslands with hard-packed soils. Regulatory personnel grew accustomed to these grasslands and adopted them as the model of good reclamation. Industry complied to satisfy requirements and avoid violations and fines. Ultimately, cultural, not regulatory, barriers led to the failure of reforestation efforts under the federal law.[3] Views about reclaiming post-mining lands have changed significantly in recent years: many landowners, coal companies, and regulators have come together in pursuit of a common goal—reestablishing the forest.

Students and faculty at UK-linked nonprofits and other universities in a cooperative effort with the Kentucky Department of Natural Resources (KDNR), the USDI Office of Surface Mining (OSM), and the coal industry to create a large-scale reforestation demonstration site that could educate diverse stakeholders. Research started in 1995 at the Starfire Mine in Perry County, Kentucky, eventually showed new reclamation techniques for establishing forests with high-value trees.[4] Ultimately, these partnerships helped pave the way for the development of important regulatory guidance documents, as well as ARRI to promote reforestation partnerships.[5] The project has provided stakeholders a more fundamental understanding of what is necessary to succeed in partnering with multiple groups that sometimes don't see eye to eye. Impacts resulting from the partnership include (1) increased acreage of forested post-mining land use on mining permits; (2) funding for development of research and demonstration areas; (3) water quality and flood mitigation improvements benefiting human, wildlife, and aquatic health; (4) heightened economic opportunities (jobs, forest products, ecotourism, carbon trading, and land value); and (5) empowerment of the community to participate in beautification and enhancement of land that is initially often abandoned. More importantly, the success exhibited by these partnerships has resulted in the formation of additional partnerships.

Building Relationships and Reciprocity

From the inception of this reforestation program, the need for partnerships was recognized as a critical and essential component for success. All coal mining operations, especially large strip mines, have multiple stakeholders. Historically, the mining community had shown some resistance toward university research due to safety and liability issues, fear of potential negative media exposure, and concern about heightened regulatory oversight and potential fines. Using a holistic approach, we formed an interdisciplinary group (forestry, engineering, economics, geology, chemistry, wildlife biology, and policy) to perform integrative studies that would potentially benefit all stakeholders. Building relationships and gaining trust with the mining community opened the door and provided a platform for UK to establish a reforestation research program on active mine sites in the region. These same sites ultimately turned into outdoor classrooms where experiential learning opportunities have been realized for thousands of students.

The role of the university reforestation team was (1) through research and discovery to develop improved techniques for restoring ecosystems impacted by surface mining; (2) through outreach to advance knowledge by demonstrating improved reforestation techniques to all partners; and (3) through scholarship and engagement to develop leaders who will carry our work forward to further protect Appalachia's environment.

The role of our partners was to (1) provide direct and in-kind funding to support large-scale outdoor research and demonstration areas (including funds for infrastructure, research personnel, technicians, and students); (2) provide assistance with regulatory permitting requirements necessary for performing research on surface-mine lands; (3) provide access to and security for research and demonstration sites that are often in very remote areas; and (4) actively participate and promote tree planting. Decision-making is shared among collaborators and often guided by critical questions important to all stakeholders. Projects are generally multifaceted with potential impacts to multiple partners. A high degree of friction can exist between inspectors, miners, and environmental activists. Therefore, it is imperative to involve partners in the decision process and to be transparent. In developing grants, we worked closely with regulatory agencies to ensure that our proposals were pertinent and legal, and with the industry to ensure that the projects are logistically feasible and not cost prohibitive. Once a project is underway, regular on-site "tailgate" meetings are held between partners so each can communicate their needs and to ensure that all parties are satisfied with the progress of the work. Partners actively participated in field demonstrations, professional presentations, and written communications.

Expanding our Engagement

People have been in search of jobs, dignity, and abundant natural resources within the heart of the Appalachian Mountains from colonial days to the present. The dis-

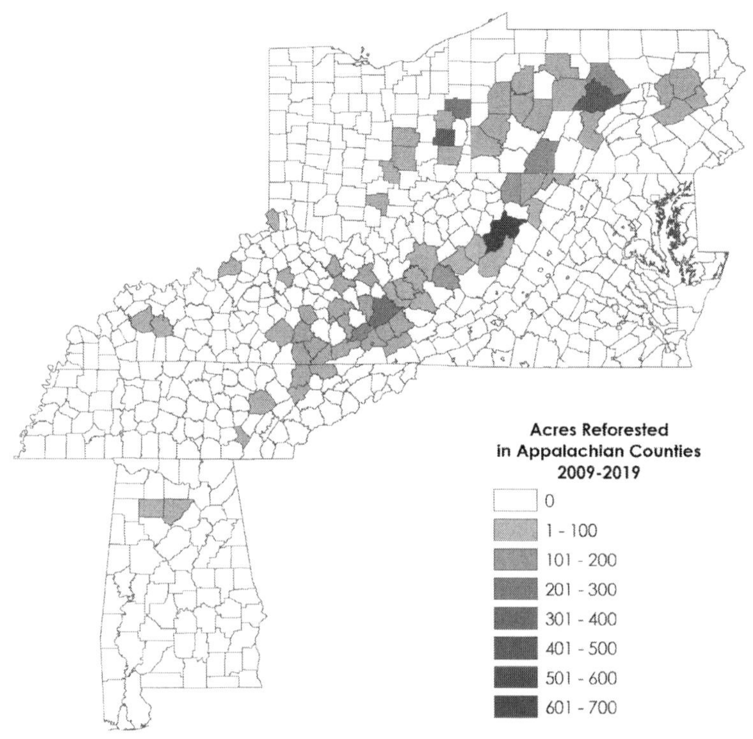

Figure 2.1. Location of Green Forests Work reforestation projects and acres planted in and around the Appalachian region. (Illustration courtesy of the authors.)

cussion of exactly where they can find those treasures is not limited to the realm of social scientists, economists, and politicians. For decades, noted artists, musicians, poets, and writers have contributed to the search. Erik Reece, author of *Lost Mountain: A Year in the Vanishing Wilderness*, wrote: "We need a New Deal for Appalachia that would return some of the region's lost wealth in the form of jobs and trees, rebuilt topsoil and resuscitated communities . . . ".[6] In cooperation with our diverse partnerships, we recognized these needs and created the Green Forests Work (GFW) program in 2009 for the citizens of Appalachia. Ancillary benefits that could develop from these restored forests include certified "green" wood products, ecotourism, biodiversity enhancement, woody biofuels, and other eco-friendly opportunities that can involve local communities as leaders. In 2009, GFW was created to expand the work of ARRI to lands that were reclaimed as grassland and are no longer the responsibility of the mining companies. The new program led to more partnerships and

Table 2.1. Impact of the Green Forests Work Reforestation Program, 2009–2019

Year Planted	Acres Reforested	Trees Planted	Volunteers
2009	37	35,155	558
2010	204	145,285	931
2011	670	352,516	1,663
2012	321	228,249	2,577
2013	381	256,182	1,949
2014	362	200,181	1,941
2015	629	374,038	1,637
2016	386	239,720	2,140
2017	350	259,305	1,817
2018	665	401,728	1,679
2019	466	318,938	2,377
Total	**4,471**	**2,811,297***	**19,249**

*Approximately 65 percent planted by contract tree planters and 35 percent by volunteers.

over 300 volunteer tree planting projects/events throughout Appalachia. Those events involved over 19,000 volunteers since 2009 and resulted in the planting of over 2.8 million trees, including 4,000 acres of legacy mined lands (Figure 2.1). College students from more than eighty campuses participated (Table 2.1). Although impressive, the importance of these volunteer events is not measured by the number of trees planted, rather by the act of putting individuals, some of whom may have opposing views on mining, together to engage in conversations about conservation, sustainability, and the future well-being of the region. These conversations, and outcomes produced from them, are the true measures of success and progress. Each volunteer planting event provides a service-learning educational opportunity to talk about the region and its natural resources. Discussions on land use in the region and its influence on ecosystems (water quality, soils, vegetation, bugs, salamanders, fish, mammals, etc.) provides volunteers insight into how impacts can be prevented and how land can be restored. Differences between environmental and economic interests dissolve in these exchanges. For example, a practical outcome of the project is that more money has circulated in local economies in the form of lodging, food, fuel, and goods and services needed to support the tree planting operations, as well as expanded opportunities for ecotourism to build on.

Cross-Institutional Outcomes

The mine land reforestation program proved to be an excellent model for bringing often diverging groups to the table to develop real solutions to tough problems. Through engagement, the number and diversity of collaborations grew, and use of this model for addressing other mining-related issues has blossomed. Teaching and scholarship arising from these partnerships have been multidisciplinary and abundant, leading thousands of hours of applied learning experiences. For the past several years, faculty at several institutions have participated in various ways in the reforestation program. The following are examples from three schools that have participated on a continuing basis.

Radford University

Faculty at Radford University (located in the New River Valley of Virginia) who specialize in Appalachian studies, biology, English, and geospatial science have organized alternative spring break trips to eastern Kentucky, in collaboration with GFW and ARRI. This extracurricular opportunity is offered to all students on campus, including both graduate and undergraduate students in a variety of disciplines, at no cost, thanks to grants and/or university support.

On the Monday of spring break in a classroom on Radford's campus, participating faculty provide students with cultural, scientific, and policy information related to the practice of mountaintop removal coalmining. Early Tuesday morning the group travels to either southwest Virginia or eastern Kentucky, depending on the planting site, to establish a "base camp" where the faculty and students will eat and sleep for two nights. Wednesday is devoted to learning about proper planting techniques and the actual planting of various hardwoods, while Thursday is a travel day back to campus, oftentimes with other educational stops included, such as the exhibition coal mine in Lynch, Kentucky, or Appalachian Sustainable Development in Abingdon, Virginia.

After the trip, students are required to submit a reflection on the experience. One student's log that captured the spirit of many students' involvement was as follows:

> *OMG, I am exhausted! Today we planted 400 trees in Robinson Forest. GO RADFORD! While that's exciting let me tell you I had some SERIOUS troubles; me and my cerebral palsy had yet another fight! Here we are on this huge reclaimed mountaintop removal site; everybody else has already made it to the top looking down at me. My legs are telling me 'You'll never make it,' feeling like spaghetti noodles with every step. I thought to myself, 'I didn't come all the way to Kentucky not to plant these trees!' So I began to hike. Left foot, right foot grabbing rocks, dirt, twigs out of breath and all while chanting in my head 'it's for the trees!' Guess who won the fight? ME!*

Berea College

Berea College, a liberal arts college located in Berea, Kentucky, was one of the first college groups that participated in tree plantings with GFW and ARRI. Involvement has included students from multiple departments (Education Studies, Agriculture and Natural Resources, Appalachian Studies, Sustainability and Environmental Studies) as well as a number of extracurricular groups (Student Government Association, Bereans for Appalachia). Brenda Richardson, former instructor at Berea College who brought homeschool and college students early on, recalls, "Planting—and learning the history of mining—had significant effects on both older and younger students."

In fall 2011, Berea College students across campus joined together for a unique planting event. Students in Education Studies (EDS) collected black walnuts, many from on campus, which were prepared for planting. The EDS students planted those walnuts in research plots (along with many additional seedlings) at the Fishtrap Wildlife Management Area in Pike County, Kentucky. The research project was aimed at finding whether walnuts planted from seed could thrive on surface-mined land, and it served as the basis for undergraduate research conducted by four students in Agriculture and Natural Resources during the summers of 2012 and 2013. In 2013 data collection involved a Sustainability and Environmental Studies class as well. While many Berea College students are from the mountains of Appalachia, many are not, and involvement in a project like this allows those who are not from the region to learn about it and connect with the land, as well as their classmates from the region. When walnuts were being prepared for the project, one student from eastern Kentucky brought her pickup truck to help haul the bucket loads of walnuts and remove the hulls (by driving over them). Other students, including a number from urban areas such as Birmingham, AL, sat around and worked to remove the loosened, blackened hulls by hand. While completing this dirty (and often amusing) task, the students shared many stories. By the end of the evening the black walnut stains on their hands and in their fingernails linked them all together as a sort of pinky swear for the trees.

The University of North Carolina

The University of North Carolina at Chapel Hill (UNC-CH) has also collaborated with the reforestation program using an innovative Course-based Undergraduate Research Experience or CURE that provides a vital and transformative step in the education and professional development of STEM majors. Since 2015, the Environment, Ecology, and Energy Program (E3P) has offered a capstone course for approximately eight advanced undergraduates with career interests in ecology, conservation, restoration, and natural resource management. E3P capstones provide a real-world and client-driven problem-solving experience to students, so UK and ARRI (i.e., the clients) meet remotely with the UNC instructor and students at the beginning of each spring semester to discuss potential research projects that can help improve Appalachian reforestation initiatives. The students then take ownership of the project by gathering information on the topic and preparing a formal research proposal for ARRI that details the experimental design they will use to address the question or problem. The research topics differ each year depending on ARRI and GFW needs and have included comparing hardwood growth performance on mined lands to areas of natural regeneration; examining the influence of climate change and stand composition (monoculture vs. polyculture with hardwoods) on mine lands for two pine species (shortleaf and loblolly); a survey of the plant pathogen *Phytophthora cinnamomi* on reforested mine soils; teasing apart the effects of headwater stream habitat modification and poor water quality from mined watersheds on salamander occupancy; and assessing the effectiveness of different timber harvest management practices on headwater stream functioning.

The UNC students travel to and live in UK's Robinson Forest over spring break to set up their experiment and gather the data that they will analyze for a written report on their findings for ARRI. While in Kentucky the students also participate in a tree-planting event, which makes their trip carbon neutral. This sustainability feature of the course conforms with the zero greenhouse gas emission goal of UNC's Three Zeroes initiative.

In all, the partnership with UNC-CH has been remarkably positive for everyone and mutually beneficial. For the students, living in Robinson Forest and working alongside ARRI and GFW professionals in natural and mineland ecosystems has a profound impact on their perceptions of Appalachia. UNC students learn about coal-mining impacts in their environmental courses but very few are from this area. Several capstone students have remarked that being immersed in this region made a stronger impression on them than their traditional courses on how dramatically mining has altered the natural, economic, and societal landscape of Appalachia. The experience has also inspired them to act. Moreover, doing research to find solutions to real-world reforestation problems creates an exciting and engaging learning experience for students where they make discoveries that are of interest to stakeholders, develop practical and quantitative skills, and learn to manage projects while trouble-shooting problems that arise.

Lessons Learned and Best Practices

Through our reforestation partnership, several cultural, technical, and regulatory barriers were identified that hindered reforestation efforts in the years following SMCRA implementation. Our group worked in partnership with Appalachian stakeholders to eliminate these. Though grassland reclamation persisted, university efforts to educate stakeholders helped to broaden support for alternatives. From a cultural perspective, great strides were made in changing the perception that tree planting is more expensive and riskier than reclamation to pastureland. This required re-education of personnel within mining companies, regulatory authorities, and the environmental community. Another major part of this effort was changing perceptions of what good forestry reclamation should look like. Landowners and conservation groups initially resisted these approaches because the sites were "ugly." With time and the emergence of a healthy forest, attitudes changed.

From a technical perspective, we worked side by side with machine operators, engineers, and miners to describe and implement Forestry Reclamation Approach

(FRA) technology. It is one thing to read about implementing a new technology, but we found that an on-site presence was needed to effectively show the industry how to prepare land for reforestation. From a regulatory perspective, we worked with state and federal authorities to ensure that FRA technologies were legal. We also worked to streamline permitting requirements for FRA reclamation. We continue to review state and federal regulations to identify and resolve impediments to reforestation and to change the perception that the regulations impede effective reforestation. Nonetheless, we achieved many tangible results. Across Appalachia, about 100 million trees have been planted on 140,000 acres using the FRA.[7] In 2009, ARRI was recognized by the United Nations Environmental Programme (UNEP) for fulfilling a pledge to plant thirty-eight million trees on surface mines—the largest pledge in North America—as part of UNEP's Billion Tree Campaign.

Establishing partnerships and gaining trust over time were key components for seeing these results. For example, the Appalachian Regional Commission (ARC) realized the importance of this work and provided the funding for establishing GFW as a 501(c)3 nonprofit organization. In that initial grant, ARC provided a modest amount of funding to initiate a reforestation project at the Flight 93 National Memorial, which was a former surface mine. The National Park Service was very skeptical about the idea of an outside group coming onto the memorial site with a large bulldozer to rip up the land for the sake of planting trees and were somewhat hesitant to move forward. GFW and ARRI engaged the National Park Service, ARC, the National Park Foundation, the Friends of Flight 93, the PA Bureau of Reclamation and others to ensure that the project would be a partnership and that input from all stakeholders was valued. Cautiously, we proceeded with site preparation and planned volunteer planting events for the public and members of families who lost loved ones in the terror attack. Over two blustery April weekends in 2012, nearly 14,000 trees were planted by 800 volunteers on twenty acres of the memorial. In all, fifty-one different partners made that first project at the Flight 93 Memorial a reality and it was a huge success. Deborah Bodley, mother of the youngest victim of the attack, Deora Bodley, participated in the planting and commented how the event had helped her heal emotionally. The slogan *"Heal the Land, Heal the Heart"* was adopted, and volunteer planting events have occurred each year since. As of May 2019, over 130,000 trees have been planted at the Flight 93 Memorial by thousands of volunteers.[8]

Through these partnerships, many economic and environmental improvements have been realized for the citizens of Appalachia. Thriving forests provide opportunities for a growing wood industry and jobs for local residents. Forests provide habitat for wildlife and support recreation activities. Forests sequester carbon, clean our air, and help offset global climate change. Forests help to lessen erosion and improve stream water quality. Forests provide an escape from the hustle and bustle of life, a place where we can think and listen. Forests improve the quality of all of our lives.

Notes

1. R. Mcilmoil and E. Hansen, *The Decline of Central Appalachian Coal and the Need for Economic Diversification* (White Paper 1, Thinking Downstream, 2010).

2. K. W. Thoemke, "Career Development: Plenty of Opportunity, Plenty of Concern: The Short Term Future of the Environmental Job Market," *Environmental Practice* 18 (2016): 75–77.

3. C. E. Zipper, J. A. Burger, J. G. Skousen, P. N. Angel, C. D. Barton, V. Davis, and J. A. Franklin, "Restoring Forests and Associated Ecosystem Services on Appalachian Coal Surface Mines," *Environmental Management* 47 (2011): 751–765.

4. Christopher Barton, Kenton Sena, Teagan Dolan, Patrick Angel, and Carl Zipper, "Restoring Forests on Surface Coal Mines in Appalachia: A regional Reforestation Approach with Global Application," in N. Bolan, M. B. Kirkham, and Y. S. Ok, eds, *Spoil to Soil: Mine Site Rehabilitation and Revegetation* (Taylor and Francis, 2017), Chapter 8, 124–145.

5. C. D. Barton, C. E. Zipper, and J. A. Burger, "Preface," in *The Forestry Reclamation Approach: Guide to Successful Reforestation of Mined Lands,* ed. Mary Beth Adams, Gen. Tech. Rep. NRS-169 (Newtown Square, PA: U.S. Department of Agriculture, Forest Service, Northern Research Station, 2017), i–iii, https://doi.org/10.2737/NRS GTR-169. See also www.arri.osmre.gov

6. Erik Reece, *Lost Mountain: A Year in the Vanishing Wilderness* (New York: Riverhead Books, 2006), 250.

7. H. Z. Angel, C. D. Barton, M. French, and P. N. Angel, "The Appalachian Regional Reforestation and Green Forests Work: Bringing Back the Forest on Surface Coal Mines in Appalachia," *Journal of the American Society of Mining and Reclamation* 4, no. 2 (2015): 91–101.

8. M. C. Tyree, J. L. Larkin, S. E. Eggerud, P. N. Angel, M. E. French, and C. D. Barton, "Flight 93 National Memorial Reforestation Project: Survival and Health Of Native Woody Plants Established on Reclaimed Mineland," *Journal of the American Society of Mining and Reclamation* 7, no. 2 (2018): 35–60, *http://dx.doi.org/10.21000/JASMR18020035.*

3

Wealth and Poverty in the Little Cities of Black Diamonds

Navigating community–university partnership in Southeast Ohio

Robert Frank, Diana Marvel, Rachel Terman, and John Winnenberg

Introduction

Located in one of Ohio's poorest counties, Ohio University is situated literally and figuratively at the intersection of wealth and poverty. Like the Appalachian region broadly, Athens County and Southeast Ohio are known as places struggling with poverty and at the same time are sites of wealth, including the university as a center of economic activity as well as the area's natural resources, built environment, history, and community. Likewise, Southeast Ohio is characterized as a rural region, which obscures the fact that Athens County is actually micropolitan and attracts a large population of urbanites through the university as well as other recreational and regional attractions. Furthermore, as the title to this chapter suggests, even some of Ohio's smallest incorporated towns share commonalities with urban places, as we will discuss later in this chapter. Thus, service-learning in Southeast Ohio provides an excellent opportunity for work that bridges divides and reveals alternative narratives about communities and Appalachia. These alternative narratives are useful when considering the often-bemoaned divisions in our society.

Although our corner of Appalachia is a space and place for breaking down dichotomous assumptions about wealth and poverty, rural and urban, there are also real disparities that are made clear from just a basic visual comparative observation of, for example, Uptown Athens, Ohio, versus Downtown Shawnee, Ohio. The former is filled with bustling shops, restaurants, and apartments adjacent to the main source of economic activity in the area: Ohio University. The latter is filled with shops, restaurants, and apartments, but many are empty and in disrepair, and the town is isolated from many workplaces in the area. This basic disparity also reflects divisions based on social class. The inequalities that exist and the impact of those inequalities on university–community relations are exigent issues requiring contin-ued and careful planning, work, and reflection. Much like our current pedagogical models for service-learning, planning, work, and reflection have helped us address the basic and fundamental questions about university-community collaboration in Southeast Ohio: what can this place give our students, and, in return, what can our students and institution give this place?

We address these questions through the perspectives of a faculty member, a com-munity organizer, and two university administrators. Rachel Terman is Assistant Professor of Sociology at Ohio University. John Winnenberg is Lead Staff Associate at Sunday Creek Associates, a nonprofit organization located in Shawnee, Ohio, responsible for the community-building experience named "Little Cities of Black Diamonds" (LCBD). Diana Marvel led Ohio University's Center for Campus and Community Engagement (CCCE) and is an advocate for asset-based community engagement. Robert Frank served as the Dean of the College of Arts and Sciences and views southeastern Ohio as a tremendous asset for student experiential learning and faculty research. We find that collaborative community–university sustainability depends on engagement "scaffolding," institutional support, and network engage-ments. We also acknowledge the challenges of long-term and continuous support for these collaborations, which can be affected by underdeveloped engagement, tran-sience, lack of critical reflection practice, community capacity, and basic structural support including changes in administration and formal systems of valuing univer-sity–community collaboration. Below, we will introduce and contextualize the Little Cities of Black Diamonds (LCBD) region and Ohio University (OHIO). Next, we describe the university–community collaboration in which we have been engaged. Finally, we discuss the successes we've had based on this work as well as what we see as the unfinished work of creating a sustainable community–university partnership and addressing inequalities in our area.

The Little Cities and Ohio University

Located in Southeast Ohio, the Little Cities of Black Diamonds (LCBD) is a micro-region within Appalachia. It is made up of more than seventy towns and named coal camps built during the coal boom of the late 1800s. Coal production declined signifi-cantly in the early twentieth century, yet the area remains impacted by the economic, social, and environmental consequences of this industrial development. There is a long history of collaboration between Ohio University and LCBD communities in Athens, Morgan, Hocking, and Perry Counties. The university, located in Athens (Athens County), Ohio, has a little over twenty thousand combined undergraduate and graduate students in residence at its main campus. Nearly 25 percent of first-year undergraduate students are first generation, and the university mission state-ment includes a "commitment to the region . . . expressed through stewardship of shared resources, access to programs and services, and contribution to economic development."[1]

OHIO was founded in 1804, and the town of Athens grew up around the school during the following two centuries. The subsequent development of the coal industry brought a diverse population of immigrants and post–Civil War African American migrants from the South into the Little Cities region seeking work in the newly opened mines. In this historical context, the town of Athens itself has always been somewhat distinct and perhaps distanced from the surrounding region given its unique position as a college town. Thus, place has and continues to be important in shaping the institutions and experiences of individuals in this part of Southeast Ohio.

However, the connection between OHIO and the Appalachian region, specifically, began during the 1960s when the region as we commonly understand it today was also beginning to crystalize. Indeed, in 1964 President Johnson first announced the plan for a "Great Society" during a speech on OHIO's campus. In this speech, the president asked students to join his efforts to confront poverty in the region.[2] The president of OHIO at that time was also interested in changing "both the image and condition of this isolated area and intended Ohio University to take the lead in spurring its economic development,"[3] and he worked with the Johnson administration in Washington D.C., Ohio, and across the country developing programs as part of the War on Poverty and promoting Ohio University.[4] Notably, just as Ron Eller finds generally in his history of development in Appalachia since 1945, these efforts in the 1960s did not yield consistent economic growth over space or time.[5] Today, the university is the main economic engine in Athens County, as well as many nearby communities in adjacent counties. However, Athens County is often listed as the poorest county in the entire state of Ohio, and the surrounding counties, including the LCBD counties, are often listed as distressed or at-risk by the Appalachian Regional Commission.[6]

Although these War on Poverty–era development initiatives did not completely restructure the economies or communities of southeastern Ohio, they did lead to and inspire many community leaders and valuable long-standing organizations in the region like the LCBD. Indeed, the LCBD Council was formed in part from frustration after seeing larger and more well-connected towns like Athens benefit from federal and state development grants and programs. Thus, OHIO has a wealth of community leaders and organizations with which to work. Although the typical "town and gown" tensions continue to be a reality, connections between the campus and the community also continue to develop and flourish.

Within the university, a development that provided support for these community–university engagements was the theme initiative started in 2014 by College of Arts & Sciences dean Robert Frank. The goal of the themes initiative was the development of multidisciplinary faculty teams that would provide a wide variety of perspectives on "big issues" through the development of new curricula and extracurricular activities. A design principle for the themes was that they be "permeable" so that students with a wide range of backgrounds and interests in a thematic area would be able to participate in formal and informal educational opportunities that would stimulate their interest in and perspectives on broad societal issues.

The development of service-learning courses, regional tours, and student research projects in southeastern Ohio along with more traditional, formal college courses provides many "on-ramps" for student engagement with a theme. One of the most successful themes is the Wealth and Poverty Theme, which brings together faculty and students from many colleges and majors. Southeastern Ohio provides numerous opportunities for tours, service learning, and research connected to the Wealth and Poverty Theme.

Around the same time the themes initiative was developed, OHIO also decided to reestablish a centralized administrative office to support campus-wide community engagement tied to the academic curriculum through the Center for Campus and Community Engagement (CCCE). The CCCE has since established a faculty certification process, a transcript designation for courses that include at least twenty hours of service, and a mini-grant program for service-learning courses. The CCCE aims to build a resource pool to help offset costs such as transportation and supplies needed when community partners don't have resources available to move engagement projects forward.

In terms of the LCBD, faculty and students have been actively engaged with these communities since 2005. John Winnenberg's role as a "bridge builder" has supported this consistency. He describes bridge builders as individuals who are from the community or region who can operate comfortably in both the university and community settings. This role is particularly useful in engagements with communities such as those in the Little Cities, where, compared to a university town, there are a limited number of residents who have attended a residential four-year college such as Ohio University. In this setting, community–university engagement means navigating cultural, educational, and class differences among faculty, visiting students, and local stakeholders. People who haven't attended college sometimes aren't familiar or comfortable with faculty members due to preconceived notions or stereotypes, and vice versa. Faculty from an academic setting and students from urban or suburban settings may be ignorant of the cultural context for people of modest means in a rural setting. Winnenberg finds that avoiding the "pity-charity" model of service and directing conversations toward asset-based development is a key way to overcome some of these barriers until folks become comfortable enough with one another to address more difficult issues such as poverty, crime, or drugs. He recalls that, initially, a few curious professors sought out the LCBD as a "museum of poverty" or "poverty tour." However, after dialogue between the LCBD and university professors produced community-driven service objectives, which we detail in the following section, meaningful and mutually beneficial hands-on projects led to administrative leaders taking note, which further advanced the partnerships and provided institutional support. This support then fostered engagement with additional faculty.

In the remainder of this chapter, we will focus on service-learning as a way of *scaffolding engagement*, a specific pedagogical approach we use to build on short-term collaborations like field trips with the goal of establishing long-term, more fully integrated collaborations like participatory action research.

Figure 3.1. Students join community members to paint a caboose, the focal point of the entrance to the village of Shawnee, Ohio. This two-day service project is an example of a short-term event that supports the long-term partnership. (Photo credit: Rachel Terman.)

Little Cities as a Classroom: Building and Using the Scaffold

The incremental and long-term nature of our work guides success in our particular university–community relationship. One way we put this objective into practice is to create what we have called a "scaffold" system of engagement.[7] Through this system, some engagement activities are lower-investment, short-term, or one-time-only events (see Figure 3.1), which ultimately support longer-term, deeper investments in the university–community partnership.

For example, we organize field trips, funded through the Wealth & Poverty Theme initiative and the CCCE, which are open to anyone at the university, to the LCBD nearly every semester. We call our planning process for these excursions "Unmaking the Poverty Tour."[8] One of the main ways in which we "unmake" the poverty tour is by focusing on the assets of the communities while acknowledging some of the struggles they face. For example, our "Alternative Economies in Appalachia" field trip involves stops at the Tecumseh Lake (see Figure 3.2) and historic Tecumseh Theater in Shawnee, Ohio, in the LCBD to highlight recreational and history-based assets along with a stop at a rural produce auction to highlight local food assets. As John Winnenberg often notes, he has seen only economic decline in these communities during his lifetime, which began after the coal boom days. Thus, these examples of economic activity serve as important lessons in Appalachian community resilience.

Figure 3.2. Students attend a pre-service field trip to Shawnee, Ohio, where an Americorps volunteer talks about the history and current recreational promotion of Tecumseh Lake and adjacent Buckeye Trail. (Photo credit: Rachel Terman.)

These trips can have over seventy students, faculty, and staff participate, which is almost twice the population of the smallest Little City, Rendville! We believe this type of engagement would be inappropriate on its own given that a field trip is generally a one-time-only visit, and there is minimal benefit to the community. Therefore, we combine the field trips with service-learning projects in the same communities. In terms of the scaffolding system, professors can require the field trip for students currently enrolled in service-learning courses as an initial introduction to the community. Participating faculty and staff also gain a more nuanced understanding of the regional context and history, as well as being afforded opportunities to meet with potential community collaborators in the LCBD. These supportive "scaffolding" engagements, combined with more robust engagements like service-learning allow university stakeholders an opportunity to be more familiar and engaged with the community and also shows the community that the university is a consistent and long-term partner.

These long-term relationships are made possible by resources invested and administrative support at the university level. Continuity of university support over time is critical to success. The relationship of Ohio University to its surrounding community is a great example. No other institution in southeastern Ohio provides greater prospects for continuity of commitment and contribution of human and financial resources. Commitment from the top of the organization is necessary because collaborative programs with community partners require the development of durable, trusting relationships that go beyond the personal relationships between individual faculty and community members. Collaborative programs built on individual relationships are inherently vulnerable to retirements, resignations, changes in personal circumstance, or the end of grant funding. A more durable foundation is needed to ensure that the interests of the university and community are sustained over time.

We use this scaffold approach as a guiding principle, along with the pedagogical perspective of service-learning provided by Andrew Furco, who explains that service-learning is distinct from other types of university-community collaborations by its "intention to equally benefit the provider and the recipient of the service as well as to ensure equal focus on both the service being provided and the learning that is occurring."[9] In this way, the service objectives and learning objectives described below form the structure of the community–university engagement through service-learning. Creating clear service and learning objectives as part of the planning process for the service-learning project helps ensure that benefits exist for the students and the community and that they are balanced appropriately as agreed upon by those involved.

Although the objectives of each service-learning project will be unique to the specific project, we use the following community-driven service objectives to gauge successful campus-community engagements which are worthy of consideration regardless of specifics:

1. Benefits the community
2. Is mutually beneficial to university and community partners
3. Recognizes assets of community, rather than focusing on deficits
4. Sustainable over time, as opposed to "one-and-done"
5. Respects local wisdom, and involves listening
6. Identifies and solves problems collaboratively
7. Takes place in settings outside the classroom
8. Engages and explores as opposed to lecture-style presentation
9. Researches and documents, while sharing those results with community
10. Celebrates and recognizes successes, individuals, and stories
11. Collaboratively designed and implemented wherever possible
12. Incremental in nature and in it "for the long haul"

Importantly, these twelve objectives were developed by the LCBD Council as "rules for engagement," and Winnenberg emphasizes the importance of their use with faculty and units within the university as a key element for building results that are lasting. He sees the need for developing a "learning community" among partners on campus and in the region as an ideal trajectory for sustained engagement success through realizing the above attributes. A learning community would provide opportunities for engaged faculty and community partners throughout the region to learn from one another by sharing their experiences and what they learned from them, as well as sharing ideas on thematic and geographical projects. The ultimate goal of the learning community would be that the university has a growing group of faculty who know and understand the community and region, and the community partners better understand the university's needs, resources, and priorities. Likewise, he again sees the role of bridge builder as particularly helpful in guiding projects toward these service objectives. He also touts engagements beyond service-learning courses that range from faculty research to the university band, theater, or sports teams participating in community events. Deeper and multifaceted engagements build familiarity and trust.

Like the service objectives, the learning objectives will be unique to the specific project. Nonetheless, there are three main themes around which we construct our learning objectives:

1. Academic: students should be able to connect the project to academic course content—for example, apply theoretical ideas to a specific place or compare knowledge from the classroom with knowledge from the community.
2. Professionalization: students should be able to practice professional skills through the project—for example, project management, research methods, experience working with diverse populations, and presentation and communication skills.
3. Citizenship: students should learn citizenship skills through the service-learning project—for example, general principles of citizenship as commonly integrated into a liberal arts education. Our A&S College mission statement includes, "The College's faculty, staff, and students aspire to meet the imperatives of tolerance, curiosity, and deeply informed engagement with a diverse and changing world."[10]

Learning objectives for service-learning projects can be tied directly to these values of citizenship. We can also connect learning objectives to ideas from progressive and popular education perspectives on the link between democracy and education. Writing in the 1920s, John Dewey argued, "The essential need . . . is the improvement of the methods and conditions of debate, discussion and persuasion. That is *the* problem of the public."[11] Some sixty years later, Paulo Freire and Myles Horton discussed the idea that "the more people participate in the process of their own education . . . the more the people participate in the development of their selves. The more the people become themselves, the better the democracy."[12] Now, in the late 2010s, these ideas about the link among citizenship, democracy, and education are still relevant, especially given the pressures on students and educators to focus on job skills and profit, sometimes to the detriment of "debate, discussion, and persuasion" and participation in one's own education. Indeed, service-learning is often understood to be part of a larger civic engagement movement within higher education.[13] In his book

Community: The Structure of Belonging, Peter Block has suggested the health and vitality of our communities is directly related to the extent that we, as community members, feel connected to those around us.[14] Block's ideas on community are applicable to service-learning collaborations in that they provide relevance for conceptualizing the service-learning experience itself as an exercise in community-building. Well-designed, equitable, community-engaged learning can foster social capital, which in turn can strengthen community cohesion.[15] Furthermore, service-learning is intrinsically about relationships, and faculty, community partners, and administrators can promote service-learning as part of a broader relationship between the community and the university.[16] Thus, service-learning provides an opportunity for students to invest in their capacity as academics, professionals, and citizens.

Case Study: Little Cities of Black Diamonds Day and the Sociology of Appalachia

Rachel Terman: I teach Sociology of Appalachia. I usually have a mix of students with some background in sociology as well as students with very little or no background in sociology from a variety of majors including journalism, media and communications, psychology, social work, child and family studies, economics, political science, and history. During the first week of class I collect information about where each student grew up, and I consistently find that almost all of my students are from Ohio, and usually about 85 percent of the class grew up outside Appalachia, with most clustering around the Cincinnati, Cleveland, and Columbus metro areas. Moreover, the vast majority of all my students have very little knowledge about Appalachia coming into the class.

One of the challenges I face each semester teaching this class is described well by Emily Satterwhite in her chapter "Navigating Myths of Appalachian Exceptionalism."[17] Satterwhite explains the process of getting students to critically think about both negative stereotypes and romantic notions about Appalachia that they have entering the class. Similarly, I also look for ways to navigate the false dichotomy of wealth and poverty. It can be easy for students, faculty, administrators, staff, and community members to assume that programs related to Appalachia under the banner of the Wealth & Poverty Theme are relevant only to poverty, not wealth. Thus, in order to meet the learning objective of critical thinking, I need to design the content in the course to disrupt our common assumptions and definitions about Appalachia, wealth, and poverty. One of the best ways I've found to achieve this objective is through the service-learning component of the course. After four years of collaboration with the LCBD, this component has developed from students presenting posters at the annual LCBD Community Day (see Figure 3.3) to giving short talks on the theme of the day, to administering an evaluation of the day and presenting the results to the LCBD Council. Using the scaffolding built by the ongoing university–community partnership, I have been able to add onto it with my students and additional support from the Appalachian Teaching Project grants sponsored by the

Figure 3.3. A student talks with a community member at the 2016 Little Cities Day where the theme was "Temperance and Taverns." Students got into the "spirit" of the day by dressing up in prohibition-era clothing and talking about their research with community members on topics ranging from the economic history of moonshine to current economic diversification and tourism strategies related to local beer, wine, and spirits. (Photo credit: Rachel Terman.)

Appalachian Regional Commission (ARC) and East Tennessee State University, which allow students to deepen their engagement with the project, develop their professional skills and knowledge of the ARC, and connect with other engaged students and faculty across the region.

I consider my students' work with the LCBD to be an overall success so far based in part on the students' and community feedback and in part on our ability to meet the service and learning objectives. For example, one student described their experience with the project this way:

> There have been very few times during my 5 years at OHIO where I have been given the opportunity to share what I learned in the classroom with the community. Not only did my research further my understanding of the economic climate of Appalachia over the years, but I was able to apply it to a community event and connect other citizens of Appalachia to their history and culture as well. The project was very time consuming, [but] the hands-on work, time spent teaching others, and benefit to the community in Shawnee certainly outweighed any negatives.

As the above example affirms, students are able to reach the academic, professionalization, and citizenship objectives of the project, and we come close to meeting all twelve of the service objective attributes outlined earlier by our community partner, the LCBD Council. Indeed, the community has invited us to return every year, former students have gone on to become integral members of the LCBD Council, and we are in the midst of carrying out participatory action research in collaboration with a community in Scioto County, Ohio, and Ohio State University. Although we have yet to scientifically measure the numbers of students who stay involved in the community after participating in curricular and cocurricular university–community programs, community engagement research suggests that these programs provide a fertile environment for continued civic engagement post-college.[18] Still, we continue to view this aspect of the course as a work in progress as we discuss in the section below.

Work in Progress: Reinforcing the Scaffold

As we celebrate our success, there are still several areas of our collaboration we consider to be works in progress. Part of the long-term nature of our university–community collaboration means that we are revising our programs on an ongoing basis. One example is our work to find ways to collaborate via a regional "experience economy" development project underway in nine southeastern Ohio counties, branded as *The Winding Road: Ohio's Rising Appalachia.* This initiative involves the creation of a network of experience entrepreneurs such as adventure guides, local food purveyors, historians, artists, outdoor recreation producers, and tourism-related businesses joining with institutional partners such as the Wayne National Forest, Ohio University, and an array of nonprofits. Although the Winding Road Network's partnership with OHIO is just getting underway, an investment from OHIO's Sugar Bush Foundation is encouraging OHIO leaders to take on a significant role in advancing the goals of the Winding Road through field-based study and service at OHIO as content for tours, programs, and other experiences. Southeastern Ohio's diverse ecology, forests, local foods movement, and rich history all provide experiences that can shape the local economy and enhance the Winding Road brand. As this example illustrates, these community–university collaborations are an opportunity to develop additional wealth based on the assets of our region.

As we continue to work on these developments, we realize one of the barriers to the long-term nature of our collaboration is the transience of those involved. As Jacoby (2015) points out, one of the drawbacks of community-based research is the structure of the university timeframe, which means that work often needs to happen within the confines of the semester.[19] Students will certainly move on after one, maybe two classes, although there are examples of students who then become more involved in the community as a result of these experiences, as we noted earlier. Faculty can also be inconsistently available given the transitory nature of the academic job market as well as the semester time frame, tenure, and sabbatical systems.

Administrators also tend not to stay in their positions over an entire career. For all these reasons, support, enthusiasm, and human capital can ebb and flow on the university side of the collaboration.

Likewise, community members may be transient, although this has not been true in our case. Community members can also experience university burnout after poorly planned or unsupported collaborations, which may lead to attrition. The capacity of community partners to host students and faculty varies greatly, particularly in rural, underdeveloped areas. The availability of a pool of resources from the university is critical to success in the majority of instances where the community partner may be a great fit for service-learning but lacks resources to advance a meaningful experience. These needs range from student transportation, food, and lodging to equipment for carrying out mutually beneficial projects. Issues of supervision and safety concerns also must be taken into account.

Finally, while we acknowledged earlier the sources of institutional support that have helped us succeed, there are also ways in which the informal nature of the university–community collaboration can create exclusive and inequitable conditions. First, the creation of the partnership and consistency required for maintaining it can leave out individuals and organizations. Not all community organizations have a bridge builder with an ongoing capacity to work with the university. Second, the work required to maintain the collaboration is not always adequately recognized or compensated. This issue manifests in different ways for those in the community and those in the university. For example, community members involved in service-learning may take on the role of a coteacher for a portion of the semester. Yet they are expected to provide this labor voluntarily in exchange for the service performed by the students while the professor is likely earning a substantial salary for her part in teaching the course. The question of fair exchange of labor, service, and compensation is an ongoing one as service-learning troubles institutional boundaries of the university as distinct from the community and vice versa. The tensions created by these boundaries may impact the longevity of the university–community collaboration. For those in the university, the development of service-learning as a legitimate pedagogy and practice is also a crucial and needed institutional support for long-term university–community partnerships. For faculty to be able to incorporate community collaborations into their courses, there must be acknowledgement and support for service-learning and other engagement pedagogies at the department, college, and university levels. For tenure-track and other long-term contract faculty, this means university–community work, which often demands extra hours and commitments outside of the workday, should be rewarded as part of the teaching, research, and service portions of the faculty member's job assignments. As Jacoby (2015) points out,

> Until institutions value engaged teaching and scholarship, many junior faculty members on the tenure track . . . will continue to find that their mentors strongly advise them not to become involved in service-learning

or community-engaged scholarship until they have achieved tenure. Particularly in such environments, junior faculty are discouraged from service-learning teaching because it is more time-consuming than "regular" teaching and may take precious time away from research.[20]

For graduate students, adjunct instructors, and other faculty in more precarious positions, community–university collaborations might be difficult to incorporate at all given the lack of support for these instructors and long-term investments.

Conclusion

As we've considered our community–university collaborative success as well as the work ahead, we again return to the theme of wealth and poverty. In a broad sense, the work we do through our community–university collaboration is in response to existing inequalities based on class, place, race, and ethnicity. As we seek to teach our students about these disparities in our region and, moreover, to do something about them, we also need to be aware of how our work might reinforce inequalities. Returning to our question, what can this place give our students, and, in return, what can our students and institution give this place? We know that the Little Cities of Black Diamonds here in Southeast Ohio offers a special opportunity for students to learn about numerous topics, including labor and industrial history, inequality, community, and sustainability, while also practicing valuable job skills. In return, Ohio University helps support community sustainability efforts through continued investment in student engagement.

However, as we seek to support sustainability by reducing inequalities, we know that our current form of community–university collaboration is not enough to achieve this goal. In a community with assets and needs, how are assets distributed? Who is responsible for addressing the needs? And how is the labor involved compensated? As an institution, we struggle to give this place financial support. This imbalance of monetary resources has implications for the sustainability of the collaboration and can reinforce the existing tensions linked to wealth and poverty in our region. In terms of sustainability, these facets of the community–university collaboration are just as vital as the structures and resources outlined above that have given us success so far.

Throughout this chapter, we discuss our finding that, given our work and experience in the context of our region and existing knowledge, collaborative sustainability depends on "scaffolding" through engagement, institutional support, and community–university networks. Our work and experience also lead us to acknowledge the challenges of long-term and continuous support for these collaborations, which can be affected by underdeveloped engagement, transience, lack of critical reflection practice, community capacity, and basic structural support including changes in administration and formal systems of valuing university–community collaboration. We see these factors as challenges that can be overcome or mitigated when acknowledged and confronted—as collaborators. Collaborations between communities and universities are crucial to the success of service-learning endeavors, but they are more than a means to educate college students. Partnerships that are democratic, equitable, and mutually beneficial can bolster community development, nourish citizen education, and support citizen action. Keeping these ideals in mind, we use service-learning as a means for connecting faculty and students to Appalachian places for research and teaching beyond the classroom, working toward the ultimate goal of sharing wealth and assets and reducing inequality in our communities.

Notes

1. "Focus on Ohio," Ohio University, 2018. https://www.ohio.edu/focus/ (accessed October 16, 2018).

2. "U.S. President Lyndon B. Johnson Visits Ohio University, Film, May 7, 1964," Ohio University Archives, https://media.library.ohio.edu/digital/collection/archives/id/40947 (accessed October 16, 2018).

3. Betty Hollow, *Ohio University: The Spirit of a Singular Place: 1804–2004* (Athens, OH: Ohio University Press, 2003), 188–189.

4. Hollow, *Ohio University*, 188–189.

5. Ronald D Eller, *Uneven Ground: Appalachia Since 1945* (Kentucky: The University Press of Kentucky, 2013).

6. "Maps," Appalachian Regional Commission, https://www.arc.gov/research/Mapsof Appalachia.asp (accessed October 16, 2018).

7. "Diana Marvel, Rachel Terman, and John Winnenberg, "Unmaking the Poverty Tour" (Presented at the 2017 Midwest Campus Compact Conference, Chicago, IL, June 6, 2017).

8. Marvel, Terman, and Winnenberg, "Unmaking the Poverty Tour."

9. Andrew Furco, *Introduction to Service-Learning Toolkit: Reading and Resources for Faculty* (Providence: Campus Compact, 2003), 9–13.

10. "Mission & Vision," Ohio University College of Arts & Sciences. https://www.ohio.edu /cas/about/vision/index.cfm (accessed October 16, 2018).

11. John Dewey, *The Public and Its Problems* (Swallow Press: Ohio University Press, 1954), 208.

12. Myles Horton and Paulo Freire, *We Make the Road by Walking: Conversations on Education and Social Change* (Philadelphia: Temple University Press, 1990), 145.

13. John Saltmarsh and Edward Zlotkowski, *Higher Education and Democracy: Essays on Service-Learning and Civic Engagement* (Philadelphia, Temple University Press, 2001).

14. Peter Block, *Community: The Structure of Belonging* (San Francisco, CA, Berrett-Koehler, 2008), 5.

15. Steven A. Henness, Anna L. Ball, and MaryJo Moncheski. "A Community Development Approach to Service-Learning: Building Social Capital Between Rural Youth and Adults," *New Directions for Youth Development* 138 (2013): 75–95.

16. Sandra Enos and Keith Morton, "Developing a Theory and Practice of Campus-Community Partnerships, in *Building Partnerships for Service-Learning*, eds. Barbara Jacoby & Associates (San Francisco, CA: Jossey-Bass, 2003) 20–41.

17. Emily Satterwhite, "Intro to Appalachian Studies: Navigating Myths of Appalachian Exceptionalism," in *Appalachia in the Classroom: Teaching the Region*, eds. Theresa L. Burriss and Patricia M. Gantt (Athens, OH: Ohio University Press, 2003), 3–32.

18. Dan Richard, Cheryl Keen, Julie A. Hatcher, and Heather A. Pease, "Pathways to Adult Civic Engagement: Benefits of Reflection and Dialogue Across Difference in Higher Education Service-learning Programs," *Michigan Journal of Community Service Learning* 23, no. 1 (2016): 60–74.

19. Barbara Jacoby, *Service-Learning Essentials* (San Francisco: Josey-Bass, 2015), 263.

20. Jacoby, *Service-Learning Essentials,* 263.

4

Collaborating for Conservation

Monitoring the hemlock woolly adelgid in the Allegheny National Forest

Jonathan Heck, Sarah Johnson, Bethany Kier, and Denise A. Piechnik[*]

Introduction

The eastern hemlock (*Tsuga canadensis*), found in forests across the eastern United States and in abundance in northern Appalachia, is an ecologically and socially important keystone species. The eastern hemlock provides food and shelter for many game species, as well as a habitat for wildlife such as birds, insects, and spiders. Humans rely on the eastern hemlock to perform many ecosystem services, such as regulating stream flow, water volume and temperature, forest decomposition rates, and air quality, as well as preventing forest soil erosion, particularly in sensitive riparian zones. However, the recently introduced insect pest known as the hemlock woolly adelgid (HWA; *Adelges tsugae*) attacks the eastern hemlock trees, changing the biodiversity of Appalachia's forests.

This chapter examines a three-year project partnership (2014–2016) between the University of Pittsburgh at Bradford (UPB) and the Nature Conservancy (TNC) to provide HWA monitoring in a high-impact area: the Allegheny National Forest (ANF), one of the nation's largest federal forests east of the Mississippi River. UPB students were trained and formed into monitoring teams that contributed important new data to a larger monitoring effort. UPB faculty integrated monitoring into biology course curricula and student retreats organized by UPB's Environmental Studies program. Training and data collection were implemented in relevant biology courses and through student–faculty retreats to the forest led by UPB's Environmental Studies program. We learned that student-led monitoring activities and leadership skills, developed through such initiatives, are effective training opportunities for citizen scientists and are important for supporting broader conservation efforts in the future.[1] More broadly, this chapter takes stock of how "student-citizen science" fits within the paradigm of citizen science, which has become a widely used strategy for public participation, data collection in conservation, and preservation efforts of nonprofit agencies and other entities.[2] This project demonstrated key advantages in applying a citizen science model that is specific to the university setting, including teaching student motivation and development of students' skillsets and responsibility, while also addressing problems faced by the local community. By contrast, the constraints of any citizen science project also apply to the student population as citizen scientists, including the necessity of infrastructure, personnel capacity, funding, and use of established protocols and ensuring data quality.[3] Constraints for this citizen science project were small and manageable, but the project yielded high rewards for all stakeholders—students, faculty, NGOs, and the local community.

The Eastern Hemlock, Invasive Species, and Threats to Biodiversity

Like the famous chestnut blight of the twentieth century, HWA is changing Appalachia's forests. HWA attacks and kills eastern hemlock, and it is found in 90 percent of the eastern hemlock's range across the eastern United States.[4] When invasive species kill their host plant, the effect creates changes that ripple through the fabric of our local ecosystems and economies. Eastern hemlock is a foundation species and plays an important role in local ecosystems by way of its long lifespan, high level of shade tolerance, and its distinctive physiology that creates rather unique leaf and tissue chemistry.[5] Hemlock tends to form dense stands, especially in sensitive areas near streams (riparian zones). In areas where HWA has caused significant mortality in hemlock-dominated stands, water quality has suffered, erosion has increased, and stream flows have been altered. Climate change has exacerbated these problems.[6] Recreational use has declined in the once magnificent old-growth hemlock forests, causing associated local economic impacts. Eastern hemlock is not only foundational ecologically but also socially and economically in many areas of Appalachia.[5] McKean County, home to UPB and a large portion of the ANF, and neighboring Potter and Elk counties have the highest wood market value of any Appalachian county. Moreover, an Appalachian Regional Commission study of the social and economic impacts of Appalachian forests found that Pennsylvania communities placed higher cultural value on their forests compared to communities of most other Appalachian states.[4] The HWA attack on this foundation species that is highly relevant to humans and ecosystems alike underscores the importance of hemlock conservation efforts from ecological, economic, and cultural perspectives.

Natural systems create the economic, social, and recreational backdrop for Appalachian communities. Appalachia boasts some of the most biologically diverse ecoregions of North America.[7] We devote little thought to our daily dependence on species like the eastern hemlock, or to the value of species diversity and the ecosystem services that they provide. However, invasive species have the ability to alter the biodiversity of Appalachian ecosystems in dramatic ways, thereby negatively impacting the human populations that rely on these ecosystems.[8] HWA in particular has caused severe mortality to eastern (and Carolina) hemlock populations in many areas, especially southern

Appalachia. Many communities in these areas are economically dependent on outdoor recreation opportunities and provision their economies with forest-related livelihoods, and sometimes multiple types of natural resources.[9] Although hemlock is no longer considered a timber species in many areas of Appalachia, it is a crucial component of healthy, functioning forest ecosystems.[5] Healthy, functional, and resilient forest ecosystems are a sustainable source of timber and other forest products that many communities in rural Appalachia depend on. Other forest commodities include nontimber forest products (NTFPs), which are experiencing a resurgence in Appalachia, in production, harvest, and usage among local populations.[10] Hemlock-dominated forests are found in rich, calcareous sites that are key habitats for NTFPs like black cohosh, ramps (wild leeks), various types of edible fungi, and ginseng. Dieback of the overstory hemlocks due to HWA will threaten the protective shading and change the particular soil chemistry, such that opportunistic competitors, such as nonnative herbaceous and shrub species, may outcompete these NTFP species.[11]

The hemlock woolly adelgid was introduced to the United States in the 1950s on infested nursery stock from Japan.[4] Many other nonnative invasive species have been unwittingly introduced by the horticultural plant trade, and even more enter the United States in solid wood packaging material (SWPM) transported with goods shipped on a global scale.[12] As an aside, SWPM was the most likely introduction method for emerald ash borer, Asian longhorned beetle, and other invasive pests. The reality of a global economy lends convenient transport for insects, fungi, and plant diseases, which travel along with the goods that people demand. The federal government and port-of-entry border security lack the resources to inspect for pests or other threats in every shipment container, trade item, piece of packaging, and transport vessel. Though the vast majority of introduced species do not become invasive, many do regularly arrive to this country in packaging material or by other means.[13] However, a potentially large impact on native species and ecosystems occur when a species is moved at the appropriate time, in the appropriate life stage, on the appropriate material, and spreads from the point of introduction to an acceptable host or habitat. Once HWA infests a hemlock, it dies in only four to eight years. Thirty years after the HWA introduction, we see evidence of the HWA becoming established and killing hemlock trees by the thousands.[14,15]

Eastern hemlock was once a larger component of many eastern forests, and in the 1800s hemlock was a highly valuable resource to the tanbark industry for its high tannin content in its tissues.[14] A large number of hemlock were harvested for their bark, and hemlock wood was turned into rail ties, mine shaft beams, and home and barn construction materials, or simply left in the woods in favor of the more valuable bark.[14] Hemlock tannins were extracted from the bark and used for tanning hides to make leather, a very important material for clothing, furniture, and other goods.[14] Though hemlock forests regrew, its high tolerance to shade resulted in many dense stands without much overstory diversity.[16] Therefore, hemlock is less common on the landscape today compared to other tree species, but there are many dense stands without other overstory species. Hemlock lost its value to the tanbark industry, and the wood is not as economically valued as much as the wood of other, more common species. Many landowners do not manage hemlock stands at all, because it is often located in hard-to-access areas, like those with difficult topography or sensitive moist/hydric habitats. Hemlock regeneration after harvest is minimal in some cases, such as during an outbreak of hemlock native pests, but on most federal and state-owned lands in Pennsylvania, all hemlocks are retained in harvest operations. Though hemlocks are managed to promote the species in Pennsylvania, populations are declining throughout its range due to native pest outbreaks, effects of climate change, and invasive insect pests such as the HWA.[17]

Native to Japan, the HWA was introduced on infested nursery stock in 1951, near Richmond, Virginia.[4] The HWA can affect large tracts of hemlock forestland and can disperse across great distances by many vectors. Adelgid crawlers and eggs can be transported to new locations on human clothing, vehicles, animals, and the wind.[15] Treatments to control the invasive HWA include chemical pesticides and biological control agents (predators), but such treatments are difficult to implement, monitor, and manage at such a large scale as a forest.[18] Biological control predators, such as *Laricobius osakensis* and *Laricobius nigrinus* (beetles). have shown promise; however, decades may be required to establish a self-sustaining population.[18] The HWA itself spreads at the rate of seventy-five meters per year on average; however, colder temperatures can slow the invasion front of this species.[18]

Case Study

As Pennsylvania's state tree, the eastern hemlock can occur in considerable densities, especially in northwest Pennsylvania forests. Compared to many areas of the state and the eastern United States, the forests of northwestern Pennsylvania are relatively intact. Though hemlock was once a much larger component of the High Allegheny Unglaciated Plateau sub-ecoregion, consisting of 40 percent of the basal area in what is now the ANF, hemlock is still found in dense, connected stands across landforms, and is a prevalent species in higher-gradient or steep riparian corridors across the plateau.[19] As the threat of HWA infestation grew, some federal assistance was available for treating infected hemlock trees. Concerned citizens were the main driving force of the federal funding provided to the Nature Conservancy (TNC) to develop a plan. Identifying and targeting important hemlock areas that require assistance of federal resources to treat hemlocks for HWA infection was TNC's plan. A cooperative agreement between TNC and the United States Forest Service initiated and managed coordination and cooperation of landowners, nonprofit recreational and outdoor groups, and academic institutions.

Subsequently, a UPB–TNC partnership emerged from a networking interaction at the August 2013 HWA Stakeholder Meeting on UPB's campus organized by the TNC's S. Johnson. This meeting brought stakeholders, such as landowners, together to share data on local hemlock stands and recent observations of the invasive HWA. From this opportunistic networking interaction, a training workshop on HWA monitoring was hosted by UPB to benefit the campus and the surrounding communities in the Allegheny National Forest (ANF). UPB is ideally located near the Marilla Reservoir, which is a very high-priority hemlock conservation area. This chance proximity and easy site access by way of a nearby popular hiking destination created the opportunity to introduce a high-profile, local conservation issue to students and to start a long-term monitoring collaboration. TNC gained an additional data source and annual monitoring in a high-priority conservation area, while students gained training in monitoring, and data collection in a high-priority location.

UPB Biology faculty and students were excited about joining the existing collaborative effort between TNC and the US Forest Service (ANF). UPB is conveniently located in the heart of the eastern hemlock's range, and the campus is near highly accessible legacy stands of hemlock. As a member of the Tree Campus USA program that promotes recognition of communities with diverse tree species, UPB aims to engage the entire campus and surrounding community in its promotion of regional biodiversity. Cultivating a community of concerned learners, UPB promotes and supports its student body to be very service-oriented. As a result, UPB students were both motivated and enthusiastic about monitoring for HWA, and they quickly adopted the collaborative spirit by monitoring the nearby hemlocks in the Marilla Reservoir area. Student enthusiasm was charged by the training process in invasive species monitoring, and contributing to research efforts relevant to a real-world problem that they may not have otherwise known about. In short, the project provided a connection to place, in a way that students could relate to.

Beginning in 2014, UPB students and faculty anticipated the arrival of the HWA, and started searching for the pest locally. Armed with GPS units and binoculars, UPB students mapped, monitored, and reported on eastern hemlocks, and HWA presence and absence to regional NGOs (e.g., the Nature Conservancy) and federal agencies (e.g., USDA-US Forest Service; Figure 4.1). Monitoring the HWA invasive pest has also connected students to the places and the habitats that the eastern hemlock created.

The applied learning of HWA monitoring overlapped well with the UPB Biology curricula. UPB offers a Conservation and Population Biology course that covers a broad background of conversation issues and monitoring techniques, making it well suited for invasive species monitoring. This monitoring project presented an opportunity for students to increase the depth of their understanding of complex biological interactions, such as the effects of species invasions on ecosystems and societies. The project met the course goals of teaching monitoring techniques, how to conduct accurate measurements in the field, understanding the importance of invasive species, and how to use GIS as an ecological tool to marry location or place information to a species and its biological information. Additional biology and environmental studies/sciences courses designed for the junior or senior levels were also identified as suitable for the type of field research that HWA monitoring entailed.

There were key traits to our approach that promoted successes in this citizen science project. Adopting a monitoring system that could be taught in a way to ensure

Figure 4.1. *UPB Back Hike,* Black and White, Digital Photography, 2020. (Photo by Anna K. Lemnitzer.)

a consistent method of data collection. Fortunately, a validated sampling protocol was already available and accessible to all levels of undergraduates in ecology, environmental studies, and forestry to participate in the search for HWA.[20] Small student groups collected data during a single lab class by carpooling to the Marilla Reservoir to collect data. Following data collection, faculty (Piechnik) pooled the student data and verified its content and accuracy prior to analysis by the students. In the next few lab periods, students analyzed the verified GIS data that they collected, with the goal of producing a map. Students appreciated the opportunity to both use and build skills in ArcGIS, the most commonly used subscription software for geographic information systems. Students from the 2014 and 2016 Conservation Biology course at UPB collected data for more than 200 hemlocks found in the Marilla Reservoir watershed.

More broadly, this multiday project encouraged students to exhibit individual responsibility to collect accurate information, and to work collaboratively on the overall project goals. For example, students divided up the report goals into isolated tasks, then worked on each task independently. After three lab periods, students produced monitoring reports for the USFS that summarized their findings on the presence or absence of HWA. Students produced a collaborative report on the findings and voted on the best student-made map to include in the report.

With a finished product, the students packaged up the GIS data files of hemlock coordinates. They shared presence-absence data with the US Forest Service, and with regionally active NGOs interested in the project. Local monitoring for HWA gave students an opportunity to "do" an ecology study from start to finish, while contributing valuable and timely data that tracked the invasion front of the HWA. Monitoring eastern hemlock for HWA developed a connection between the students and the surrounding community entities, reinforced their attitudes of protecting and sustaining natural ecosystems, and increased their awareness of ecological threats and environmental problems that scientists and managers must confront.

CHALLENGES AND OPPORTUNITIES POSED BY CONNECTING STUDENTS TO PLACE THROUGH MONITORING

The HWA monitoring project undoubtedly connected UPB students and faculty to place, particularly that of the rich ecological diversity of northwestern Pennsylvania. Though surrounded by the forest, monitoring—or careful observation—of hemlock stands invited an even greater awareness and understanding of the natural assets that define an ecosystem. The monitoring process introduced students to the importance of riparian areas to hemlock associated plant and animal species. Though TNC and the US Forest Service did not interact with UPB students for any substantial amount of time, the training techniques and technical GIS support were communicated during a single workshop, jointly led by TNC and the USFS. Most of the remaining communication between the university and its collaborators were carried out by UPB faculty via email. The hemlock monitoring project did not encounter many unforeseen problems, in part due to good communication as the project progressed, the access to established monitoring and data checking protocols, and a focused set of objectives within a narrow project scope, all of which fit the ability and availability of students. Nor did it have any unmet project goals.

Working with students trained in careful monitoring techniques expanded the scope of project goals and objectives. Collaborating with students encouraged and further engaged these learners to develop a deeper interest in the impacts of invasive species. These student leaders increased their engagement by leading and training other students in the HWA monitoring process. There are many challenges to working in effective partnerships. Of the utmost importance is ensuring both the quality and accuracy of the HWA presence and absence data. This quality control was essential to this collaborative forest conservation research whose primary focus was to monitor the eastern hemlock and HWA. However, depending on the individual skills of each volunteer, many times when engaging citizen scientists, the need to limit data requests and the amount of data collected is key to continuing a higher level of interest and involvement.[21]

Working with universities offers a wonderful opportunity for students and conservation partners to offer and provide meaningful experiences to students, and to obtain more data. Indeed, this is one way to increase community engagement in nonprofit and conservation group efforts, as this type of collaboration offers the expertise of faculty specialists and university resources in the training of students to become citizen scientists. Interinstitutional collaborations, like between NGOs and universities, can leverage the limited staff and resources to address a pressing problem with a native ecosystem, such as the problem posed by a nonnative species invading native habitats. Such collaborative projects are more likely to succeed when caution and oversight are applied while training students to collect and interpret data.[22]

Broader Lessons

Acknowledging the project limitations of connecting students directly to UPB's partner institutions, the hemlock monitoring project nonetheless facilitated deeper connections between faculty, TNC, and the US Forest Service. This was a common thread of value observed in the university–community–agency partnership. An important lesson gained was that collaborations can both share common goals and provide opportunities specific to each partner. Project success for the different entities were measured in different ways. The TNC gained reliable data on important hemlock locations in an area that might not otherwise receive attention by other monitoring entities due to lack of resources.

Continuing student involvement was an important marker of success for this project. Several students involved in the project continued with invasive species work in one way or another. Twelve students expressed further interest in learning more about invasive species identification and other skill-building opportunities, in addition to those gained during the monitoring effort. Some students signed up for GIS courses offered at UPB. Other students opted to do their senior capstone research project on the HWA or the ecological and economic ramifications of invasive species. From the perspective of UPB, our students had yet another opportunity to conduct out-of-classroom learning, receive skill-building training, and get involved in a project that had a scope much greater in magnitude than the UPB campus and the regional forest. Thus, the types of continued student interest and involvement beyond the defined project timeline also indicates that students were making broader connections, linking biological phenomena to economics, leadership, and community capacity.

Involvement by other stakeholders fortified the success of the project. TNC relied on project participants to assist with data collection and transmission, while the USFS provided expertise on forest-related conditions and management practices. Though each entity had a unique set of responsibilities, each played a role in increasing the acquisition of more data on ANF hemlocks and the presence of HWA.

The desired goals and outcomes of each partner and project responsibilities between UPB faculty and TNC were asymmetrical, as UPB's data contribution was one of several TNC data collection efforts. TNC needed reliable and usable data, so it was imperative that communication was open and clear about project and data collection parameters. An open dialogue between UPB faculty and TNC ensured there was little misunderstanding in our approach and prioritized areas for data collection, and how to implement the monitoring protocol. TNC identified potentially supportive assets through advertising, training seminars, and by recruiting different community groups to survey and monitor priority hemlock areas. Many participants were recruited by word-of-mouth connections within Pennsylvania's conservation community. Of large importance was identifying collaborators who were "go-getter" citizens motivated to both monitor and help with organizing monitoring efforts. A valuable element of leadership development also emerged from the project. Students active in UPB's Environmental Studies Club were interested in this project for the opportunity to gain hands-on experience with monitoring an invasive species. Faculty (Piechnik) trained the club officers (Kier and Heck) on how to perform monitoring techniques. In turn, the officers then planned and organized monitoring workshops at Environmental Studies Club retreats. They produced "cheat sheets" on the tell-tale signs of HWA presence on a hemlock tree for the students who lacked experience in entomology and spotting insects. Student-led monitoring opportunities were set up for retreat attendees to engage in field monitoring exercises, allowing attendees to gain valuable insights on methods used to identify the HWA. Students also gained background knowledge on why hemlock trees are important as an ecological and economic asset. As one student leader reflected, "Leading the trip was an important first step in bringing the community together to monitor HWA, and made it obvious that future leaders are necessary in order to drive community action towards monitoring invasive species." Additional feedback from students took the form of an informal discussion between Conservation Biology students and Environmental Studies Retreat student attendees. Students valued the opportunity to get any experience that they perceived as "hands-on experience." They were incredibly enthusiastic and energetic about monitoring an invasive species, which placed them in roles of responsibility and leadership within a larger conservation effort.

Conclusion

For Appalachian communities to respond to ecological changes, such as those resulting from invasive species, we offer a model of engagement that brings together university expertise, nonprofit activism, and organization to train students to do necessary yet labor-intensive monitoring and data collection. Students, in turn, transformed their strong desire for hands-on learning into tangible data collection and leadership skills, which increased their confidence in their abilities and hope for the future.

In this time of unprecedented human population growth, our commerce and mobility are bringing impactful ecological change to our natural ecosystems by the introduction of invasive species. Scientists researching disturbances of natural systems, such as the HWA attacking eastern hemlock, greatly benefit from the additional data collection from reliable, citizen-based sources, as demonstrated from this case. Developing multi-entity collaborations (i.e., university—governmental agency—nongovernmental organization) to promote data collection on an applied problem also enhances students' understanding and sense of place and agency.

Including students in investigating conservation-based problems, like invasive species monitoring, provides a unique and valuable opportunity to understand the depth of problems caused by invasive species. By empowering students to be part of the investigative process of solving an environmental issue, students are more likely to engage in future science and citizen-science activities.[22]

Notes

* Authorship determined alphabetically.

1. Rick Bonney, Caren B. Cooper, Janis Dickinson, Steve Kelling, Tina Phillips, Kenneth V. Rosenberg, and Jennifer Shirk, "Citizen Science: A Developing Tool for Expanding Science Knowledge and Scientific Literacy," *BioScience* 59, no. 11 (2009): 977–984.

2. Heidi L. Ballard, Lucy D. Robinson, Alison N. Young, Gregory B. Pauly, Lila M. Higgins, Rebecca F. Johnson, and John C. Tweddle, "Contributions to Conservation Outcomes by Natural History Museum-Led Citizen Science: Examining Evidence and Next Steps," *Biological Conservation* 208 (2017): 87–97.

3. S. Haklay, M. Hecker, A. Bowser, Z. Makuch, J. Vogel, and A. Bonn, *Citizen Science: Innovation in Open Science, Society and Policy* (London: UCL Press, 2018).

4. Carol Cheah, Michael E. Montgomery, Scott Salom, Bruce L. Parker, Scott Costa, and Margaret Skinner, *Biological Control of Hemlock Woolly Adelgid* (Forest Health Technology Enterprise Team, 2004).

5. Aaron M. Ellison, Michael S. Bank, Barton D. Clinton, Elizabeth A. Colburn, Katherine Elliott, Chelcy R. Ford, David R. Foster, Brian D. Kloeppel, Jennifer D. Knoepp, Gary M. Lovett, Jacqueline Mohan, David A. Orwig, Nicholas L. Rodenhouse, William V. Sobczak, Kristina A. Stinson, Jeffrey K. Stone, Christopher M. Swan, Jill Thompson, Betsy Von Holle, Jackson R. Webster, "Loss of Foundation Species: Consequences for the Structure and Dynamics of Forested Ecosystems," *Frontiers in Ecology and the Environment* 3, no. 9 (2005): 479–486.

6. Mikko Kuussaari, Riccardo Bommarco, Risto K. Heikkinen, Aveliina Helm, Jochen Krauss, Regina Lindborg, Erik Öckinger, Meelis Pärtel, Joan Pino, Ferran Rodà, Constantí Stefanescu, Tiit Teder, Martin Zobel, Ingolf Steffan-Dewenter, "Extinction Debt: A Challenge for Biodiversity Conservation," *Trends in Ecology and Evolution* 24, no. 10 (2009): 564–471. https://doi.org/10.1016/j.tree.2009.04.011.

7. Craig R. Groves, Deborah B. Jensen, Laura L. Valutis, Kent H. Redford, Mark L. Shaffer, J. Michael Scott, Jeffrey V. Baumgartner, Jonathan V. Higgins, Michael W. Beck, and Mark G. Anderson, "Planning for Biodiversity Conservation: Putting Conservation Science into Practice," *BioScience* 52, no. 6 (2002): 499–512.

8. Xiaoshu Li, Evan L. Preisser, Kevin J. Boyle, Thomas P. Holmes, Andrew Liebhold, and David Orwig, "Potential Social and Economic Impacts of the Hemlock Woolly Adelgid in Southern New England," *Southeastern Naturalist* 13, no. 6 (2014): 130–146.

9. Thomas P. Holmes, Juliann E. Aukema, Betsy Von Holle, Andrew Liebhold, and Erin Sills, "Economic Impacts of Invasive Species in Forests: Past, Present, and Future," *Annals of the New York Academy of Sciences* 1162 (2009): 18–38.

10. Rebecca J. McLain and Eric T. Jones, *Nontimber Forest Products Management on National Forests in the United States* (Portland, OR: U.S. Dept. of Agriculture, Forest Service, Pacific Northwest Research Station, 2005).

11. James L. Chamberlain, *Assessment of Nontimber Forest Products in the United States under Changing Conditions* (U.S. Government Printing Office, 2018).

12. W. Keith Moser, Edward L. Barnard, Ronald F. Billings, Susan J. Crocker, Mary Ellen Dix, Andrew N. Gray, George G. Ice, Mee-Sook Kim, Richard Reid, Sue U. Rodman, William H. McWilliams, "Impacts of Nonnative Invasive Species on US Forests and Recommendations for Policy and Management," *Journal of Forestry* 107, no. 6 (2009): 320–327.

13. Timothy T. Work, Deborah G. McCullough, Joseph F. Cavey, and Ronald Komsa, "Arrival Rate of Nonindigenous Insect Species into the United States through Foreign Trade," *Biological Invasions* 7, no. 2 (2005): 323–332.

14. Ashbel Hough, *Silvical Characteristics of Eastern Hemlock (Tsuga Canadensis)* (U.S. Government, 1960).

15. Katherine J. Elliott and James M. Vose, "The Contribution of the Coweeta Hydrologic Laboratory to Developing an Understanding of Long-Term (1934–2008) Changes in Managed and Unmanaged Forests," *Forest Ecology and Management* 261, no. 5 (2011): 900–910.

16. Marc D. Abrams and David A. Orwig, "A 300-Year History of Disturbance and Canopy Recruitment for Co-Occurring White Pine and Hemlock on the Allegheny Plateau, USA," *The Journal of Ecology* 84, no. 3 (1996): 353.

17. Robert T. Brooks, "Early Regeneration Following the Presalvage Cutting of Hemlock from Hemlock-Dominated Stands," *Northern Journal of Applied Forestry* 21, no. 1 (2004): 12–18.

18. Bradley Onken and Richard C. Reardon, *Implementation and Status of Biological Control of the Hemlock Woolly Adelgid* (U.S. Government Printing Office, 2011).

19. H.J. Lutz, "Original Forest Composition in Northwestern Pennsylvania as Indicated by Early Land Survey Notes," *Journal of Forestry* 28, no. 8 (1930): 1098–1103.

20. Scott Costa and Bradley Onken, *Standardizing Sampling for Detection and Monitoring of Hemlock Woolly Adelgid in Eastern Hemlock Forests* (U.S. Government Printing Office, 2006).

21. Marianne E. Krassny and Rick Bonney, "Environmental Education through Citizen Science and Participatory Action Research," in *Environmental Education and Advocacy*, eds. Edward A. Johnson, Michael J. Mappin (Cambridge: Cambridge University Press, 2005), 292–302.

22. Heidi L. Ballard, Colin G.H. Dixon, and Emily M. Harris, "Youth-Focused Citizen Science: Examining the Role of Environmental Science Learning and Agency for Conservation," *Biological Conservation* 208 (2017): 65–75.

5

Documenting the Past to Sustain the Future

Appalachian Teaching Project in Unicoi County, Tennessee

Rebecca Adkins Fletcher, Johnny Lynch, and Ron R. Roach

In this difficult time of failed public expectations, when thoughtful people wonder where to look for hope, I keep returning in my own mind to the thought of the renewal of the rural communities. I know that one revived rural community would be more convincing and more encouraging than all the government and university programs of the last fifty years. And I think that it could be the beginning of the renewal of our country, for the renewal of rural communities ultimately implies the renewal of urban ones.

—Wendell Berry, "The Work of Local Culture"[1]

Introduction

The street names in Erwin, Tennessee, county seat of Unicoi County, still reflect the community's industrial past. Driving through the town today, one will cross in succession Carolina, Clinchfield, and Ohio Avenues, vivid reminders of the C.C. & O. Railroad (the "Clinchfield"), which laid out these streets in the early 1900s. For about a century, the Clinchfield (later subsumed by CSX Transportation) was the major employer and driving force in this community, transporting coal from Kentucky and Virginia to the Piedmont South. In 2015, however, CSX abruptly closed its facilities in Erwin, with the loss of more than 300 jobs. This closure was not only an economic blow, but a cultural one, as so much of the community's identity had been tied to the railroad for so many years. How the community responded to this challenge is a lesson in determination, pride, and resiliency.

This chapter describes three projects in Unicoi County, Tennessee, that represent different community concerns, approaches to asset development, and viable outcomes. In so doing, this chapter highlights the ways we have sought to answer the call to proactively participate in shaping Appalachia's future through university-community engagement. In particular, projects that draw upon cultural arts, farming and agritourism, and cultural heritage shape and support community visions for sustainable economic and community development. As the case studies attest, students and community partners find ways to identify problems, innovate, and discover tangible ways to effect change. The authors also focus on challenges to community engagement in effecting sustainability of university–community partnerships and community transitions.

Project in Context

Economic challenges are not new to Unicoi County. Like many communities across Appalachia, the economic history of Unicoi is one of highs and lows, of transition, and of periodic struggles to overcome adversity. While the center of Unicoi's economic life, the railroad also provides context for two of Erwin's pivotal historic events that remain lasting pieces of Erwin's identity. Perhaps best known as the town where the elephant was hanged, Erwin was the site of a 1916 circus publicity stunt involving the use of the railyard crane to hang Big Mary the elephant after she killed her trainer in neighboring Kingsport. Two years later, the Erwin Expulsion of 1918 saw the forced removal of Erwin's Black population, many of whom worked as railroad laborers, after the killing and public burning of Tom Devert, a young Black property owner. The mob, although dissuaded from burning the Black homes by L.H. Phetteplace, the C.C. & O. general manager, gave Erwin a long-standing reputation as a Sundown town. Although these events occurred a century ago, they continue to exert a strong influence in public memory, amplified by the Internet, and remain part of the challenges still faced by this community in terms of reckoning with injustices amid social and economic transformation.[2]

The railroad was not only the town's major employer for decades but also the chief force in developing the town of Erwin—donating land, labor, materials, and funds for schools, power and water plants, a hospital, churches, and the YMCA. The Clinchfield also actively recruited industry and agriculture to the region, including the A.P. Villa and Brothers Silk Mill, a feldspar mill, orchards, and, most famously, Clinchfield (later Southern) Potteries. From the 1920s to the 1950s, Erwin became the pottery capital of the southern Appalachians, home to Blue Ridge dishware, which achieved fame for its bright, hand-painted designs. At its height in the 1940s, Southern Potteries employed more than a thousand workers, most of them women, making it the largest hand-painted pottery facility in the United States. Although the plant closed in 1957, the legacy of the pottery remains vibrant in local culture, and Blue Ridge Pottery is highly sought after by collectors.

Unicoi County has continued to face economic obstacles in more recent years. According to the Appalachian Regional Commission, between fiscal year 2011 and 2012 Unicoi County's economic status decreased from "transitional" to "at-risk," a status the town retains today. This is reflected in the county's three-year (2019–2021) average unemployment rate of 5.1 percent (129 percent of the U.S. average), its per capita market income of $23,706 (only 51 percent of the U.S. average), and its poverty rate of 18.1 percent (135 percent of the US average). Indeed, in 2018, the county poverty rate hit 22.5 percent, the highest rate recorded since 1980.[3]

Such challenges are all too common across rural America, and both the coming and going of industries have brought their own kinds of distress. As Helen Lewis writes, "With both industrialization and de-industrialization, we have experienced the erosion and destruction of communities." How a community responds to these kinds of economic challenges can have a significant impact on the future of the community—demographically, economically, and culturally. In recent years, an increasing number of observers have concluded that the most effective and sustainable response to such challenges is a broad-based approach that begins with the community itself and develops a diverse range of cultural and economic initiatives, rooted in place-based and asset-based development, transitioning to what Anthony Flaccavento has called "bottom-up, local living economies." Such a transformation has begun taking place in Unicoi County, driven by a diverse group of people from both the public and private sector. These efforts are supported by the Appalachian Regional Commission's Five-Year Strategic Plan for Capitalizing on Appalachia's Opportunities, 2016–2020.[4]

As coauthor Lynch has pointed out, a key factor in such community development is the forging of successful partnerships. Since 2007, the Department of Appalachian Studies at East Tennessee State University has enjoyed just such a partnership with several community partners in the towns of Erwin, Unicoi, and elsewhere in Unicoi County, in upper East Tennessee. Through the department's Documenting Community Traditions (DCT) course, faculty members and students have fostered a long-term university–community partnership that seeks to respond to the Appalachian Teaching Project question: "How do we build community capacity in order to shape a positive future for Appalachia?" Through these collaborations, the DCT graduate course documents and honors community history and local culture through oral history collection, trains students in teamwork and community engagement professionalism, and assists community partners in their efforts to build a more diverse and sustainable economy.

Case Studies

CASE STUDY ONE: CULTURAL ARTS-TANASI ARTS AND HERITAGE CENTER

Fall in the East Tennessee mountains is glorious, as the trees reveal hues of orange, yellow, red, and brown and the hills prepare for a winter's sleep. With a view of the mountains and guinea hens roaming the yard, the three coauthors sat in an office at the I-26 Welcome Center in the town of Unicoi, sharing stories and reflecting about the Department of Appalachian Studies' decade of collaboration with community partners in Unicoi County, Tennessee, and the towns of Unicoi and Erwin. Drs.

Roach and Fletcher are Director and Assistant Director of ETSU's Center for Appalachian Studies and Services, respectively. Johnny Lynch served as the mayor of the town of Unicoi for sixteen years and is a long-time community partner with the DCT course. Now home to the Tanasi Arts and Heritage Center (2013) and Mountain Harvest Kitchen (2017), the story of the Welcome Center complex is intertwined with many iterations of the DCT course, which has been taught as part of Appalachian Teaching Project (ATP), funded by the Appalachian Regional Commission (ARC).

The idea for the ATP itself had its genesis in the DCT course. The course was developed at ETSU in the late 1990s by Jean Haskell (at that time the director of the ETSU Center of Excellence for Appalachian Studies and Services), Dr. Theresa (Tess) Lloyd, and Dr. Ted Olson. The concept was so successful in promoting community engagement that it was then developed by a consortium of college and university Appalachian Centers and implemented as a grant program by the Appalachian Regional Commission in 2001. The program has since expanded to include sixteen institutions from Alabama to New York state, led by Kostas Skordas, Director of Research and Evaluation at the ARC, and by two successive directors of the ETSU Center, Dr. Roberta Herrin and Dr. Ron R. Roach. Since the program's founding, more than two thousand students have taken part in the ATP.

The first Documenting Community Traditions project in Unicoi County was led by Tess Lloyd and began in 2007, when the "Tanasi" group, which was planning the development of a local arts and crafts center, reached out to Appalachian Studies for help. The project grew out of the fact that arts and crafts are an important cultural resource in the community, but the community lacked a center to promote and sell local artwork. From 2007 to 2009, DCT students interviewed artists and craftspeople, conducted community and cultural surveys, compiled data, helped to plan a conference in arts and business development, helped to develop a website, and provided data for grant applications. The project hoped to promote the arts, enhance marketing opportunities for regional artisans, and use the arts to foster sustainable development.

In 2013, the Tanasi Arts and Heritage Center successfully opened when the town of Unicoi offered the use of space in the new I-26 Welcome Center. After purchasing the Welcome's Center property about six years ago, Lynch states, "We realized that there was room in the building, we could go ahead and help out the Tanasi project . . . . So, we [the town of Unicoi] had sponsored it, but we didn't have a home for it. So, that way it gave them a home."

CASE STUDY TWO: FARMING AND AGRITOURISM—MOUNTAIN
HARVEST KITCHEN

From 2010–2013 (Tess Lloyd, instructor), DCT students documented the history of local farming (1945–2013) and the rise of sustainable agriculture and agritourism in Unicoi County. With the Town of Unicoi as community partner, the project goals included the preservation of Unicoi's farming heritage and the promotion of sustainable agriculture for increasing job opportunities. As Lloyd describes:

> We gave the community a product that they could use, you know? We gave them a lot of interviews that they can use, we gave them museum exhibitions that they can use . . . . I saw it as like, you know, a direct exchange there. What can we give you guys? And it took a little while to kind of get something to give to them. Although Johnny [Lynch] always felt, and I always felt too as a folklorist, I always felt that simply preserving this information for the community is like a big gift right there.

In the final year of the project, students created a museum exhibit from the collected oral histories and exhibited it at the renovated Bogart-Bowman Cabin in Unicoi County and at the Reece Museum at ETSU.[5]

In October 2014, this project culminated in *Unicoi County's Farm Heritage, 1945–2014: Seeds of the Past, Seeds of the Future,* which focused on the past seventy years of agriculture in Unicoi County. The exhibit, which was on display at East Tennessee State University's Reece Museum for several months, was well attended and drew a great deal of attention to the history and current role of agriculture in Unicoi County. The opening reception, which was attended by many Unicoi County residents, who reminisced and shared their own stories of the agricultural traditions of the community, demonstrated the community's pride in its farming heritage.[6]

Students interviewed fifty-five people in the county who were either currently involved in agriculture or had been in the past. About fifteen of these interviews were then used to develop biographical panels that highlighted the narrator and his or her role in the agricultural history of the county. The exhibit also included about thirty carefully chosen historical photographs. Community members got into the act and loaned many of their own items to the exhibit, such as farm implements and artifacts, including a highlight of the exhibit: a 1949 Farmall Cub tractor that was driven into the museum for display.[7]

The project documented the decline in small-scale family farms—the number of farms in Unicoi County decreased from 1,068 in 1945 to only 86 in 2007. The decline in the number of farms was partly due to the rise of larger commercial operations, with the average size of a farm increasing from thirty-nine acres in 1945 to fifty-five in 2007. The students also found that small farms typically produce a more diverse range of crops and livestock. For example, in 1945, 55 percent of farms in the county had hogs, which declined to 0 percent in 2007; likewise, in 1945, 84 percent of farms raised cattle, which dropped to 47 percent in 2007.[8] The project's findings reinforced the belief expressed by small farmers in Unicoi County that diversified farming helps to maintain the sustainability of the land, increases economic benefit, contributes to local food security, and preserves cultural traditions.

It was through the sponsorship and development of the farming and agritourism project that the town of Unicoi began making plans to build a community kitchen. Lynch described the kitchen's development thus:

> Then we start looking for grants and ways of building this kitchen . . . . I thought at first, "you know, we could probably build a nice little kitchen that the Ruritan can use to make their preserves in and then the people in the community could also use it." And so, that's how I got started on the idea of the kitchen . . . . Got some people on board, got some people to go out in the community and do surveys, worked with the people at ETSU. In fact, one of the students at ETSU is one of the main people that got our survey material together. And we realized, not only is there a need for a kitchen for somebody to go into to do their strawberries or their apple butter, but there's also a need for a kitchen for somebody that really wants to get into the business of it and be able to sell it on the open market. And so, things kind of went up into another gear then. And we started looking at it in a different way and realized that there's probably a bigger need for a job creator than there is anything. And that's when we started focusing more on entrepreneurship and that sort of thing. And as we did that, I think it actually helped us to qualify more for grants because we were, a multitude of ideas there thrown into one and different way it would serve the people. And sure enough, it worked out that way.

An important outcome of the DCT community interviews was the realization that a community kitchen would serve multiple purposes. Thus, the Mountain Harvest Kitchen (Kitchen) is not simply a commercial kitchen; it is a business incubator. Lynch describes the Kitchen as a "food processing facility with classes, instructions, seminars on proper food preparation as well as some basic business classes." Moving far beyond the initial idea of supporting the Ruritan Club's strawberry and apple butter projects, the Kitchen opened in the summer of 2017 and now offers community members a commercial-grade food preparation facility and business support center. Indeed, in its first four months of operation, the kitchen had "500 visitors; hosted eight classes attended by more than 100 people, including 'budding entrepreneurs;' supported 15 entrepreneurs in their development of food businesses; and assisted in the launch of one new business." With full-time director Lee Manning, the Kitchen also encourages other agribusiness, with a permanent farmer's market in the plans and economic diversification that honors local farming and food traditions involving strawberry farms and apple orchards.[9]

CASE STUDY THREE: CULTURAL HERITAGE—CLINCHFIELD RAILROAD MUSEUM

For three years (2015–2017), DCT students sought to honor Clinchfield Railroad's history and cultural importance for Erwin and Unicoi County within the context of looking forward. To do this, the classes, led by Ron Roach and Rebecca Adkins Fletcher, partnered with Unicoi County Economic Development Board (Tish Oldham, director) and The Unicoi County Heritage Museum and Clinchfield Railroad Museum (Martha Erwin, curator). Cultural heritage tourism offers potential for the community as one strategy toward sustainable economic development. Oral histories documented the experiences of multigenerational railroad families, including the difficulties and hardships of family separation, seniority and job placement, the reality of the dangers of railroad jobs, and the work-culture changes resulting from corporate ownership fluctuations. By collecting Clinchfield Railroad oral histories, students documented aspects of railroad work and culture and family railroad legacies. They also described the influence the railroad had on other local industries, such as supporting a fish hatchery, orchards, a lumber mill, silk mill, feldspar mine, and hand-painted pottery industries that employed several thousand workers and artisans.

When CSX closed its operations in 2015, during the second year of the project, the Clinchfield oral history project took a dramatic turn. The elimination of the last railroad jobs in Erwin, a town founded by the railroad, was a blow to the community not only economically but also in terms of identity. As Lynch, a member of a third-generation railroad family, put it at the time, "It breaks your heart. It's like someone pulled out a piece of your heritage and dropped it." Suddenly, preserving the oral history of the railroad's role in the life of the community assumed new importance and became not only therapeutic for residents who wanted to share their stories but also became a way to document the changing cultural and economic landscape.[10]

Community leaders recognize the importance of cultural heritage tourism as one aspect of economic sustainability. Drawing upon the importance of the railroad in this community's history and identity as a "railroad town," students collaborated with Martha Erwin and members of the museum board to create a rack card to offer a measurable difference in visibility for the Clinchfield Railroad Museum and make a positive contribution in promoting cultural heritage tourism in Erwin and Unicoi County.

Looking Back: DCT Successes and Challenges

By working with the community to document oral histories about many aspects of life, DCT students have recorded community legacies from many voices and perspectives. The importance of this lies not only in recording and archiving oral histories but also in providing information that community leaders, often along with students, have used to shape tangible changes that better the community. Lynch describes the importance of the university–community partnerships in these terms:

> We worked, actually we work pretty well with ETSU on most everything, you know, that we've done. And very grateful to have a partner like that.

That can come in and give us support like that from the students. The students like it, students love to do things like that. So, they come in and help us a whole lot on just about everything we turn around and get ready to do.

Lynch gives much credit to the ETSU students for their excitement and hard work in the community, acknowledging the involvement of students from several ETSU classes, including Marketing and Public Relations, as vital partners in the development of strategies that have been implemented to promote sustainable economic diversity that respects cultural heritage. For example, Lynch described the service of one particular DCT student as "very instrumental and very, very helpful in her volunteer time that she put in over here in going out to all the farmers markets and interviewing and getting, gathering information for us as we developed this kitchen."

By engaging students in a community-based ethnographic learning experience, the ATP project works to "build the capacity and skills of current and next-generation leaders and organizations to innovate, collaborate, and advance community and economic development" (ARC 2016–20 Strategic Plan Goal Five). By creating and maintaining community partnerships across one county, the Department of Appalachian Studies and the DCT courses have built continuity and rapport that allows for a new group of students to enter the community and keep the process going. We see this as exemplifying participatory development through long-term participatory research. Following Keefe, this research method "involves community members in theorizing, organizing, and implementing research on issues of interest to the community." Importantly, community members are active cocreators of projects that not only serve specific local needs but also train students in collaborative community engagements.[11]

Strengths of the DCT Model

In many ways, the Documenting Community Traditions course model is ideal for collaborative community engagement. First, and most importantly, it is community based. Each course begins by assessing the needs expressed by community members. Each course also works with one or more community partners, who serve as liaisons between the community and the students. This grounding in a community also ensures that the course utilizes place-based learning. Students learn the history, culture, politics, and landscape of the place. As many examples of community participatory engagement attest, Appalachia exists as a "place of knowledge," where forms of economic and community development work best when local ideas and knowledges are understood and applied as resources for positive change.[12]

Second, this model is grounded in community stories. While students in the DCT course carry out a lot of tasks, ethnographic fieldwork forms the core of the course, as students collect oral histories from community members. Wendell Berry wrote that communities have no more important tasks than to care for their environment and for their stories: "A human community, too, must collect leaves and stories, and turn them to account. It must build soil, and build that memory of itself—in lore and story and song—that will be its culture. These two kinds of accumulation, of local soil and local culture, are intimately related."[13] To this end, with participant permission, collected oral histories are deposited in the Archives of Appalachia to preserve the voices and stories of local community members.

Third, the DCT model embodies experiential learning. Students get out of the classroom and are exposed to a broad array of experiences in the community. They not only learn ethnographic research methods, but they put them into action by collaborating with project planning, conducting participant-observation and interviewing. Students often see similarities between the issues in the research community and their home community, creating a sense of ownership and attachment to the project.

Fourth, this model generates new opportunities. These community engagement projects have repeatedly opened new doors for collaboration and for networking with many different people. This is one reason our projects have deliberately moved from place to place within the county. These projects also spur on new ideas in the community, such as the creation of the Mountain Harvest Kitchen. As Lynch pointed out, one of the best outcomes of these projects has been the high level of publicity and public interest generated by the students' work.

Fifth, the model is linked to sustainable development. Sustainability is not just about the environment; it is about cultural, economic, and social sustainability as well. Projects are chosen that will not only create economic opportunities but also that are respectful of local assets and needs and respectful of local culture.

Sixth, the model is based on a long-term relationship with a community. For more than ten years, we have worked with community partners in Unicoi County. This has helped to build trust and relationships that would not be possible if we were moving into a new county each year. Such a relationship allows faculty members to get to know the community intimately, including its strengths, challenges, and opportunities. Additionally, the familiarity of the DCT projects within the community makes getting up to speed with a new group of students each year more manageable.

Seventh, in addition, the breadth of the community projects that have been tackled in the course demonstrates the wide range of vibrant natural, cultural, and economic assets that are available in rural Appalachian communities.

Challenges of the DCT Model

In addition to its strengths, the DCT model has inherent challenges that must be addressed. First, the model must work within the time constraints of the academic calendar. Faculty members face a heavy burden to ensure that students complete the work assigned during the semester but also must make sure there is adequate follow-through with the community after the semester ends. Getting students familiar with local culture and context early in the semester is difficult. To mitigate this challenge, instructors must plan carefully and proactively and sometimes organize follow-up activities in the ensuing semester.

A second challenge is the fast turnover in students. DCT is a graduate-level course in ETSU's master's degree program in Appalachian studies. Students are in the course for one semester and in the program for only two years. This means that the professor and the community partners have to work hard to orient new students to the community each year. Students also come to the class from a variety of majors and backgrounds, and not all students have Appalachian studies knowledge. This leads to very unique interdisciplinary class personalities that can be both creative and difficult to guide for effective project collaboration.

A third challenge is the need to find a balance to ensure that student projects truly benefit the community as well as provide an excellent learning experience. Supporting a collaborative, community-based learning project is hard work, and faculty members have to take care that the course is not an undue burden on the community partner. Building strong relationships and maintaining frequent communication with the community partner is essential to overcoming this challenge.

A fourth challenge is to develop projects within the constraints of a federal grant. Since its founding in 1965, the primary focus of the ARC has been economic development and job creation. While the ARC strategic plan also acknowledges the importance of leadership development and of the region's natural and cultural assets, all ATP courses must demonstrate that their community engagement is linked to economic development. Some projects lend themselves more easily to this linkage than others. In recent years, the ARC and ATP leadership have worked closely with faculty directors on each ATP campus to help them strengthen and better communicate the economic development aspects of their projects. In addition, the ARC has taken a broader view of economic development, recognizing, for example, that issues such as health care and the opioid crisis have a tremendous impact on development.

A fifth challenge is to maintain effective communication with the community partners and ensure that there is adequate input and feedback from the community. When asked to identify challenges that have faced past projects, this is the one that Lynch pointed out as the most difficult. Faculty face added responsibility to maintain community engagement and foster relationships throughout the year beyond the limits of the class. This work is often underappreciated in regard to faculty expectations of teaching, service, and research.

A sixth challenge is finding ways to meaningfully represent marginalized voices and difficult histories that remain damaging and hurtful within the community, including reckoning with the negative elephant imagery (associated with the hanging of Mary the Elephant) and the virtual absence of Black representation in the community. Conversely, one of the best ways to address such difficult issues is by engaging in inclusive discourse with a wide range of community members, which is precisely what the DCT model encourages. Thus, while faculty members must work carefully to prepare their students to handle such challenges, the DCT model provides an excellent way to start the conversation in a safe environment and, hopefully, help communities to begin a process of healing.

Long-term university–community collaborations are difficult to maintain but the rewards for the efforts are substantial. These efforts of the ATP ventures endure through continued communication, reflection, and long-term commitment to positive transformations in Appalachian communities. For us, this is how we "build community capacity in order to shape a positive future for Appalachia."

In addition to the economic developments directly related to the ATP projects, students also documented several additional community efforts toward economic transformation. As the oral histories highlighted the historical importance of interconnecting industries for local job opportunities, interviews also documented ways in which residents reimagined the future. For example, the second- and third-year students in the Clinchfield project noted a more active role of Erwin Downtown Merchants Association toward new businesses, including the Bramble (wedding and event venue) and Steel Rails (coffee shop). A recently formed civic group, "RISE Erwin" ("rejuvenate, invest, support and energize" Erwin), includes millennial-aged business and civic leaders who are determined to revitalize their community by working with established leadership and developing and organizing new attractions, events, and businesses to draw visitors and shoppers into the town. These include a new farmers market in Erwin that supports local farmers and several small festivals of which the most prominent was the "Erwin Elephant Revival." Importantly, this festival also seeks to directly transform the negative community reputation Erwin has held for one hundred years following the hanging of Mary the Elephant by supporting an elephant sanctuary in Middle Tennessee. Erwin also invested in infrastructure, including broadening sidewalks and broadband.

While this chapter reflects on a decade of community engagement in this community, we are not done yet. In 2017–2019, the DCT course expanded its community ties to exploring land use and natural resource assets through a partnership with Lamar Alexander Rocky Fork State Park in Unicoi County. DCT students, park rangers, and community members document and preserve significant aspects of the park's cultural heritage and natural history assets. In so doing, DCT students and community partners directly address sustainable development by using strategies that identify local assets and assist in building community capacity. To this end, developing Rocky Fork as an economic and cultural asset in keeping with ecotourism requires asset identification and community buy-in if sustainable development efforts will strike a balance between preservation and change, increase diverse participation and inclusion efforts, and honor livability, affordability, and ecological preservation.

We began this chapter with Wendell Berry's invocation of the ways in which "thoughtful people" seek alternative means and narratives to sustain rural communities. We agree with Berry that local communities and thoughtful people are the true agents of sustainable change. However, we also argue that university programs, such as the Documenting Community Traditions course and Appalachian Teaching Project, can effectively serve in community rebuilding in ways that respect local perspectives, assets, and traditions. This is the decades-long lesson Unicoi County residents and ETSU students have to share with Appalachia and rural people engaged in the vital work of community development and placemaking. As Flaccavento says, "Building a 'public life' requires that we cultivate vibrant local economies and communities where very different sorts of folks both interact with each other and guide the decisions that impact their lives."[14]

We see this in thoughtful and innovative ways in which local traditions and land use are reconfigured into modern small business ventures of local artistry (Tanasi Arts and Heritage Center), local agriculture and foodways (Mountain Harvest Kitchen), and industrial heritage (Clinchfield Railroad Museum). We see this continuing in the work to create and sustain Lamar Alexander Rocky Fork State Park and in the annual Upper East Tennessee Fiddler's Convention at Flag Pond, founded in 2017. Together, community residents, university students, and Appalachian Studies faculty brought together old-time musicians and dancers, university students, and the Friends of Rocky Fork State Park as they created a new "old-time" tradition. Finally, we see this reflecting the success of the DCT model in embracing such a broad range of community engagement modes, and in 2020 we revised the course name to Appalachian Community Engagement (ACE). ACE reflects the outgrowths of experiences and the dynamics between past and present, culture and environment, and capacity-building for just and sustainable communities. This change reflects our understanding that the course was never just about "documenting community traditions" but was rather about engaging with a community, helping its members to document their stories and find new ways to build on their cultural and natural assets.

Notes

1. Wendell Berry, "The Work of Local Culture," in *What Are People For? Essays,* ed. Wendell Berry (Berkeley, CA: Counterpoint, 2010 [1990]), 153–169.

2. Charles Edwin Price, *The Day They Hung the Elephant* (Johnson City, TN: Overmountain Press, 1992); Carrie A. Russell, "Reckoning with a Violent Past and Lawlessness Past: A Study of Race, Violence and Reconciliation in Tennessee," (PhD diss., Vanderbilt University, 2010); James W. Loewen, "Sundown Towns: A Hidden Dimension of American Racism," http://sundown.tougaloo.edu/sundowntownsshow.php?id=302 (accessed August 3, 2020).

3. Appalachian Regional Commission, "County Economic Status in Appalachia, FY 2022," https://www.arc.gov/map/county-economic-status-in-appalachia-fy-2022/ (accessed June 9, 2022); "County Economic Status in Appalachia, FY 2018," https://www.arc.gov/map/county-economic-status-in-appalachia-fy-2018/ (accessed June 9, 2022).

4. Helen M. Lewis, "Rebuilding Communities: A 12-Step Recovery Program," *Appalachian Journal* 34, no. 3/4 (2007): 316–325, 216; Anthony Flaccavento, *Building a Healthy Economy from the Bottom Up: Harnessing Real-World Experience for Transformative Change* (Lexington: University Press of Kentucky, 2016), 114; Appalachian Regional Commission, "The Appalachian Regional Commission's Five-Year Strategic Plan for Capitalizing on Appalachia's Opportunities, 2016–2020," https://www.arc.gov/about/arc2016-2020strategicplan.asp (accessed August 14, 2020).

5. The Bogart-Bowman Cabin is a log cabin from the late 1700s or early 1800s purchased in 2008 and renovated to original condition (http://www.unicoitn.net/bogart-bowman-cabin/). The cabin is used for educational events for children and as a meeting place by local musicians.

6. *Unicoi County's Farm Heritage, 1945–2014: Seeds of the Past, Seeds of the Future,* Oct. 21–Dec. 12, 2014, B. Carroll Reece Museum, East Tennessee State University, Johnson City, TN.

7. Brad Hicks, "Farm Exhibit Looks to Cultivate Interest in History of Local Agriculture," *Johnson City Press* (October 12, 2014), www.johnsoncitypress.com/beta.johnsoncitypress .com/frontpage/2014/10/12/Farm-exhibit-looks-to-cultivate-interest-in-history-of-local-ag-riculture (accessed August 14, 2020).

8. *Unicoi County's Farm Heritage, 1945–2014: Seeds of the Past, Seeds of the Future,* Oct. 21–Dec. 12, 2014, B. Carroll Reece Museum, East Tennessee State University, Johnson City, TN.

9. Sue Guinn Legg, "Mountain Harvest Kitchen Building Steam," *Johnson City Press,* January 1, 2018, http://www.johnsoncitypress.com/Government/2018/01/01/Mountain-Harvest -Kitchen-building-steam.html?ci=stream&lp=6&p=1 (accessed February 20, 2018).

10. Sue Guinn Legg, "Brutal Change: Still Reeling from CSX Blow, Erwin Looks to Rebound," *Johnson City Press,* October 17, 2015, www.johnsoncitypress.com/Local/2015/10/17 /Erwin-still-reeling-from-CSX-blow-looking-to-rebound.html (accessed August 14, 2020).

11. Susan Keefe, "Introduction: What Participatory Development Means for Appalachian Communities," in *Participatory Development in Appalachia: Cultural Identity, Community, and Sustainability,* ed. Susan Keefe (Knoxville: University of Tennessee Press, 2009), 1–44.

12. Rebecca Adkins Fletcher, "(Re)Introduction: The Global Neighborhoods of Appala-chian Studies," in *Appalachia Revisited: New Perspectives on Place, tradition, and Progress,* eds. William Schumann and Rebecca Adkins Fletcher (Lexington: University Press of Kentucky, 2016), 275–290, 286.

13. Berry, "The Work of Local Culture," 154.

14. Flaccavento, *Building a Healthy Economy from the Bottom Up,* 254.

6

Roots with Wings

Oral history project in Floyd County, Virginia

Mary Dickerson, Barry Hollandsworth, Kathleen Ingoldsby, Angela Myers, Catherine Pauley, and Melinda Bollar Wagner

Introduction

The Roots with Wings project plants the *roots* of intergenerational community relationships while affixing state-of-the-art technology *wings*. Together these ends cultivate resilience for youth and the community. Roots with Wings is an outreach of the nonprofit Floyd Story Center at the Old Church Gallery, in partnership with Floyd County High School and Radford University in southwestern Virginia. Two quotes from Floyd County High School students represent two goals of the Roots with Wings: Floyd County Place-based Education Oral History Project: the heart piece—making community connections, and the head piece—building skills:

> Now when I see someone on the street in town, I think, 'I wonder what his story is.' (FCHS Student #001)
>
> The project was full of learning. Although our mentors ran us down on the basics, we often had to piece together the details and experiment to figure things out or get them to work. The movies especially were hands-on learning, as we had to find workarounds to an issue, or just to make the quality better. (FCHS Student #004)

Floyd Story Center volunteer directors, Radford University mentors, and their professor spend every spring semester working with Floyd County High School students and their teacher to instruct them how to conduct ethical, methodologically sound interviews, record using audio and video equipment, transcribe, archive, discover themes, and create movies. From 2007 through 2018, 222 Floyd County High School students have interviewed either World War II veterans and their families or representatives of local communities and neighborhoods, and created seventy video movies, assisted by ninety-seven Radford University mentors, while 340 community members followed the weekly activities via the Floyd Story Center blog (http://www.floydstorycenter.blogspot.com).

Our community partner site, Floyd County, Virginia, is described by some as "old Floyd" and "new Floyd," or at times old Floyd versus new Floyd. The quick description refers, on the one hand, to Floyd's agrarian roots, with families that go back nine generations on the same pieces of land, and on the other hand, newcomers who have settled in Floyd for a variety of reasons—as commune dwellers, artisans and craftpersons, Y2K survivalists, retirees, and commuters to out-of-county jobs (largely at the two nearby universities). The county's population "has grown by over 25 percent in the past 20 years, the fastest rate in the region," increasing 10.5 percent from 2000 to 2010, and stands at 15,650.[1]

The population mix has advantages and disadvantages. It has led to some controversies and has made the cultural differences and stereotyping of Appalachian communities more visible. The relatively affluent brought-ins have caused real estate prices to increase sharply. Most farms have shrunk to less than 150 acres, and, as a consequence, employment in agriculture has dropped 34 percent since 1970. "Diversity in economics" is reflected in high home ownership rates (79%), but nearly 2 percent of homes are without indoor plumbing. Further, many residents spend more than 30 percent of their income on housing costs, indicating that home ownership is not affordable. Every measure of community concern has increased over recent years and has outpaced both the New River Valley and the state of Virginia as a whole, with teen pregnancy being the only exception.[2]

Theoretical Foundations

Local stresses fostered by rapid culture change are joined by burdens faced by young people nationwide: too little resiliency and too much technology. As the fall 2016 semester rocketed into action, universities across the nation began "adulting" efforts to help their students cope. Why would institutions of higher learning add yet another task to their already full plates? As just one example of the alarm that prompted the response, East Carolina University's counseling office noted a sharp rise in counseling appointments, especially "those involving a crisis." "It felt like something very different was going on—a lack of resiliency and the ability to cope." Resilience—the ability to bounce back, to figure out a way out or a way through, to adapt, to improvise—is missing. The Roots with Wings Project targets youth resiliency at an earlier age, with an intervention via celebration of local history. Research has shown that "children's resilience [is] enhanced by a strong sense of belonging to a vibrant community that 'celebrates its own culture and history'" This goal meshes with the primary finding of Floyd County's Land Policy Task Force: that in the wake of challenges and change, what matters most to county residents includes "preservation of rural character, Appalachian heritage, and community identity."[3]

Children who are most resilient in the face of challenges such as negative stereotyping, community and family dysfunction, or culture change have a "strong intergenerational self." They identify as part of something larger than themselves that spans generations. Roots with Wings provides a forum for intergenerational lessons of past hardships and demonstrations of coping skills. The project shines a light on oral tradition and storytelling because "stories provide a way of talking about stressors and change that can enhance resilience." Narratives serve to foster resiliency by linking "the generations, transmitting knowledge, values, and a sense of shared identity. The act of storytelling and listening itself is a way to connect people and create a sort of communitas—a lived sense of belonging and solidarity."[4]

For populations who have labored under the weight of negative stereotyping, this "'indigenous psyche' provides a counter-model and form of resistance against mainstream representations . . . that serves as 'identity protection.'" The Roots with Wings project plants the *roots* of the "web of meaningful relationships" found to be a factor in community resilience.[5]

The Roots with Wings project uses technology to foster these relationships. But recent research is raising alarms with regard to the effects children's screen time might have. The dangers of the overuse of technology include a narrowing of diverse experiences and consequential effects on young people's emerging identities. That is, narrowed experiences and fewer unstructured opportunities for imagining shrink the fodder for creating identity. The Roots with Wings project turns this problem on its head, using technology in a positive way. This *particular* use of technology *broadens* the students' experience with diversity, ameliorating the potential "diminishing experiences" danger of some uses of technology. It connects young students to a generation whose experiences—at the same ages—were very unlike their own.[6]

Along with resiliency as a predictor for adaptation and success, recent research has emphasized the importance of self-control in children and youth. We and high school administrators have observed improvements in self-control among the young people in our project, as they have taken on the important roles of *interviewer, audiographer, videographer,* and *photographer.*[7]

The Roots with Wings Team

The Roots with Wings team members share the common goals of developing intergenerational connections for community resilience and sustainability, conserving local history, fostering pride in Appalachian cultures, building technology and communication skills, and promoting interest in higher education. However, they see those goals through the lenses of their particular roles. Who the partners are and what they bring to the project are important to understanding why the project works. The partners will be introduced as their voices become part of the chapter. All of the partners live in Floyd County.

Our Educator

Mary Dickerson, with long family roots in the county, teaches sixth grade at Check Elementary, one of four K–7 schools in the county. Mary received degrees in sociology and education from Radford University, and while she was a student became an expert on place-based education and served as a mentor and super-mentor/assistant for the project.

Place-based education is an alternative educational approach that allows students to connect with their communities and develop a sense of place, all while drawing upon the local history, culture, and environment of a place as a curriculum source that seeks to connect students to their community. Students use resources within the community to supplement the curriculum and rely on student-guided learning. Teachers and community members serve as support systems and colearners throughout the process.

The curriculum must be clearly grounded in local issues and possibilities, reflecting the needs of the community. Teachers must exemplify a willingness to step beyond standardization and textbooks, and into specifically designed instructional plans to implement place-based education. Teachers must ask students to become creators of knowledge and to exercise their own voices by fostering a model that encourages students to rely upon inquiry and action, rather than recitation and memorization. Much of this happens when teachers create opportunities for other adults to share in the education of their community's youth. Partnerships with local agencies, like the Floyd Story Center at the Old Church Gallery and Radford University, are essential to constructing successful programs that give students a chance to appreciate and highly regard the place in which they live. A successful collaboration is important—not just cooperation or coordination—in order for place-based education to ever work. When students are taught to learn in this manner, the community benefits from a body of learners who are active citizens and willing to better the place in which they live.[8]

Our Principal

Floyd County High School principal Barry Hollandsworth is a native of Floyd County and has been an administrator in the county's public school system for twenty years. In 2007, he and Joe Klein, an innovative counselor for at-risk students, sought ways to connect disaffected youth to their community. Mr. Hollandsworth remains a stalwart supporter of the project. His support includes encouragement to teachers and students, enthusiastic communication to other administrators, and quick fixes to logistical problems.

Overall, the benefits far outweigh the negatives, which are logistical in nature (and described in the Challenges section below). Our students have discovered talents they didn't know they had. The project fosters their ability to speak to someone they didn't know, and builds confidence. We have seen improvements in behavior and academics for our at-risk students. We have observed the opportunities for learning that high-impact practices bring to all the students who participate. Closing the generation gap is a bonus. The project has strengthened our relationship with Radford University, where we send a good number of students every year, as well as our relationship with the Floyd County community, which is very important to me.

Our Classroom Teacher

Angela Myers is a native of Floyd County who is a high school Career and Technical Educator both in the classroom and online. Angela's Video and Media Technology classes worked with the project for four years, during which her classes were a model of the kind of collaboration required for the successful operation of place-based education. During those years, World War II veterans were the focus of the interviews.

Let me describe my students' experience in the project by contrasting "before and after" interview day. Alongside the community partners and the university mentors I train the students in interviewing and movie-making skills, using the Roots with Wings 158-page *Project Manual*. During that process the students can be, "Okay, yeah, ho hum," with the generation gap looming large. There is nothing that the students think they have in common with their assigned WWII veteran—until interview day. All of this preparation comes to fruition on that big day. The moment their veteran begins talking, they are engrossed. During the interview they cannot take their eyes and ears off of the interviewee. Then, their person is no longer "their old person"—but now "their veteran." They become first name, last name; they become an individual. Their stories become real. The students start to imagine themselves in the situations the interviewee is describing. And they think, "Gosh, they were the same age I am," and, "Wow, their life was so different." This is when they start to appreciate a generation that has preceded them.

I see the appreciation and the respect that they develop. Toward the end of the semester, they so want to perfect the transcription and movie products because of that relationship they have with their veteran. They want to honor the veteran that they interviewed. They don't want to just get a grade. In this situation, for the first time in their school careers, it's not all about them. The focus is on helping people, on preserving stories—on giving the family members something they will keep forever. We are giving them life skills. These students are transformed.

High school students' writings verify Mrs. Myers' observations:

> My experience in this project has, indeed, changed my view of the older generation. I have come to realize, that at one point, we were all young. Everyone was a kid, we all played with our friends, got into small arguments (and sometimes fights), and we all suffered hardships. It makes me think that no matter how old someone is, they probably aren't that much different from you. (FCHS Student #004)
>
> Roots with Wings was an amazing project that I am so thankful to have participated in. I think it helped better me as a person, because I realized

that though things may not be rainbows and sunshine all the time, I am so blessed that I did not have to endure the things they did. I learned that things get hard but they could be worse, and they will always get better. (FCHS Student #100)

The relationships the students develop with the Floyd Story Center volunteers and the university mentors is a bonus. Before this experience, the students may or may not have had a connection directly to a college student or a college professor. Some of them have. Some of them will be nurtured at home; some of them have parents who are professors or have older brothers and sisters who have gone to college. But for those who don't, just being with and carrying on a conversation with a professor and college students makes a big difference. The university student mentors realize this and share information about their college lives. Some even brought financial aid applications to the high school students during their weekly visits. They too are investing in the lives of those around them; they are adding value to "their students."

Our Community Partner, Organization Founder

Catherine Vaughn Pauley is the heart piece of the project. She describes herself as "a mountain girl from Willis, Virginia, located in Floyd County." Catherine is codirector of The Floyd Story Center and a founder of the Old Church Gallery, nonprofit organizations in Floyd County with all-volunteer staffs (https://www.oldchurchgallery.org). Catherine's position in the county is iconic. She recently received the New River Valley's Leading Lights Lifetime Achievement Award. She does not like to be labeled a culture broker, but being a native, a beloved retired high school art teacher, and an accomplished artist, she does have a foot in both of Floyd County's worlds of longtime residents and newcomer artisans. She says, "Welcome. Settle in beside us. We can hold hands and be good neighbors." Catherine agrees with what Supreme Court Justice Sonia Sotomayor wrote: "Every people has a past, but the dignity of a history comes when a community of scholars devotes itself to chronicling and studying that past."

My own journey of discovery came along with Kathleen Ingoldsby. She moved here and has become a very good friend. She has helped me to appreciate my history more than anyone, because *she* actually appreciated it. And then Dr. Melinda Wagner, from Radford University, was the same way.[9]

My passion for this work extends to developing ways to instill cultural appreciation in young people. If you do not teach young people at high school and college level, or guide them in this direction, and help them with some instruction, then they may never realize the potential of studying and appreciating the beauty of the cultures that are actually around them.

Just as Catherine discovered the beauty of her own culture initially through the eyes of others, just so the Roots with Wings Project creates a multi-generational company of scholars focused on community. The students' own words demonstrate that they understand the overall importance of the work:

This semester is one that I will remember for the rest of my life. (FCHS Student #010)

This project is definitely something I will remember and take with me when I leave the high school. I think this was a great experience to have and could help me prepare for jobs I may have when I'm older. It's also really an honor to do such a great thing for the interviewee's family by preserving their stories and their history with these interviews and movies. I feel proud to have been involved in such an important project. (FCHS Student #030)

Our Community Partner, Archivist and Technical Expert

Floyd Story Center's volunteer codirector, Kathleen Ingoldsby, as our "data wrangler," leads the project's effort to render the students' products long-lasting and useful to the community, by ensuring digital continuity and community access for the collections. Coming to Floyd County from the Boston area, Kathleen was impressed by the generational memory of her new neighbors. She gained the trust of longtime residents and became dedicated to cultural conservation efforts. She completed training in filmmaking and in archival methods. Her work provides the creative and technology-based "wings" for the project.

What sets this program apart from many other school oral history projects is the community component. An accessible community archive, a long-term goal, keeps cultural history alive for future generations. In 2015, we began a major reassessment of our digital archives in preparation for public access and distribution. We had to decide what should be saved for final archival storage. At the top of the list, according to recent National Endowment for the Humanities advice, are our *paper* files. The wealth of preservation guidelines for acid-free paper makes this an easy choice. We keep an archival copy of each interview's products, and we also present the interviewees with a similar binder containing the printed transcript, permissions, project information, and selected copies of photographic prints, as well as DVDs of recordings, images, and movies.

An equally important preservation priority is the digital audio. Original voice confirms the contextual importance of any oral history collection. Next are the transcript files, content logs, and copies of original materials provided by each respondent: photographs, documents, media, and artifacts. Closely following are the uncompressed full-length interview video recordings.

In 2017, we secured a Virginia Foundation for the Humanities grant, "From the Front Porch to the Front Lines," to produce the thirty-nine short films of our World War II series into DVD sets, with extensive liner notes, for local libraries. We are working to digitize, reformat, and organize our digital holdings, anticipating migrating the data to a final repository and creating a web-based catalog listing with narrative summaries of each interview. One high school moviemaker hoped for this availability, blurting out, "I want my kids to see this!" The best way to *save* cultural heritage material may well be to *share* it—developing cooperation and collaboration with larger audiences to keep the stories alive.

Our University Connection

Melinda Wagner, professor emerita of anthropology and Appalachian studies at Radford University, has roots in the Appalachian region, but some genealogy is required to find them. More salient for her interest in the project is growing up on a farm in Indiana, being a cultural anthropologist, having an aspiration to lead undergraduate students into challenging and meaningful research of value to communities, and a desire to meet and learn from residents young and old from Floyd County, her new home. She brings to the project resources—Radford University students—and theoretical context.

When university professors link with local communities, they should be willing to become a bridge. The BRIDGE can serve as an acronym for successful engagement. **B**e willing to cross **B**oundaries; **R**educe jargon/relate/communicate; attend to **I**dentities—keep yours and pay attention to your community partners'; **D**on't compromise your method or theory; **G**et Connected; **E**ngage. The importance of communicating was underscored when Catherine Pauley said while listening to students discuss Foucault, "Let's take these lofty ideas and put them on a hay bale." Notice that she did not say, "Let's take these lofty ideas and throw them into the cistern." She didn't want them to be thrown out. She wanted them to be communicated.[10]

We are guests in a Floyd County High School classroom. We—Kathleen, Catherine, Melinda, and about ten Radford University mentors—bound into the classroom every Thursday. We hope that the teacher and the students have read the lesson for the workshop of the day from the 158-page *Project Manual* curriculum guide that we have painstakingly developed. But we don't know what else the teacher might have been required to do in her class on Monday through Wednesday. We don't know how the kids are feeling that day. We don't know how many students will be called away to athletic practice or club activities. Will prom decorations take up space in the classroom? Will the computers be working? How many snow days have thrown off-kilter our semester's tight schedule? In short, we are not in control. Flexibility is the word of the day, every day, for all mentors. Persons who need a tightly structured predictable environment need not apply.

Challenges of Place-Based Education

Just as project stakeholders see the rewards of the project from their own viewpoints, they recognize challenges from the perspectives of their particular pillars. Our educator and place-based education expert noted that the problem with place-based education is there is no playbook that can be used to guide lesson planning or unit structuring. By its very nature, place-based education cannot be standardized or centralized because the activities, projects, and learning must reflect the unique characteristics and opportunities within the place itself.

Our principal, who originated the project, saw logistical challenges. He noted that one of the things he did not at first realize is the time it does require:

Fortunately, I've had assistance. But if I had to spend all this time on it myself administratively, there is no way that I could do it. You need someone who is very committed to it. You need some outside assistance like the Floyd Story Center and Radford University have provided. This becomes bigger than most people can handle. Look at the logistics. There is acquiring the necessary technology. Then just trying to get a group of people together to interview, trying to figure out a time and date and place, providing transportation for fifteen-year-olds because they can't drive. We require parent permission for a student leaving campus to interview an individual. So it entails quite a bit more than I originally had thought. Over the years we have had teacher turnover that of course affects our continuity.

Diversity among the high school class presents the challenges that it typically does in the classroom setting. The Floyd County High School class in which the project is embedded includes students ranging from those needing remediation to gifted, from at-risk students to those headed for college. During a recent spring semester, two of the students had anger management/self-control issues. One was on the autism spectrum. Others were quite shy. Mentors worked one on one with students, and without specific instructions to do so, tended to gravitate toward those requiring the most help and encouragement.

Our archivist's recent efforts highlight the challenges of keeping current with fast-paced changes in technology. For one, our appetite for collecting oral histories outpaced our archival organizational capacity. We also face the dilemma of long-term digital preservation. We seek a path for an archival process while navigating through various digital constraints: digital image files with no universal filename formats; cassette tapes, floppy discs, and media cards with limited lifespans; unreadable software formats; and legalities of content ownership. We strive to end each semester with products as perfected and archivable as possible. But often we walk a tightrope between pedagogical outcomes and professional products, and in those times, generally pedagogy is favored.

Overcoming the challenges of a complex project requires effort—collaboration—from all of the participants: community nonprofit, public school, and university. Participants' written evaluations and our own observations convince us that the project provides this set of Floyd County's youth with roots and wings—a strong appreciation for the wisdom of their county's elders, and technological skills to carry into the future.

A purpose of this volume is to offer inspiration and suggestions to others who want to develop university–community projects. From our experience, what is transferable? The idea of place-based education can be applied in any place, although the particulars cannot. Place-based education offers a foundation for forming relationships among people within a community who otherwise might not meet: high school students, World War II veterans, and founders of alternative communities, for example. Joining university students into the mix adds an in-between age group from far-flung places.

Working with technology adds more than bait for young students' interest. It demands innovation and ways to make it work better toward an end goal. Technology that needs to be used in groups requires team skills that our principal noted students did not come in with. (He noted that not only did they not know how to relate to members of an older generation, they didn't know how to relate to each other.) Place-based education and use of technology can be joined with concerted efforts to share the results with the community at large in a variety of ways. The local library's community room was filled to overflowing when the "From the Front Porch to the Front Lines" series of student-made movies of WWII veterans was presented. The local newspaper covered the event in print and online; the telephone and cable television cooperative broadcast it. The Floyd Story Center at the Old Church Gallery's enhanced website (https:// oldchurchgallery.org) now provides another means of sharing with residents. If other communities find, as Floyd County's Land Policy Task Force did, that what matters most is "preservation of rural character, Appalachian heritage, and community identity," place-based education is one tool for meeting that goal.

Notes

1. "Communities in Schools of Floyd Virginia," (unpublished community report, 2012).

2. "Communities in Schools of Floyd Virginia." Nearly half (43%) of the 2,032 students enrolled in the county's school system participate in the federal free and reduced lunch program. Increase in methamphetamine use has led to higher incidence of child-abuse-by-neglect cases. The measures of community concern include high school alcohol incidents, high school drug incidents, high school dropouts, suicides, homicides, drug deaths, and court intake complaints due to alcohol, tobacco, drugs, and weapons.

3. Susan Donaldson James, "College Teaches Anxious Students Not to See Failure as 'Catastrophic," *NBC News,* September 4, 2016, *http://www.nbcnews.com/feature/college-game-plan/college-teaches-anxious-students-not-see-failure-catastrophic-n641521?cid=sm_fb*; Sharon McKay and Shelley Thomas Prokop, "Identity, Community, Resilience: The Transmission of Values Project," in *Putting a Human Face on Child Welfare: Voices from the Prairies,* eds. Ivan Brown, Ferzana Chaze, Don Fuchs, Jean Lafrance, Sharon McKay, and Shelley Prokop (Regina, Ontario: Prairie Child Welfare Consortium, 2007), 25–57; Laurence J. Kirmayer, Megha Sehdev, Rob Whitley, Stephane F. Dandeneau, and Colette Isaac, "Community Resilience: Models, Metaphors and Measures," *Journal of Aboriginal Health* 5, no. 1 (2009): 62–117; Land Policy Task Force, "Common Sense Meets Home Ground," *The Floyd Press* (Floyd, Virginia, February 21, 2013).

4. Kirmayer et al, "Community Resilience," 81, 72; Nancy MacDonald, Joan Glode, and Fred Wien, "Respecting Aboriginal Families: Pathways to Resilience in Customs Adoption and Family Group Conferencing," in *Handbook for Working with Children and Youth: Pathways to Resilience Across Cultures and Contexts,* ed. Michael Ungar (Thousand Oaks, CA: Sage Publications, 2005), 357–370; Christopher C. Sonn and Adrian T. Fisher, "Sense of Community: Community Resilient Responses to Oppression and Change," *Journal of Community Psychology* 26, no. 5 (1998): 457–472. See also Caroline S. Clauss-Ehlers, "Reinventing Resilience: A Model of Culturally-Focused Resilient Adaptation," in *Community Planning to Foster Resilience in Children,* eds. Caroline S. Clauss-Ehlers and Mark D. Weist (New York: Kluwer Academic Publishers, 2004); Caroline S. Clauss-Ehlers and Liliana L. Lopez-Levi, "Violence and

Community, Terms in Conflict: An Ecological Approach to Resilience," *Journal of Social Distress & the Homeless* 11, no. 4 (2002): 265–278; Bruce Feiler, "The Stories that Bind Us," *the New York Times,* March 15, 2013.

5. Kirmayer et al, "Community Resilience," 81, 72; MacDonald, Glode, and Wien, "Respecting Aboriginal Families;" Sonn and Fisher, "Sense of Community."

6. "Media use is the amount of time per day spent using media such as television, computers, and audio devices. Adolescents (ages eight to eighteen) spend an average of seven-and-a-half hours per day using such media." That doesn't include talking or texting on a mobile phone or using a computer for school. The Pew Internet Project and other reports found that teenagers' average text count for a month was 4,000 texts. U.S. Department of Health and Human Services, "Teen Media Use Part 1—Increasing and On the Move," *The Office of Adolescent Health,* November 2013; Vivian Vahlberg, *Fitting Into Their Lives: A Survey of Three Studies About Youth Media Usage* (Arlington, VA: Newspaper Association of America Foundation, 2010); Susan Pinker, *The Village Effect: How Face-to-Face Contact Can Make Us Healthier, Happier, and Smarter* (New York: Random House, 2014); Susan Greenfield, *Mind Change: How Digital Technologies are Leaving Their Mark on Our Brains* (New York: Random House, 2015).

7. Terrie E. Moffitt, Louise Arseneault, Daniel Belsky, Nigel Dickson, Robert J. Hancox, HonaLee Harrington, Renate Houts, Richie Poulton, Brent W. Roberts, Stephen Ross, Malcolm R. Sears, W. Murray Thomson, Avshalom Caspi, and James J. Heckman, "A Gradient of Childhood Self-Control Predicts Health, Wealth, and Public Safety," *Proceedings of the National Academy of Sciences of the United States of America* 8, no. 7 (2011): 2693–2698. This study led by researchers from Duke University and King's College London followed 1,000 children from birth to age 32, plus twins from birth to 12 years, with subject retention rates of 96%. The research design enabled parsing out the effects of childhood and adolescent self-control, intelligence, and social class on adult outcomes of physical health, substance dependence, personal finances, and criminal offenses. The study showed that self-control is indeed a predictor of these measures of healthy adulthood.

8. Simon Beames, Pete Higgins, and Robbie Nicol, *Learning Outside the Classroom: Theory and Guidelines for Practice* (New York: Routledge, 2012); Gregory Smith and David Sobel, *Place- and Community-based Education in Schools* (New York: Routledge, 2010); Larry E. Decker, Virginia A. Decker, and Pamela M. Brown, *Diverse Partnerships for Student Success: Strategies and Tools to Help School Leaders* (Lanham, MD: Rowman & Littlefield Education, 2007).

9. Sonia Sotomayor, *My Beloved World* (New York: Alfred A. Knopf, 2013), 149. View this video to hear Angela Myers discuss Roots with Wings: https://youtu.be/Tt8EMLTP8zM.

10. Melinda Bollar Wagner, "Celebrating the Local," in *Reinventing and Reinvesting in the Local for Our Common Good,* ed. Brian A. Hoey (Knoxville: University of Tennessee Press, 2020).

7

Breaking the Chains of Addiction through University, Nonprofit and Community Partnerships

The story of Pollen8

Louis Gaunch and Cheryl Laws

Introduction

A popular slogan used to describe the state of West Virginia is "Wild and Wonderful, Almost Heaven." However wild, wonderful, or beautiful, Almost Heaven is in deep crisis. Driven by opioid addiction, the state is an epicenter of a national drug crisis, which is an extension of a longer poverty crisis. Poverty's cyclical forces of underdevelopment, low education, and poor health often limit job opportunities and public services alike. Equally important, the gravity of poverty/addiction grounds some West Virginians more than others; gender, race, and disability differences can translate into varied levels of preparedness and support to climb higher. Yet "wild and wonderful" can also be applied to the people of West Virginia, including a history of resiliency and an aptitude for community support.

Located on the northern edge of the Appalachian Mountain Region, West Virginia is the only state whose boundaries are entirely encompassed within the area served by the Appalachian Regional Commission (ARC). This chapter presents a community-based partnership approach to tapping into the resiliency of individuals to escape the pull of poverty/addiction. While acknowledging significant challenges ahead, it evaluates the early success of Pollen8, a South Charleston, West Virginia, nonprofit formed to promote holistic recovery strategies, as well as an evolving collaboration between Pollen8 and the University of Charleston (UC) to expand the capacity of Pollen8's mission. South Charleston is part of Kanawha County, whose population is nearly 89 percent white, per capita income is $29,253, and 15.7 percent of resident live below the poverty line.[1] The specific mission of Pollen8 is to work with vision and values to break the cycle of addiction by providing prevention, treatment, and reintegration programs for women and children. They envision an Appalachia where women are no longer bound by addiction and children never know addiction. The first section provides historical context on the interrelated issues of poverty and addiction in West Virginia communities. The Continuum of Care program includes communications across organizations to monitor and adjust recovery support and services as needed and to coordinate joint-venture projects that avoid the duplication of services to scale up this work.

A History of Poverty/A Fast Track to Addiction

West Virginia has a long history with poverty, dating as far back as the nineteenth century when war destroyed Appalachia's agrarian economy and self-sufficiency declined in parallel with local land ownership during a period of rapid industrialization. The mountainous land that shaped identities and livelihoods was still present, but most people were now working in, on, or under it, rather than with it, for survival. Subsequent generations became increasingly dependent on government subsidies when industrialization—the coal industry—went bust, a by-product of underdiversification in the state's economy. One can understand the rationale for the growth of the welfare state in West Virginia, but programs from Lyndon Johnson's War on Poverty to the deregulatory federal disengagement of Ronald Reagan have not appreciably brought the state closer to the American Dream. West Virginia is currently ranked in the bottom five in the nation for education, qualify of life, economic development, and in the top five for unemployment, obesity, and hopelessness.[2] The hollowed shell of "One hundred fifty plus years of industrial progress" remains in West Virginia, yet the most visible exploitation of human and natural resource are its people. Women in Appalachia have been particularly marginalized by economic modernization and social underinvestment following federal policy shifts on welfare beginning in the 1980s.[3] Perhaps the most tragic sign of the toll of underdevelopment in West Virginia is the opioid crisis. The problem has become the subject of national reporting and massive lawsuits, yet much of this is focused on individual tragedies and not the cumulative impacts on communities.[4]

This story is no truer than in the city of South Charleston. Union Carbide turned South Charleston into an industrial center in the 1920s when it began buying up property along the Kanawha River. "Carbide," as it was called locally, grew into one of the world's largest chemical companies, and for the next three-quarters of a century the fortunes of the company and the city were intertwined. In 1949, Union Carbide developed a technical center above its South Charleston plant, drawing highly educated scientists from all over the world. Union Carbide employed approximately 10,000 people in the area at its height, and South Charleston's population peaked at 19,180 in 1960. But changing markets in the 1980s and the tragic industrial accident at the company's Bhopal, India, facility in 1984 undercut Carbide's future. Dow Corporation acquired Union Carbide in 2001 and substantially reduced employment. With large cuts in chemical and manufacturing jobs, South Charleston moved to diversify its economy. In the late 1990s, city redevelopment created the region's main shopping district, new sports facilities, and the only ice-skating rink in the area.[5]

Another industry leader, Purdue Pharmaceuticals, came on the scene in 1996. Purdue introduced OxyContin, an opioid pain medication that was aggressively marketed and highly promoted. Sales grew from $48 million in 1996 to almost $1.1 billion in 2000.[6] By 2001, West Virginia had the highest rate of opioid overdoses in the country. It became the first state to take the OxyContin robber barons to court, later settling for a mere $94 million in restitution. The fallout had major impacts on West Virginia's politics and health care. Rival political parties accused each other of being manipulated by the drug companies, the media raised questions about conflicts of interest, policymakers criticized the state's former attorney general for spending settlement money on special interest projects, and state examiners found money was mismanaged while state bureaucrats fought over how to allocate the awards. Of the state's settlement funds, "$24 million was spent on legal fees to private attorneys and more than $20 million went to drug treatment facilities."[7]

Improved policies and procedures cut down on the abuse of doctors writing prescriptions, including computerized systems that monitored for prescription fraud and misuse. By cutting off the source but not addressing the underlying problem, some users were driven to the illegal drug market, resulting in a spike in heroin-related deaths. With such an underwhelming and acrimonious response to the crisis, the only clear outcome of these interventions has been addiction. To date, West Virginia has the highest age-adjusted rate of drug overdose deaths involving opioids. In 2017, there were 833 drug overdose deaths involving opioids in West Virginia—a rate of 49.6 deaths per 100,000 persons. This is double the rate in 2010 and threefold higher than the national rate of 14.6 deaths per 100,000 persons. The sharpest increase in opioid involved overdose deaths was seen in cases involving synthetic opioids other than methadone (mainly fentanyl): a rise from 122 deaths in 2014 to 618 deaths in 2017.[8]

Substance use disorder does not only affect adults; it also affects children. From 2004 to 2014, the rate of infants diagnosed with NAS rose 433 percent in the United States.[9] Largely driven by the opioid epidemic, this national crisis hit hardest in West Virginia. Our state has the highest rate of Neonatal Abstinence Syndrome (NAS), with a rate of 5 percent, which is more than six times the national average.[10] In 2018, the West Virginia Department of Health and Human Resources (DHHR) released county-level NAS data for 2017 showing the overall incidence rate of NAS was 50.6 cases per 1,000 live births (5.06%) for West Virginia residents.[11] There has been a 46 percent increase in the number of children taken into custody, and 84 percent of all child protective service cases involve drug use. In 2016, the founder of Pollen8 stated in her thesis there were 4,600 children in protective custody in the state of West Virginia. As of 2020, that number has risen to 6,938.[12] Children across our state have suffered more than anyone because of the drug epidemic.

These data suggest a stark message. Whatever the intentions of state lawmakers and others to confront the opioid epidemic in West Virginia, the outcomes of intervention to date have largely neglected the issues of poverty that undergird and perpetuate drug addiction. There are strong links between the challenges of poverty (joblessness, homelessness, gender inequalities, poor health care access) and substance abuse across America. Regrettably, West Virginia is a case study in the problem.

In March 2020, just prior to the COVID-19 outbreak, the National Conference of State Legislatures reported that West Virginia had the second-highest unemployment rate in the United States at 6.1 percent.[13] An article in *Business Insider* states that addiction professionals linked joblessness with illegal drug use; prescription opioids, heroin, and methamphetamines currently represent the recreational drugs of choice. Our communities have experienced continued decline with the shifts in coal and manufacturing industries and the closing of several major plants. The result has been a downward spiral in national rankings for West Virginia. Housing continues to age without repair; health care ranks forty-eighth; schools continue to decline, ranking forty-fourth; the tax base continues to shrink, ranking fiftieth economically; and residents succumb to hopelessness, which results in a range of social problems including substance abuse and violent crime.[14]

The history of industrialization, economic decline, and poverty in West Virginia speaks to the deep roots of these problems, yet also indicates the great resiliency of its communities over time. The next section examines how a South Charleston nonprofit and the University of Charleston have collaborated to foster this human potential through holistic programs for rehabilitating individuals and families. Our model takes *follow-up* care to substance abuse treatment as essential to addressing West Virginia's drug epidemic. By grounding the work in the *place* of South Charleston through interorganizational partnerships with community organizations, Pollen8 encourages long-term sobriety by teaching other life changes that mutually support recovering individuals and their communities.

Pollen8: A Nonprofit Case Study

The idea for Pollen8 first took root in 2011 when Cheryl Laws, a native of West Virginia accepted a part-time position at Kanawha County (West Virginia) Drug Court. She was hired to enter all of the information from the applicants who had come through the program (over a hundred to date) into a computerized system. Privy to their criminal backgrounds, mug shot pictures, drug screens, and biopsychosocial histories (stories of their lives), Cheryl began to realize that adverse childhood experiences (ACEs) play a significant part in substance use disorder. She uncovered that almost every young woman in this process had been molested by a significant male in her life (father, grandfather, uncle, mom's boyfriend/stepdad). Furthermore, almost every young man involved had been abused or abandoned by a significant male in his life (father, grandfather, mom's boyfriend/stepdad), leaving a small pocket of middle-class, white students who had been injured during a college sport and became addicted to the pain medication. This experience supports a sociological understanding that behaviors are consequences of an individual's interpretation of what they believe about themselves and their environment.

After high school graduation, in 1987, Cheryl attended Marshall University for one year, but her own brush with drug addiction caused her to leave school after her freshman year. At age 21, Cheryl was attending cosmetology school in Charleston, West Virginia, and in June 1990 she gave birth to her son. She practiced cosmetology for twenty years, created several businesses but nothing truly inspired her until 2011. After that part-time position at Kanawha County Drug Court, Cheryl returned to college at West Virginia State University in Institute. In 2014, she graduated from West Virginia State University, summa cum laude, with a Regents Bachelor of Arts and a minor in sociology.

Knowing that she wanted to change her community on a systematic level, Cheryl felt that understanding the culture of West Virginia would help address her state's addiction/poverty challenge. In 2014, Cheryl and her daughter (born in 2004) relocated to Boone, North Carolina, where she began her graduate degree at Appalachian State University. By December 2015, she had formulated a plan grounded in scholarly literature, comparisons of best practices from national and international recovery programs, and original research. She used that information to write her thesis, "Reintegration Strategies to Mitigate Child Abuse and Neglect by Substance Abusers in West Virginia Communities." In May 2016, Cheryl graduated from Appalachian State University with a master of arts in Appalachian Studies. The literature, research, and statistics from her degree and thesis were used to create the programs of Pollen8. Since 2016, Pollen8 has operated as a nonprofit organization to create holistic programs for women in recovery from substance use disorder.

Throughout said literature, it has been identified and proven that there is a direct link of poverty to drug usage with the underlying causes as ACEs. The three habitual environmental factors that lead to a relapse of those who are in recovery are (1) monotony of life, (2) returning to an unsafe living environment, and (3) returning to the same low socioeconomic status. In a highly poverty-ridden state such as West Virginia, the removal of these barriers is pertinent for successful reintegration and recovery from substance use disorder. Without removal, a perpetuating cycle of drug use will continue until the gaps in services are filled. Philosophically, Pollen8 has used a "communitarianism" approach to nonprofit service, which is based on the idea that if a social agent within a community does not succeed, there are multiple contributing factors. This holds the entire community responsible. To heal that social agent, it takes the entire community's contribution. Pollen8 is based in downtown South Charleston in a former church that has been renovated to include office space, public meeting space, a large open kitchen, and an outdoor food garden. To address the dual issues of addiction and poverty, the organization's mission is to reduce adverse experiences of women and children through a continuum of care recovery strategy. The program includes communications across organizations to monitor and adjust recovery support and services when/as needed and to coordinate joint-venture projects to avoid the duplication of services.

Our ReIntgr8 program provides continued support for women in recovery that consists of employment training, housing, personal development, and intensive inpatient and outpatient treatment. Admission to ReIntegr8 shows no discrimination of protected classes, such as but not limited to race, color, national origin, religion, sex, age, or disability. Through this relationship building and healing, we provide women in our ReIntegr8 program three "chapters" of treatment. ReInterg8 provides social and behavioral assessments and a continuum of care that is person focused. Once a participant is accepted into Chapter 1 of ReIntegr8 they come to live with us at Appalachian Behavioral Healthcare.

In February 2020, Pollen8 was awarded $384,407 in state funds from the Jobs & Hope Grant Program administered through the West Virginia Bureau for Behavioral Health to create a treatment center set to open in September 2020. Appalachian Behavioral HealthCare is a 9,966 square foot, 24/7 supervised treatment facility located in South Charleston, West Virginia. The women have access to public transportation and local churches, while nestled in a protective environment that historically was a rock quarry and then Rock Lake Pool from 1942 to 1986. The facility is currently owned by one of our community partners, Rock Lake Presbyterian Church. The facility is situated on over 2.6 acres of beautiful outside space barricaded by rock cliffs, which allows for a holistic and healing environment.

Chapter 1 of the program consists of intensive levels of care, administered by our Appalachian Behavioral HealthCare (ABHC) treatment team, consisting of a licensed clinical psychologist, addiction counselors, case managers, and a peer recovery support specialist, which will work with the women to alleviate any barriers they may have to successfully completing the program chapters. The team works with the women in the ReIntegr8 program to mentor and aid them in a successful transition back into the community by providing support with social, legal, and financial resources.

ReIntegr8 aspires to impede the stress of securing safe and sober housing by allowing women that have successfully completed Chapter 1 to remain in our community-style recovery home environment and advance to Chapter 2. Chapter 2 begins their job skills training at our social enterprises—Cafe Appalachia, Cafe Appalachia Catering, and Cafe Appalachia Express. Participants will gain culinary skills ranging from barista to event planning, as well as resume building and interview skills. While in job training, the women will acquire techniques that can not only be utilized in the workforce but in their home as well to prepare healthy meals for their families. They will also earn a state certified Food Handlers Card. They are required to acquire, at bare minimum, their General Education Development (GED) and also follow a curriculum that is compiled of the 12 Steps, basic life skills (Adult Roles/Responsibilities, ACEs Reduction, Effective Communication, Finance, and Health/Wellness/Nutrition), and job skills training that will allow them to change the trajectory of their future through permanent employment and education. Successful graduates of ReIntegr8 will be assisted in obtaining full-time employment through one of our Community Hiring Partners (businesses trained in Recovery Friendly Work Environment training).

Pollen8 envisions an Appalachia where women are no longer bound by addiction and children never know addiction. The organization honors the values of purpose, health, and community by realizing these ideals through programs and services. Given the roots and scale of the problem, in fact, the high goals of Pollen8 can only be reached in partnership with private, governmental, religious, nonprofit/community-based, and educational collaborations. Rather than growing out and up, Pollen8 seeks to grow deep roots that bring South Charleston's and Kanawha County's many voices together. With this in mind, Pollen8 has partnered with local municipality, schools, banks, churches, and area business owners to create collaboration for community-wide healing and collective participation in the successful recovery and reintegration of those of our community members who have fallen through the cracks. This is done through recruiting local businesses to participate as a Community Hiring Partner.

Community Hiring Partners are local businesses that are trained by Pollen8 to understand Trauma Informed Peer Support (TIPS), which is a training that educates the community and employers on the employment needs of someone who is recovering from substance use disorder and the importance of safety, accountability, and dependability for the women in the program. Pollen8 aspires to create a "continuum of care" for recovering women. One essential objective is to build a network of community partners who are educated about the needs of recovering addicts to assist clients throughout every stage of recovery. Among Pollen8's partners to date are Adult Drug Court, detox programs, fellow Residential Treatment Facilities, the Cabin Creek Health Clinic, Thomas Health Systems, Rock Lake Presbyterian and St. Johns United Methodist Churches, the South Charleston and Charleston Housing Authorities, WVARR, Ascension, SOAR, medical professionals, and Jobs & Hope.

However, motivating the greater community to get involved, such as volunteering at one of our social enterprises or at one of our grow sites, continues to be a challenge. As Pollen8 has reached its operational capacity in some areas, the need for broader partnerships and additional expertise has also grown. A budding collaboration with nearby University of Charleston, described below, offers the potential to meet these goals.

Growing Capacity by Fostering Partnerships

Pollen8 is grounded in the idea that interorganization collaborations and community partnerships are necessary to lessen the prevalence of addiction and eradicate poverty. As the organization has grown into a role that matches community needs, it has also been apparent that educational partnerships are a missing link. There is some rationale for this disconnect. Educators decide what should be taught and how; in most disciplines, the business and industrial sectors do not shape curricula. Many educational institutions across West Virginia from public schools to vocational and technical programs to colleges and universities face similar challenges to building community-based partnerships: low funding, lack of personnel resources, and pressure to meet systemic accreditation standards. We would add that educators and higher education administrators may at times lack a sociological context for engagement, and that this "inward view" of academic culture must also change. This perspective may likely be far less common in Appalachian studies circles—that is, in Appalachian colleges and universities with established traditions of place-based curricula and community engagement. However, there are dozens of campuses in the region that have no such tradition and yet could play a vital role in local regeneration for sustainability though localized partnerships. Not only valuable in extending the proximity of higher educational resources to more Appalachian communities, these underutilized networks could broaden the types of projects and partnerships that are available to the region. Appalachia needs this greater capacity to confront issues like poverty and addiction.

The University of Charleston (UC) is now working with Pollen8 to meet this demand. Founded as the Barboursville Seminary of the Southern Methodist Church in 1888, UC moved to its present campus in Charleston across the river from the State Capitol in the 1940s. By the 1970s, the university began to heavily reinvest in campus facilities and add more academic programs, including a pharmacy school and, most recently, a business/technology Innovation Center. The small campus of approximately 2,400 students is organized around six learning competencies that suggest the potential for a significant outreach role in West Virginia: Citizenship, Communication, Creativity, Critical Thinking, Ethical Practice, and Innovation. Several graduate and undergraduate programs of study, including Business and Leadership, Education, Communications, Accounting, Nursing, Pharmacy, and the Arts & Sciences, indicate specific directions community collaborations might go. Like many other campuses, however, UC lacked a history of community-centered engagement, or an established institutional culture that validated and prioritized applied and/or place-based learning on behalf of students, faculty, and communities alike. As UC realized that it was training and educating students who were then leaving the state for jobs and careers, a plan was established to combat the exodus.

A board of advocates was created to open a line of communication about opportunities and needs in Kanawha County. The learning outcomes for each class, program and major were reevaluated, though largely in terms of internal goals and objectives. Then an accidental confluence of events began the change; Innovation met Leadership. This was a literal event as the leaders of the Leadership programs met with a new vice president of the Innovation Center to ponder the question: "How do we take this out there?" A UC-Pollen8 partnership to place students in community development roles was one outcome of these discussions. Not only providing UC students with real-world experience in leadership and innovation, this project added a missing piece to Pollen8's puzzle: bringing young, inspired, transformational-minded students to intern within the programs in various fields such as business administration and marketing. The hope is to reverse the brain drain that is instilled in most middle to upper-class West Virginian parents to "get your children educated and get them out." A multifaceted program like Pollen8 will only be successful because of coordination with the wider communities of South Charleston. The partnerships contributing to Pollen8's holistic recovery service include area churches, student interns from several universities, Thomas Health Systems, and multiple nonprofit organizations. In government, the City of South Charleston, West Virginia's drug courts, and the Appalachian Regional Commission have contributed to our work in different ways.

Within Pollen8, the project seeks to inspire graduates to stay by exposing them to the power of place-based learning, applying their knowledge and skills to the immediate needs of West Virginians. How do we do this? We are supporting programs where the Appalachian history and culture (music, language, art, folklore) can be explored and understood as a point of pride and understanding rather than a source of embarrassment. In the fall of 2019, the UC Master of Business Administration (MBA) program chose Pollen8 as their Capstone project. Twenty-one MBA students began an 18-month program to aid Pollen8 with marketing, research, businesses projections, and outcome assessments. Through extending the educational arms into the community and forming partnerships that are like-minded, philanthropy and nonprofit organizations can begin to make educated business decisions grounded in research and scholarly literature. In May 2020, graduating during the uncertainty of COVID-19, the students were unable to present to Pollen8 in person, and instead submitted a thirty-two-slide PowerPoint with financial forecasts, recommendations on management style, opportunities for potential growth, and strategic recommendations for the future.

Conclusion: New Opportunities, Old Challenges

The next step is to reverse the roles and have Pollen8 pour into UC. Currently, the university is exploring internship opportunities for business and pharmacy students and special topic speakers in those programs with Pollen8 participants. What better way to share knowledge with tomorrow's leaders than to give them real life information from both a truthful and challenging perspective? We believe this will not only be positive for UC and Pollen8 but for the state and all of Appalachia. If we can keep our best and brightest home, then our future should have hope to eclipse both our past and our present. So, why is South Charleston, and West Virginia, seeing success in building community, restoring hope and breaking the chains of addiction? Simply put, PARTNERSHIPS. To quote former President Harry S. Truman, "It's amazing what you can accomplish when it doesn't matter who gets the credit."

Notes

1. United States Census Bureau QuickFacts: Kanawha County, West Virginia, https://www.census.gov/quickfacts/kanawhacountywestvirginia (accessed January 24, 2022).

2. U.S. News, "West Virginia," *U.S. News,* n.d., https://www.usnews.com/news/best-states/we,st-virginia (accessed June 21, 2020).

3. For research on the intersection of federal policy, women, and addiction in Appalachia, see: Lesly-Marie Buer, *Rx Appalachia: Stories of Treatment and Survival in Rural Kentucky* (Haymarket Books, 2020). For a historical perspective on women and work in Appalachia, see: Connie Park Rice, and Marie Tedesco, eds. *Women of the Mountain South: Identity, Work, and Activism* (Athens, OH: Ohio University Press, 2015).

4. Emily Allen, "W. Va. Attorney General Files Lawsuits against Two More Opioid Manufacturers," *West Virginia Public Broadcasting,* November 20, 2019, https://www.wvpublic.org/post/w-va-attorney-general-files-lawsuits-against-two-more-opioid-manufacturers#stream/0 (accessed July 8, 2020).

5. Scott Finn, "South Charleston," *e-WV: The West Virginia Encyclopedia,* January 15, 2019, https://www.wvencyclopedia.org/articles/518 (accessed February 27, 2020).

6. Art Van Zee, "The Promotion and Marketing of OxyContin: Commercial Triumph, Public Health Tragedy," *American Journal of Public Health* 99 (2009): 221–227.

7. Debbie Cenziper, Emily Corio, Kelly Hooper, and Douglas Soule, "They Looked at Us Like an Easy Target," *Washington Post,* October 18, 2019, https://www.washingtonpost.com/graphics/2019/investigations/west-virginia-opioid-legal-battle-foster-care/ (accessed June 21, 2020).

8. National Institute on Drug Abuse, "West Virginia: Opioid-Involved Deaths and Related Harms," *National Institute on Drug Abuse,* June 8, 2020, https://www.drugabuse.gov/drug-topics/opioids/opioid-summaries-by-state/west-virginia-opioid-involved-deaths-related-harms (accessed June 21, 2020).

9. Wendy Holdren, "Although Overdose Deaths Up, WV Health Officer Cautiously Optimistic about Future," *Register-Herald,* Beckley, WV, March 7, 2017, https://www.register-herald.com/news/although-overdose-deaths-up-wv-health-officer-cautiously-optimistic-about/article_eb38b7df-09b3-52ac-b3a0-4811c2347f62.html (accessed June 21, 2020).

10. Amna Umer, Sean Loudin, Stefan Maxwell, Christa Lilly, Meagan E. Stabler, Lesley Cottrell, Candice Hamilton, Janine Breyel, Christina Mullins, and Collin John, "Capturing the Statewide Incidence of Neonatal Abstinence Syndrome in Real Time: The West Virginia Experience" *Pediatrics Research* 85, no. 5 (2019): 607–611.

11. WV DHHR, "DHHR Releases Neonatal Abstinence Syndrome Data for 2017," *WV DHHR,* April 11, 2018, https://dhhr.wv.gov/News/2018/Pages/DHHR-Releases-Neonatal-Abstinence-Syndrome-Data-for-2017-.aspx (accessed June 21, 2020).

12. Adopt Us Kids, "West Virginia Foster Care and Adoption Guidelines," *Adopt Us Kids,* n.d., https://adoptuskids.org/adoption-and-foster-care/how-to-adopt-and-foster/state-information/west-virginia (accessed June 21, 2020).

13. Zach Herman, "April Unemployment Numbers: Higher in All Fifty States," *National Conference of State Legislatures,* April 23, 2020, https://www.ncsl.org/research/labor-and-employment/state-unemployment-update.aspx (accessed June 21, 2020).

14. U.S. News, "West Virginia."

8

Students Leading the Way to Social Change

Engaging students in applied sociological research in Eastern Kentucky

*Dylan C. Burns, J. Jared Friesen,
James N. Maples, Stephanie M. McSpirit,
and Shaunna L. Scott*

Introduction

Educators who are committed to making a positive change in the world, providing students with a quality education, and making our disciplinary work relevant to the public have found that campus–community partnerships can be beneficial in many ways. Partnerships have the potential to assist local communities to achieve their goals, contribute to the public good, increase skills and self-efficacy among our students, and catalyze a broader rethinking of hegemonic hierarchies of power/knowledge that automatically privilege academic "experts" over citizens. These goals characterize the interdisciplinary field of Appalachian studies and have increasingly become legitimized at institutions of higher education.[1]

This chapter examines two university–community partnerships in eastern Kentucky from our perspective as educators and students, with a primary focus on whether and how these partnerships contributed to the achievement of our course learning goals and student learning outcomes, including research skills, mastery of substantive material, and increasing student efficacy as citizens and agents of social change.[2] In addition, this chapter outlines the challenges and benefits to community engagement as an educational process and offers suggestions to instructors contemplating using this technique in their own classrooms. Our decision to collaborate in this reflection of multiple projects at two fields sites is an extension of our multi-course collaboration for the past seven years. Throughout this time, the three instructors have shared our research results with one another and our students; we have cowritten reports for our communities; and students from Eastern Kentucky University (EKU) have visited classes and conferences at the University of Kentucky (UK) and participated in UK research field trips. This collaboration has worked, in part, because we are all working together to support communities in Eastern Kentucky as they attempt to negotiate the transition away from coal mining and to find more diverse and ecologically sustainable economic livelihoods. In addition, each campus–community partnership focused on adventure tourism development—one involving an investigation of rock-climbing in the Red River Gorge and the other focusing on a variety of class-based projects in support of the Elkhorn City Area Heritage Council's economic diversification goals. Both build on community-based research principles, including focusing our research on issues identified by the communities we serve, involving members of the community in designing research and analyzing the data, building action priorities based upon the evidence, and evaluation of the effectiveness of those actions.[3] As much as we shared in common, there were also significant differences in research methods and the number of students directly involved in fieldwork and data collection, which also made comparison and contrast worthwhile.

Engagement Sites: Elkhorn City and Red River Gorge, Kentucky

Kentucky's Red River Gorge (henceforth, the Red) is located along the Outer Bluegrass and Cumberland Plateau regions of Kentucky, approximately an hour going east from Lexington. The Red's Corbin Sandstone offers a unique variety of overhanging sandstone that makes the Red a highly desirable global destination for rock climbing.[4] Today, an estimated 7,500 climbers visit the Red annually, equating in several hundred thousand climbing visits per year from around the nation and globe. Local residents have mixed feelings about climbers, some describing them as dirt bags, hippies, and outsiders.[5] The culture shock is understandable even if reactions are sometimes stereotypical. The sheer number of climbers visiting the gorge is remarkable given the small populations in the surrounding counties of Menifee, Powell, and Wolfe, which averaged 8,698 residents in 2018. Still others now see the benefit of climbing as a viable economic resource for the region, an area largely beyond eastern Kentucky's coalfields and experiencing dramatic economic decline. Median household income in the three counties ranges between $22,458 and $39,905, all below national averages; in contrast, the poverty rate ranges from 22 percent to 31.4 percent, all of which are above the national rate. High school and bachelor's degree (plus) completion rates are as high as 80.5 percent and 17.6 percent, and as low as 69.9 percent and 14.7 percent, respectively, yet none match or exceed national averages.[6]

Elkhorn City, Kentucky (pop. 952), located in the Russell Fork River area of southwestern Virginia and southeastern Kentucky (estimated pop. 11,300), sits along the banks of the Russell Fork River and adjacent to the Breaks Interstate Park, the "Grand Canyon of the South."[7] Located within a three-hour drive of cities such as Lexington, Kentucky, Knoxville, Tennessee, and Charleston, West Virginia, its close proximity to hiking, cycling, and horse trails, the Breaks gorge, and world-class whitewater make it a potentially desirable but currently under-utilized tourist destination. Elkhorn City, once a bustling railroad town, now struggles to provide basic services, jobs, and a good quality of life to its residents because, once the switchyard closed in 1981 and the town's high school was closed in 2002, the town suffered economic, social and demographic decline. Pike County, home to Elkhorn City, also witnessed steady population declines in recent decades, including a 10 percent population loss between 2010 and 2018 (down to 58,402). The county median household income is $34,081, and nearly 24 percent of residents live in poverty; 76 percent have obtained a high school degree and 13 percent have obtained a bachelor's degree or higher.[8]

Partners and Projects

The Red River Gorge Climbers' Coalition, an advocacy group for climbers in the region, contacted James Maples with the goal of expanding local knowledge about the regional economic impact of rock climate and actual facts about the climbers themselves. Maples' team worked together to design a survey that measured climbers' economic impact and established facts about climbers to inform local understanding about this group and about the climbing/adventure tourism economic sector. Data collection began in spring 2015 and finished around Thanksgiving that year. The study resulted in an economic impact study that has since been used nationally to campaign for climbing access, while the demographic data from the study has radically altered how local residents see climbers.[9] To date, several new businesses have developed in the region aimed at climbers, creating local jobs and tax dollars that benefit the community.

The Elkhorn City Area Heritage Council (ECAHC), incorporated in 1999 to "preserve the history, culture, and natural beauty," likewise wanted to learn more about adventure tourists to their area as well the as attitudes of local residents toward the promotion of tourism as part of the town's economic diversification planning.[10] ECAHC contacted researchers affiliated with the Appalachian Center at Eastern Kentucky University in 2012 for support in developing the outdoor recreation and adventure tourism sector of their economy. EKU held a meeting with the community and invited Appalachian Center affiliates from the University of Kentucky to join them. As a result, four faculty members from EKU and one faculty and one staff member from UK became actively involved in the collaboration with the ECAHC. From 2012 to 2013, community and university partners worked together to create surveys of visitors to the area and of local residents. Additional interviews were organized with community stakeholders in support of its quest for Trail Town certification from the Kentucky Department of Tourism, which was accomplished in September 2015. In addition, our collaboration resulted in the development of numerous community assets: a pedestrian plan for the downtown area; a report documenting the flora and fauna of the Breaks Interstate Park; an online oral historical archive of local history; a video on the history of the railroad in Elkhorn City; a mobile local railroad history exhibit; and student-authored reports, business plans, and policy papers.[11]

Challenges and Obstacles

As Shaunna Scott continued her collaborative relationship with the ECAHC, subsequent classes did not have the benefit of months of planning. Rather, planning, instruction, and execution of the community-based research projects occurred "on the fly," sometimes simultaneously. One semester, when the community and instructor could not identify a single project for the class, students were divided into small groups of about four students each, and given some options of directions or issues upon which to focus, including conducting additional interviews of stakeholders, developing an online funding campaign to construct a rock-climbing wall at the town's riverside, and collaborating with local schools to involve students in heritage activities and oral history collection. Students sorted themselves into teams based upon the project that interested them the most. For a number of reasons, including a key student's withdrawal and the community's underestimation of the costs and liabilities of the rock-climbing wall proposal, we were unable to complete these tasks. So, Scott pivoted the course midstream to conduct oral histories focusing on the role of the Russell Fork River in community life.[12]

As a result, some students found the democratic, participatory class/community decision-making processes inefficient and demanding. They would have preferred more "top down" direction and unilateral decisions from the instructor. However, the primary negative aspect from the student perspective was a perceived lack of instructor organization; the need to adjust project process, expectations, goals, and schedules were seen by the students as the result of instructor indecisiveness rather than the inevitable result of balancing the needs and goals of multiple social actors, including a community organization off-campus. Students with anxiety disorders might find this type of class overwhelming, with its emphasis on discussion and presentation both within the classroom and outside of it and its requirement to travel off-campus into unknown territory. Finally, students working with Elkhorn City expressed frustration—even shock—that such a small town lacked agreement on development strategies and were bitterly divided on whether the sales of alcohol should be legalized.[13] Driving back from a 2015 oral history field trip, students discussed their surprise and dismay about community polarization and dysfunction, concluding: "How can we help this community when they aren't even on the same page?" It is important to note that some of the "negative" aspects of the service-learning experience were nevertheless learning experiences, encouraging students to be creative, flexible and resilient while also disabusing them of stereotypes of rural communities as inherently homogenous and harmonious.

Maples' study of the Red River Gorge offered pedagogical challenges as well. Utilizing students as part of data collection efforts meant putting them in an uncontrolled and unpredictable setting. Whereas teaching the methodology of survey administration is direct, students also need to be prepared for unexpected experiences that often come with data collection. For example, students needed to be ready to explain measures in the survey (e.g., differences in measuring sex vs. gender or race vs. ethnicity). It is anecdotal, but Maples (a leading figure in climbing research) finds that climber respondents generally ask more questions than respondents in nonclimbing studies do. Although he has not analyzed this, Maples feels this could be because many climbers are employed as researchers (e.g., professors, scientists) or in problem-solving professions, which make them particularly inquisitive.

Still other challenges abound based on terrain. Students had to navigate backcountry areas where cell phone reception was unpredictable, meaning they needed to be self-reliant. As the study area crossed multiple counties, they also required adequate training in how to get to their destinations, where they could legally park, and ensuring they followed landowner (sometimes Forest Service) rules and regulations while there. Students were also expected (and taught) how to be good advocates for their university while also representing the climbing community during data collection. There are also important safety protocols to consider, such as learning how to safely travel through active climbing areas or not speaking to persons while belaying or climbing. Each of these challenges go beyond what is typically required in a research design course.

This study also presented the challenge of working with multiple community partners. Data collection efforts involved engaging the United States Forest Service, the Red River Gorge Climbers' Coalition, Muir Valley, and local landowners. Each had their own scheduling requirements and options for collecting data. Although students were minimally involved in the overall scheduling, they did work occasionally with contacts for specific days, such as collecting at a trail day. This helped lead to scenarios where students were either welcomed warmly or arrived and no one expected them. In some cases, the weather completely closed out data collection efforts, making trips result in zero surveys collected. In other cases, there were far more climbers than anticipated, meaning students had to work extra hard in collecting data as pairs. Regardless, students learned to adapt to circumstances, taking advantage of the situation as best they could when things did not work as planned.

Learning Goals and Outcomes

In addition to our desire to integrate education, research, and service in an effort to facilitate positive social change and empowerment of the communities with whom we partnered, we emphasized the potential of such community engagement to provide our undergraduate and graduate students with experiential education in historical and social science research methods, data analysis, communication, and teamwork—all valuable citizenship and career skills.[14] So far, we have engaged approximately seventy students (both graduate and undergraduate) at two campuses in data collection, analysis, and public presentations, through independent study credits, summer internships, regular courses, and graduate seminars. As a result of our shared disciplinary background and our commitment to scholar-community collaboration in our research and service, our teaching objectives were similar across campuses, semesters, and courses. The challenge was translating these into similar and positive learning outcomes. Courses were ostensibly designed to hone our students' research, analytic, and critical thinking skills, their public presentation skills, and their ability to collaborate, compromise, and listen to and respond to the perspectives and ideas of others. As you will see below, we varied in our success reaching these goals, even when our projects represented hundreds of hours of field experience for students and faculty.

FIELD RESEARCH EXPERIENCE

Students and instructors both agreed that field research experience was one of the most valuable aspects of our courses. Across all of our projects, Scott, Maples, and Stephanie McSpirit have transported over seventy students—undergraduate and graduate alike—on at least one field trip to an Eastern Kentucky community. These trips included overnight stays, visits to key attractions, local theater performances, museums, and local history sites, three survey sweeps in Elkhorn City and the Red, and weekend visits to conduct oral history interviews and focused interviews of stakeholders. Many of our students attended ECAHC or Trail Town Task Force meetings to collect observational data and, also, to collaborate with community members and present research (see below). Scott's students conveyed, in both written course evaluations and in face-to-face communication, that the group field trip experience was the most productive aspect of the course; students recommended that field trips occur as early as possible in the semester in order to increase their commitment to the community and build class rapport. For Scott's students, trips to the field were a required class experience.

In contrast, Maples' undergraduate students helped with focus group testing the survey and refining the original draft of questions, with only a select few undergraduates assisting with data collection. Dylan Burns got firsthand experience with the obstacles and frustrations that can occur during field research. The plan was to collect data from climbers at a trail maintenance event, but word that the research team was coming had been lost between the organization sponsoring the event and the person organizing it. Dylan explains how the researchers adapted:

> We arrived at a camp of climbers who were wholly unaware that we would be visiting them. The climbers were gathering to discuss trail cleanup and gorge preservation, and we were there to distribute surveys. There was no formal process for handing out the surveys, partly because we were not expected, and partly because the setting was informal and having an official process for surveying climbers may have dampened the atmosphere. Instead, we were tasked with going about the camp when the climbers were relaxing at their sites and talking to them about their experience in the climbing community.

As a result of learning to adjust to field research situations, the research team reached their survey quota for the day and learned a valuable lesson about the importance of effective communication with the contracting organization and prospective survey respondents prior to the survey collection process. Scott's students encountered a similar problem when conducting their Elkhorn City residents' survey during a 2014 spring break weekend. They found that, on the Saturday door-to-door distribution date, many local residents were attending an elementary school basketball tournament. When no one was home, students dropped off the surveys at the house and returned the following day to collect them. (Self-addressed, stamped envelopes and instructions about how to return surveys by mail were also provided.)

Collaboration Skills

Collaborative skills and teamwork constitute a central emphasis of Scott's courses at the University of Kentucky, both because she values these skills and because her courses fulfill the university's core general studies "citizenship" requirement.[15] As a result, she always incorporates small group assignments into her courses, assignments which require students to analyze data and collaboratively write short summaries or reports of their findings. To work successfully, there must be at least a minimal level of trust and mutually agreed-upon safeguards against "free riders" (those who seek to benefit from the work of others without contributing to the product). Scott discusses accountability and collaboration with her students throughout the first week or two of each semester and works with students to develop course-specific guidelines for identifying and sanctioning free riders. In conventional classroom-based courses, Scott normally has one to three students who are identified as free riders and must, therefore, face the students' penalty—usually additional work or a grade penalty. While that is an annoyance in a conventional course, it is much more important that students develop collaborative skills in a community-engaged course. To encourage this, we set the foundation early by modeling collaborative deliberation with our communities before the class even started and then reporting this to our students. At the start of the course (and with regular reminders) we communicated to our students that ours was not a "regular" course, but a team effort and that communities in eastern Kentucky were depending upon us. In Elkhorn City, students attended community meetings and worked side by side with local residents to make decisions and plans. Collaboration between the university and the community organizations was successful, by and large, and was the most important priority of our work.

Jared Friesen particularly valued the opportunity to work in a region that had experienced exploitive relationships with experts, employers and developers. This provided him with experience in negotiating researcher–subject relationships that were valuable for his dissertation research. For example, researchers may collect data without releasing the findings to the public or simply using it to advance their own careers with no concern for the persons being studied. Approaching this course, subject matter, research, and field site as cocreators of knowledge with community residents was revolutionary for Friesen. He found it exciting to work alongside and learn from local people while bringing his own ideas and energy to the project. Because of the format of this course, he gained deeper knowledge of issues in the region and applied what he learned about research methods—participant-observation, interview, and participatory action research—to his dissertation research.

Much like McSpirit and Scott's study, Maples' students learned teamwork. Whereas students shared grades in the Elkhorn Study, Maples' students learned to multitask as a team. Groups often worked in threes, meaning one person could interact with respondents, one could distribute clipboards with surveys, and a third could reload clipboards and safely secure the completed surveys. Much like the Elkhorn study, this allowed students to identify individual strengths, such as letting those more comfortable with talking take that role. There was limited room for free riding (as referred to earlier in the chapter) as students were also there because they wanted research experience and the work kept them fairly busy either hiking to a location or collecting surveys.

Within Scott's classroom, students were organized into teams and given specific tasks to complete. To produce the railroad museum exhibit, student teams focused their research on different time periods and then on different tasks, such as printing and mounting pictures and captions, building the exhibit space, and traveling to the museum to identify artifacts and to install the exhibit. Finally, we also emphasized cross-course collaboration. During the spring 2013 semester, for instance, EKU and UK students worked together with the community to develop the Elkhorn City residents' survey. A Sociology of Appalachia class at UK from spring 2016 utilized a video on Elkhorn City's railroad history, produced by a UK Appalachian Center intern during the summer of 2014, in developing a mobile railroad history museum exhibit, for example. Finally, McSpirit and Scott used Maples' economic impact research on the Red to inform a December 2016 report to Elkhorn City community members.

ANALYTIC/CRITICAL THINKING SKILLS

While McSpirit's and Scott's students coded data, Maples was able to engage four undergraduate students to create descriptive statistics tables, run frequencies and crosstabs, conduct OLS regression, and create viable scales using SPSS. In student reviews at the end of the semester, several students noted the value of working with real data, particularly when they have also seen the survey from whence it came. One graduate student used the data as part of a class paper, and two used data from this project in their dissertations. As a qualitative researcher, Scott did not emphasize statistical analysis with her students; however, her students honed their critical thinking skills by interpreting the meaning and importance of statistical measures, indexing (coding) oral history interviews archived at the University of Kentucky Nunn Center for Oral History, and triangulating different data sources (surveys, interviews, newspapers, and observations).[16]

Public Presentation

All of us were committed to sharing our data with the communities with which we worked, as well as other audiences, and wanted to involve students directly in that process. We all succeeded in achieving this goal. In addition to coauthoring book chapters and articles, Scott's students created and presented posters at professional conferences, including the Appalachian Studies Association,[17] Rural Sociological Society,[18] and the Kentucky Recreation and Park Society. Students also presented at the Kentucky State Capitol as part of a student research poster day aimed at sharing student research with state legislators. Equally important, students presented at meetings of the ECAHC and the Red River Gorge Climbers' Coalition.

Likewise, the rock climber survey findings were presented to over fifty members of the public, the Forest Service, and the Red River Gorge Climbers' Coalition. Students assisted with the room organization, handing out programs, and meeting community members. Later, presentations to the public were the foundation of changing how local residents understood climbers and their interests in the region.[19] Since then, students have written articles for publication and used this data in masters theses. Students have also been involved in Maples research on economic impact of outdoor recreation in other areas. Maples now includes learning to write applied reports as objectives in two upper division courses he teaches.

Evaluation and Recommendations

We all agree that it is worthwhile to involve students in a community engagement/research project, even though it requires extra logistical work, travel, and effort from the instructor. The amount of additional work required of instructors is difficult to estimate; it includes years of networking in the service area; travel to field sites, often on weekends or during campus "vacation" times; and near-constant communication with communities and students during the semester. Students expressed a preference for community-engaged courses over conventional ones, because they gained knowledge, understood course material better, enhanced their research skills, felt empowered, and believed that universities (and individuals) should make a positive impact in the community. Students willingly gave up weekend time and time during finals week to finish projects. Finally, a few students continued to be engaged in their communities after the courses were over, either through internships, independent studies, or visiting the community to enjoy the natural scenery and tourism opportunities. A few reported that the experience influenced their thinking about future career paths.

Scott found that the grades in the community-engaged courses were better than in conventional classroom formats, with the vast majority of students earning As and Bs. Community-engaged students also demonstrated increased capacity to synthesize material from different sources in their written work, and they were better at applying theory to the explanation and action in the world than students in conventional courses. More intangibly, students took greater responsibility for their own work and for meeting deadlines, they showed superior collaboration skills than students in conventional courses, and they were more willing to hold themselves *and one another* accountable for their actions, because they were working for a greater cause than just their individual grades.[20] For instance, when students observed that one of their peers was not a skilled interviewer, they volunteered to do his assigned interviews themselves in order to produce better oral history interviews. When one of their classmates was suffering from an anxiety disorder, students assigned her tasks that she could comfortably handle and voluntarily shouldered more of the load themselves. No one was identified or penalized for free riding. Whether community engagement causes the students to behave more collaboratively or whether only the most collaborative, responsible and mature students choose to take (or stay in) such courses remains an open question.

We attribute our success to a number of factors. First, we were all approached by the community organizations with whom we partnered; therefore, we had buy-in from them, though perhaps not other groups or all the residents of their service areas. Second, each of our partner groups came to us with clear ideas about the data that they needed, their target audience, and their goals for collecting the data. Third, the instructors met with members of the community to discuss and plan for our research activities months in advance. Planning and laying groundwork before students arrive to the course is a key aspect of student learning outcome success. Once students arrived to distribute surveys, they worked in small teams to distribute surveys, talk to respondents, and to keep track of numbers of surveys delivered to which addresses, so that their team could return to the appropriate address the following day to collect surveys. In addition to working as teams on the surveys, students traveled together, took meals and shared accommodations on research trips, all of which reinforced students' bonds with one another and their commitment to the projects and community.

Another beneficial aspect was that our courses focused on a single class research project, rather than a set of service choices for individual students. While the latter arrangement has the benefit of offering student choice, the liabilities outweigh the benefits. For one thing, it is more difficult to coordinate, assess, and hold parties accountable in this course model. In addition, students working individually may feel isolated and, as a result, may be unable to refuse menial tasks that do not match the course learning goals or facilitate learning. In addition, courses of this type lack the cohesiveness and collaborative group experience that our initial classes achieved.

One advantage to these challenges was that each led to learning experiences. Students were far more comfortable with explaining why survey measures were designed a particular way when asked (and they were). Maples watched one example where an undergraduate student adequately explained the differences in measuring sex, gender, and sexuality to an inquisitive climber. As a result, student administrators were stronger at building surveys in their research methodology courses and senior theses. Students gained confidence from being self-sufficient in a backcountry setting, as well. Several students involved went on to learn about Leave No Trace minimal impact behaviors (principles for minimizing one's impact on backcountry areas). Students also learned the basics of climbing and to be aware of their work environments and gained skills interacting with persons from around the world visiting eastern Kentucky.

Based on our experience, we offer the following recommendations to instructors who wish to engage their students in community-based, action or participatory-action research in Appalachia, or anywhere. For the best results—for both your community partner and for your students' learning and quality of experience—invest time with your community partners to understand their issues, questions, and goals and also make clear to them what your goals are as an educator. It is important to maintain regular communication, invest in your relationships with your partners, be reliable in delivering on your promises, and be honest about your limitations and obstacles. For example, Scott uses email and Facebook to keep in regular contact with the community, and she turned down projects that were not relevant to the learning objectives of her sociology courses, such as invasive plant eradication. In situations such as these, we recommend politely declining, explaining why, and connecting the community with the appropriate university departments, organization, or government agencies to meet that need. The instructor is responsible for maintaining a balance between meeting the community's goals and meeting the students' learning goals within the discipline and topic of your course.

Second, focus your class on one integrated project at a time—for example, conducting a survey, creating an oral history archive, or constructing a local history exhibit, webpage, blog or vlog. Choose a project that meet the following criteria: (1) it will contribute knowledge or meet a need that the partner community has identified as important (and that they agree to), (2) it will give your students an opportunity to build research, career or citizenship skills and learn material that is relevant to your course goals, and (3) it is sufficiently complex to challenge your students and to be divided into a number of sequential stages and individual or team tasks.

Finally, acknowledge and plan for the inevitability of community-engagement conflicts and plan revisions; these will challenge and, at times, frustrate your students (and yourself), and will be particularly difficult for students with anxiety disorders and those who are less flexible, in either their class/work schedules or their personalities. Acknowledge this in your syllabus and initial class meetings while there is still time for students to change their class schedules if they feel unable or unwilling to cope with these circumstances. Throughout the course, communicate honestly and openly with your students about complications as they emerge, so that students are not caught off guard by changes to the project or timeline. In addition, you may build in "class meeting release time" to compensate for team meetings and community visits. Make contingency plans, share them with your class, and give students a choice in selecting which ones you employ. When balancing the goals of the community and your students, be sure to communicate your support for your students' well-being and learning. Above all, do not let community-driven changes negatively impact your students' grades. Be sure to include in your course sufficient individual assessment instruments (e.g., quizzes, reflective essays, etc.) independent from the community engagement product, so that you can determine a fair grade for your students no matter what happens with the community engagement product. Ultimately, the instructor can neither control every aspect of such courses nor prevent the challenges and frustrations of community-engagement. That is fine, because successfully adapting to changed circumstances and negotiating tension and conflict will be a part of your students' lives and careers in the future. By incorporating this into class, you will facilitate a valuable learning experience for your students in the realities of citizenship, civic engagement, and adulthood.

Notes

1. See Chad Berry, Phillip J. Obermiller, and Shaunna L. Scott, eds. *Studying Appalachian Studies: Making the Path by Walking* (Urbana: University of Illinois Press, 2015); Campus Compact, "Carnegie Community Engagement Classification," 2017, https://compact.org/initiatives/carnegie-community-engagement-classification/ (accessed July 25, 2017).

2. Theresa Petray and Kelsey Halbert, "Teaching Engagement: Reflections on Sociological Praxis," *Journal of Sociology* 49, no. 4 (2013): 441–455.

3. Randy Stoecker, "Are We Talking the Walk of Community-Based Research?" *Action Research* 7, no. 4 (2009): 385–404.

4. James N. Maples, Ryan L. Sharp, Brian Clark, Katherine Gerlaugh, and Braylon Gillespie, "Climbing Out of Poverty: The Economic Impact of Rock Climbing in Eastern Kentucky's Red River Gorge," *Journal of Appalachian Studies* 23, no. 1 (2017): 53–71.

5. Maples et al., "Climbing Out of Poverty."

6. United States Census, "Quick Facts," https://www.census.gov/quickfacts/powellcounty kentucky, https://www.census.gov/quickfacts/wolfecountykentucky, https://www.census.gov /quickfacts/menifeecountykentucky (accessed March 9, 2020).

7. U.S. Census blocks matched by watershed layer in ArcMap.

8. United States Census, "Quick Facts," https://www.census.gov/quickfacts/pikecounty kentucky (accessed March 9, 2020).

9. Ula Chrobak, "Not Just Dirtbags: The Economic Impact of Climbers in the Red River Gorge, Explained," *Climbing Magazine,* October 13, 2017, https://www.climbing.com/news/not-just-dirtbags-the-economic-impact-of-climbers-in-the-red-river-gorge-explained/ (accessed August 5, 2018); Alex Honnold, "Alex Honnold to Politicos: Leave Our Public Lands Alone," *Outside,* May 25, 2018, https://www.outsideonline.com/2313076/alex-honnold-politicos-leave-our-public-lands-alone (accessed August 5, 2018).

10. "The Elkhorn City Area Heritage Council, Inc.," Facebook page, https://www.facebook.com/The-Elkhorn-City-Area-Heritage-Council-Inc-249250088425018/ (accessed June 3, 2022).

11. For the online oral history project, visit https://kentuckyoralhistory.org/catalog /xt7t7659gq6v.

12. Nunn Center for Oral History, University of Kentucky, "Elkhorn City River Oral History Project," https://kentuckyoralhistory.org/ark:/16417/xt7mpg1hmj96.

13. Shaunna L. Scott, Stephanie M. McSpirit, J. Jared Friesen, and Kathryn Engle, "How about Some Collaboration?: Micro-Level Barriers to Democratic, Evidence-Based Decision-Making" *Journal of Appalachian Studies* 26, no. 2 (2020): 209–226.

14. John Dewey, *Experience and Education* (New York: Simon and Schuster, 1997); Paolo Friere, *The Politics of Education: Culture, Power, and Liberation* (South Hadley, MA: Bergin and Garvey, 1985).

15. University of Kentucky, "The UK Core General Education Requirements," 2013, http://www.uky.edu/registrar/bulletinCurrent/ukc.pdf (accessed May 16, 2020).

16. Oral history interviews can be accessed at https://kentuckyoralhistory.org/catalog/xt7mpg1hmj96.

17. Shaunna Scott, "Diversifying an Economy: Tourism and Recreation on the Russell Fork," Appalachian Studies Association, Johnson City, Tennessee, March 27–29, 2015.

18. Shaunna L. Scott and Jared Friesen, "Obstacles to Diversifying a Local Economy: An Appalachian Kentucky Community Case Study," Rural Sociological Society, Toronto, Canada, August 6–9, 2016.

19. Chrobak, "Not Just Dirtbags."

20. Noam Ostrander and Sara Chapin-Hogue, "Learning from Our Mistakes: An Autopsy of an Unsuccessful University-Community Collaboration," *Social Work Education* 30, no. 4 (2011): 454–464.

9

Town and Gown Collaborations in Southwest Virginia Post–Coal Communities

Clinch River Valley Initiative and Radford University economic diversification efforts

Theresa L. Burriss, Kasey Campbell, and Caroline Leggett

Project Context and Preplanning

As we face the end of the second decade of the twenty-first century, many communities in southwest Virginia are continuing their transition to post-coal economies. Because coal has dominated the social, cultural, environmental, and economic landscape in these counties for well over a century, communities are working toward a future that honors the past yet includes a more diverse, sustainable economic portfolio drawing on regional assets. In many regards, these communities are reinventing themselves and their identities, a difficult and sometimes painful process. Consequently, area leaders and residents are searching for partnerships with educators, grassroots organizers, entrepreneurs, and health care professionals to create fulfilling, viable prospects for young and old alike. The Clinch River Valley Initiative (CRVI), a grassroots collective created as a result of the 2010 forum "Building Local Economies in Southwest Virginia," is dedicated to diversifying the economies of southwest Virginia communities that are distressed or at-risk, as classified by Appalachian Regional Commission (ARC).[1] As a participant in the ARC's Appalachian Teaching Project (ATP) from its inception, Radford University's Appalachian Studies program has partnered with various community groups over the years to respond to the ARC's question of how to build sustainable communities for the future.[2]

In the fall of 2016, students in Theresa Burriss's APST495: Research in Appalachia, a community-based research class affiliated with the ATP, began working with CRVI to assist with the group's oral history project. With community-based research comes great responsibility for the university students and faculty to overtly eschew an historical colonial missionary mentality, whereby they enter a community believing they possess definitive answers and solutions to whatever challenges may exist. Faculty members have an ethical obligation to educate their students about such perspectives and their consequent damage. Indeed, "university as savior" mind-sets have fostered justified community distrust of the very institutions that should be listening to, respecting, and acting on residents' knowledge. Case studies abound with university exploitation of communities to further faculty research agendas, publications, and professional advancement. This chapter revisits the engagement and training processes vital to meaningful collaboration in the project and reflects on common challenges faced that might support future CRVI programs, as well as other community–university relations. In particular, the authors examine such topics as the creation of the class and community partnerships, requisite preparatory work in the classroom, engagement logistics with community interviewees, travel and time commitments, and community partner feedback, among other matters. With an intentional process-reflection orientation, the authors aim to create an easy-to-replicate model, with the understanding that each community-based research project will possess unique characteristics, successes, and challenges.

As is often the case with these types of research classes, Burriss took on some of the work well before the start of the semester as she communicated with contacts in southwest Virginia to identify a new community partner for the 2016 ATP class. Serving as the director of the Appalachian Regional & Rural Studies Center at Radford University since July 2010, Burriss appreciated the importance of having connections in all community sectors, not simply to broaden personal and professional networks but, more importantly, to decrease the likelihood of redundancy and overlap, as well as strengthen coalition work. After obtaining a lead, Burriss contacted an associate with the University of Virginia's (UVA) Institute for Environmental Negotiation (IEN), who facilitated CRVI's meetings until June 2018 when funding was depleted and the nonprofit Friends of Southwest Virginia assumed facilitation. With a mission "to mediate environmental issues and facilitate community solutions," coupled with the location of UVA's satellite campus of UVA-Wise in the Clinch River Valley, the institute aligned with CRVI's efforts to explore "ways to put the Clinch River in the center of an economic revitalization effort."[3] Such revitalization is critical as unemployment in the region increases and population decreases. According to a *Bristol Herald Courier* newspaper article dated February 16, 2019, and citing the UVA Weldon Cooper Center for Public Service, "So far this decade, every city and county in far Southwest Virginia has shrunk in population while the rest of the state—thanks primarily to urban areas—has grown."[4] Another report by the Cooper Center, although older (2014), shows a bleak southwest Virginia under the Poverty and Income category, with 19.8 percent of the region falling below the poverty line, higher than the statewide rate of 11 percent. Among the localities, the poverty rates range from 12.4 percent to 35.2 percent.[5] With the further decline in coal production over the past six years, the current numbers inevitably are worse.

At the invitation of IEN associate Christine Gyovai, Burriss attended her first CRVI steering committee meeting in the summer of 2016 in Cleveland, Virginia (Russell County), where she met various leaders from St. Paul, Virginia, among other CRVI members. Because she is from the area, she knew some of the participants but not the majority, who hailed from nonprofits, education, business, municipalities and planning districts, and state and federal agencies. Although a biology faculty member from UVA-Wise expressed an interest in collaborating on mussel health research in the Clinch River, Burriss was educated in the humanities/social sciences and not the physical sciences. Despite a long, deep relationship with the natural environment, and a desire to heal it, she did not possess the academic training to contribute to such research, nor the ability to coach her students in it. No matter a community's needs, faculty members must be forthright about their limitations in assisting. Such honesty contributes to community trust, thereby leading to stronger relationships between community members and the educational institution.

Project and Course Development

A week later, Burriss talked with members of the Downtown Revitalization, Marketing, and Entrepreneurship Action Group, who shared their need to obtain river stories/oral histories to augment their downtown revitalization and regional tourism efforts.[6] Although some may not see the connection or be skeptical of oral histories' impact on economic revitalization, such interviews have the ability, for example, to bolster community pride, which can lead to residents more willing to innovate and invest in their community. Additionally, the stories, coupled with natural resource assets, can be used to establish more remote rural communities as unique travel destinations, enticing tourists from a variety of backgrounds to discover and explore the area's distinctiveness. Having engaged in oral history collecting for many years, Burriss committed to the project and began preparing her syllabus, which remained a work-in-progress over the first third of the semester primarily due to attempts to schedule community partner meetings and the identification of new reading materials. She tried to strike a balance between sources addressing all of Central Appalachia's history, the Clinch River Valley and St. Paul, and methods/methodologies of oral history collecting. Ronald D Eller's *Uneven Ground: Appalachia since 1945* fit the first category perfectly, while Peter Crow's *Do, Die, or Get Along: A Tale of Two Appalachian Towns* and *Appalachian Genesis: The Clinch River Valley from Prehistoric Times to the End of the Frontier Era* served the second.[7] To provide students with content on oral history methods/methodologies, Burriss selected Sherna Berger Gluck and Daphne Patai's *Women's Words: The Feminist Practice of Oral History* (1991).[8] Students easily read and acquired the information in the history texts yet found Gluck and Patai's work challenging, primarily because the discourse was new to them and a couple had never engaged in oral history research or collecting before.

Reflection logs prompted students' more in-depth analysis of the content. Additionally, the logs provided students the space to question and comment on issues, such as the politics of identity, power and privilege, and representation through the spoken and written word. For example, in her chapter in Gluck and Patai's text, Claudia Salazar incorporates the collective oral history of Guatemalan Rigoberta Menchu to discuss cultural and social power.[9] Salazar asserts, "Together with the shaping of her political consciousness, Rigoberta also realizes that language and cultural representation are important weapons in fighting oppression at both the ideological and the material levels."[10] With Appalachia's long history of exploitation and stereotyping, Rigoberta's understanding is valuable to students embarking on oral history work with central Appalachian residents. Class discussions, including those focused on the inevitable power dynamics between interviewer and interviewee, as well as ethical interviewing and understanding of structural injustices, also helped students better grasp not only the content of the text but also the implications on their own oral history collecting. The authors in *Women's Words* provided strong methodological examples for the students to study and guided their thematic coding of the interviews. Because APST495 is an upper-level undergraduate class, Burriss believed it important to push students' intellectual boundaries while providing guidance in their navigation of new concepts, ideas, and discourses.

Project Challenges

A major challenge with the CRVI–Radford University partnership related to geographic distance. Radford University is located in the New River Valley in the city of Radford, Virginia, which is 125 miles east of St. Paul, a little over a two-hour car ride one-way. Unlike past community partnerships, the one with CRVI and St. Paul residents required several all-day Saturday trips for the oral history interviews. Students had to be aware of such weekend commitments before enrolling in the class because work schedules and other responsibilities could prohibit their involvement. Skype and conference calls were necessary at the start of the semester to introduce community members to the students and to begin to establish relationships. While St. Paul has reliable Internet and cell phone service, other nearby communities such as Dante do not, an issue that faculty must consider when trying to communicate with partners in the Clinch River Valley. Many remote rural mountain communities throughout Appalachia face such challenges, challenges that some other rural and many urban residents do not experience or consider. Thanks to a grant from the Appalachian Regional Commission through the Appalachian Teaching Project, all travel expenses to St. Paul were covered. In these lean times of public higher education, when legislative support is dwindling, outside support for community-based research is critical, especially in isolated southwest Virginia coal counties.

Yet another critical component of town and gown partnerships involves recruitment of students in interdisciplinary community-based research classes. The students who enrolled in this class were majoring in biology, psychology, and interdisciplinary studies, with various minors. With strict curricular standards for many majors and minors, driven by accrediting bodies, students cannot earn credits in their major or minor if the professor of a class in which they enroll does not hold at least a master's degree in their respective discipline. Although standardized curricular criteria ensure qualified graduates, limitations exist in such narrowly defined paradigms. After all, both natural and human environments do not fit neatly into prescribed channels or silos. Sure, specialization has a place in both, but interconnectedness is a reality. Accrediting bodies need to recognize this.

Students' dietary restrictions, whether related to health and/or personal choice, is another challenge faculty members may not anticipate. Inquiring about students' diets may seem beyond the purview of a faculty member in a traditional class, but not a community-based research one. In many regards, faculty in these classes assume a parental-type role as they facilitate student requests with resident cultural etiquette. If students do indeed have special diets, then it's vital the faculty member tactfully communicate with community project organizers in a way that doesn't assume food will be prepared but does alert them if they had intended to offer it. As is typical with many Appalachians, who provide food to welcome guests into their homes and communities, several Clinch River Valley residents prepared various dishes to serve the Radford group.

Student Benefits

By stepping out of their designated track of study, and sometimes their comfort zone, students gain unique experiences and perspectives that enrich their time at college. Applying textbook theory, students see beyond the page to make visceral connections with their life as it relates to others, local community, and society at large. Mary Drury describes her experience well:

> Being able to actually travel to a town once . . . owned and operated by a successful coal company and learning how things were back then . . . has truly allowed me to change my perception of Appalachia from what I have learned in textbooks and shape it around seeing the reality of what Appalachia is up against.[11]

In the class time leading up to interview days, students prepared to be off-campus leaders. They were keenly aware of being ambassadors of Radford University in particular and their generation in general, as well as potential representatives at the ATP and Appalachian Studies Association conferences. We discussed our individual backgrounds, experiences, and what biases we might have about how others see ourselves and how we see the research area's history, location, and stereotypes. As part of preproduction, we asked our community partners to provide some background details about interviewees, such as occupation, family relations, military veteran status, and whether they lived elsewhere during their life. We then combined this with class readings and some short films as prompts for discussion about our interviewees' potential biases, experiences, and fears, as well as exploring the effect both interviewer and interviewee have on the whole interview process.

Classes such as these are different from more traditional ones not involving outside partnerships. They are dynamic and organic, requiring more qualitative measures and sustained student participation, rather than many traditional disciplinary classes in which student progress is measured solely by quantitative tests. Students must be reliable, adaptive, and possess strong interpersonal dexterity—"soft" skills not typically evaluated in conventional classes. For this reason, it helps to recruit students from all disciplines with the knowledgeable assistance of colleagues, who are aware of the unique nature of the class. Thus, they can recommend students with these dispositions and who they believe will welcome and rise to the challenge.

Recording Equipment

The scope of this chapter does not allow for in-depth analysis of equipment options, only a summary of how to proceed: what you have will work and you can work with what you have. Though the general cost of digital recording equipment has become more affordable, video cameras are still more expensive than audio recorders. Because of our small class enrollment, it was not feasible to collect video as well as audio of the interviews. The extra requirements for video recording also make it less suitable for a nonintrusive way to record interviewees' stories. A camera can be very intimidating, and people may actually share more of their story if only an audio recorder is present. If students do capture video footage, they need a tripod, a good location with bright lights or supplemental lighting, and synchronized video and audio (or the ability to do this in post-production).

The advancements in technology and its permeation into everyday life means students now are likely more familiar with recording equipment than teachers are. Perhaps one day all students will have a smart phone, which now are capable audio/video recorders on their own. Our university library has several camera options, but we found it best to use Olympus DM-720 digital audio recorders. They are small, light, require only one AAA battery, have large file storage space, and are easy to learn to use.

Project and Interview Considerations

Although the interview setting is important, a soundproof box in which to work is not necessary. We were able to use well-known town gathering spots, such as the community center, museum, and learning center. However, some interviewees, though willing to participate, were unable to meet us at the specified locations due to weakened health or limited mobility. Because we had such minimal, mobile equipment, it was easy for us to go to interviewee homes and change locations on short notice. The audio goal is to minimize interruptions and background noise, but this cannot be achieved in every situation. A phone will ring, a friend will stop by, or participants will suddenly get up to stretch their legs and walk around pointing at landmarks or museum items. We considered conducting multiple interviews simultaneously in large community rooms because this is the simplest and most readily available situation. However, several pairs of people talking in each corner of a large room creates too much visual distraction and audio interference.

When coordinating many participants, scheduling conflicts are unavoidable. Though we would like to be able to spend as much time in the field as possible, consideration needs to be given for students' total class and workload, as well as community partner work and time availability. Some students traveled independently to St. Paul and were able to spend extra time in the community, which supports the need for direct student involvement with community partners throughout the whole process. Lauren Landreth describes her experience:

> I felt like I had plenty of direct contact with community partners, especially after spending the weekend with Terry Vencil. That was one of the highlights of the whole experience for me, getting to see the behind-the-scenes of what she does and her tour of St. Paul, as well as learning more about her as a person and community member. I only really met the other community partners through Skype and phone calls, but I really liked them.[12]

Just as society and the dynamics of university–community relations are changing, perhaps we need to evaluate what "traditional class time" means at the college level. Of course, the content of some disciplines necessitates traditional class structure; however, projects like this require intense student-community partner collaboration, schedule coordination, and unique application of research theory. In this case, we might ask: does traditional class time enable students to achieve learning objectives or does it limit the power of universities to leverage their assets to the best of their ability? If the goal of projects like this is to increase university-community relations and strengthen society's overall ability to adapt to change, then restructuring the approach to how universities balance nose-in-books with boots-on-community-ground could be one way we help make this happen. Although traditional classes do not typically meet on weekends, Saturdays provided the best opportunity to travel to the community and spend hours interviewing various residents. Also, place-based education practitioners, typically found in K–12 settings with a few at the post-secondary level, offer several models that seamlessly connect students with community in nontraditional formats.[13] University administrators have the ability to promote and implement varied, flexible course scheduling to accommodate the unique needs of community-based research classes, while still ensuring the requisite number of contact hours for accreditation standards.

Project Scope

Our interviews focused on collecting life stories of the past. For example, students asked, "What was it like growing up around the Clinch River and how has the community and environment changed over time?" In addition to recording lived experiences on the Clinch, we discovered that community need, and potential for university assistance, goes far beyond collecting stories to assist with cultural tourism. If university faculty and students approach a specific project with an open instead of prescribed mindset, community partners are more likely to become engaged stakeholders in town-gown collaborations. A university group could propose an initial project, but also ask residents questions about related circumstances. For example, peripheral to increasing tourism, students might ask about town trash collection, sewer conditions, Internet coverage, or less well-known impediments to community organization and action. Ideas discovered during the current project could be a topic of a semester-end university and community "Feedback and Next Steps" meeting.

Project goals should be many, but it is important to consider what can be accomplished realistically within one semester. During our one-semester project, with three student interviewers, we completed thirteen interviews. One Saturday trip included a single interview conducted by an experienced student so the students without previous experience could observe. On the other two field days, each of the three students conducted two interviews. Each interview was between one and two hours, leading to roughly twenty-six hours of transcribed audio. If more students had enrolled in the class, we may have had time for additional post-production work, such as annotating transcriptions, selecting interview sound bites for inclusion on community websites, or outlining the organization of a transcript book.

A tangential yet equally important byproduct of students' presentations at conferences exists, especially the Appalachian Teaching Project conference, where Appalachian Regional Commission staff are present. While students recount highlights of their interactions, they share residents' concerns about community challenges, including infrastructure issues and other resource shortages. Those in a position to act on these needs, who often have the financial means to assist, hear these opportunities to help and thus can initiate support and implement aid.

Challenges and Recommendations

Transcribing interviews proved to be one of the most cumbersome and time-consuming out-of-class activities. We used a free online program called oTranscribe.[14] Students said they learned to use it easily but wished they had started earlier so they would not have been burdened with a heavy workload at the end of the semester. We recommend deciding on and outlining a standard transcription format at the outset so formatting is uniform. Small details are important, including how often to insert time stamps, how to write speakers' names, how to format the heading, and how to break up long passages in response to an interview question.

All students reported they would have liked more interaction with community members. In our case, we used email, phone calls, and Skype to conduct pre-interview day meetings and early-semester collaboration. A shorter town–gown distance would have facilitated more face-to-face meetings, which for us only occurred on the three interview days. We also used technology to discuss in-progress feedback with community partners; however, we did not have a formal semester wrap-up meeting of partners, students, and teacher. This would have provided additional feedback for student progress through the semester, community partner opportunity for student feedback about the town, and a discussion of next steps to move the project forward.

The biggest challenge for this type of class at Radford University is enrollment. There are benefits to a class size of three students: it reduced travel expenses (we needed only one vehicle to travel to our community partner location), made spur-of-the-moment meeting opportunities within the community manageable, and enabled easier coordination of schedules. However, our production power was limited. More students working on the project would allow for more creativity in scheduling and arranging the scope of objectives within the project.

Building Relationships

The ability to adapt well to change is dependent on the willingness of various generations to listen to what is different from their own perspective—namely, for the young to hear how it was and the old to hear how it is now. In our climate of social discord, projects that unite younger and older generations are vital for a healthy future. Community–university partnerships are particularly suited to bridge this hyphen that sometimes represents a canyon, thus providing structure, funding, innovation, and human collaboration. Although universities are poised to facilitate intergenerational dialogues, as well as meaningful, fruitful town-and-gown relations, it is worth reiterating the necessity of university students and faculty to deeply listen to and honor the knowledge of community residents. Building sustainable Appalachian communities that thrive now and in the future means investing in and caring for one of our greatest resources, people, and encouraging those people to work together. Our project and similar ones provide opportunity and inspiration for college students to be active in their communities, bridging the gap between higher education institutions and the communities that surround them. Celeste Chorniak describes how she has done just this:

> The activities in this class really made me realize how much of an interest I have in river/watershed water quality and stream ecology. Since taking this class I have joined Dr. Lau's aquatic (stream) ecology research team. We will be researching how land use impacts fungal biodiversity and abundance in streams. I am also taking a biology seminar class this semester, which is all about how to communicate science to non-scientists. The process of researching and presenting in our (ATP) research class really influenced me to sign up for this seminar class.[15]

These types of classes encourage the formation of citizen-students, as they take what they've learned, apply it to their own careers, and continue to pursue community-based projects. Students acquire agency through their community work, learning how to participate in and contribute to democratic societies. This concept of citizen-students is in many ways parallel to the citizen-scientist initiatives promoted by such organizations as National Geographic and even the federal government.[16] College can be a self-contained bubble where students don't want or don't know how to engage with surrounding communities. Through projects like this, they become the bridge linking academics and application in society. Here is how Julia Kell is applying this project experience to her life and college career:

> After this class, I am more interested in researching and participating in conferences. I stepped out of my comfort zone in taking this class and I am glad I chose to take it because it showed me that people can make a difference in their own communities. For my Honors Capstone, I am planning on working on an African American heritage trail. In Dante, there is an African American school and church and I am planning on looking into their history.[17]

Feedback from CRVI Partners

Kasey Campbell, who was not involved in the 2016 CRVI project but had participated in previous ATP classes, learned about the collaboration largely from the perspective of the community partners. She asked a series of questions designed to prompt feedback on several aspects of the project. This was insightful to her as a former Radford University student involved in other community partnerships because she heard about the project from those with the original visions for community impact—not as an introduction like in past projects, but as a reflection. Her goal was to have a different discussion with community partners from those that took place during the project, with the hope of obtaining ideas that will contribute further to CRVI's efforts and inform Radford University's continued community involvement.

Communicating with community partners is always thought provoking when assessing a project for its impact, and the reflections obtained from our questions provided a good basis of support for the students' work thus far while planting the seeds for many projects to come. Though there will be more obstacles to face as far as scheduling and other logistical concerns, the momentum so far is promising, and the CRVI partners seem beyond enthused for the future of their community. One partner noted:

> I am very impressed with CRVI's progress and relations with our community. At first, I thought the process was too overloaded with meetings and process vs action but when the action plan was implemented, it gathered much traction . . . In summary I was a CRVI skeptic turned fan. It's great to be wrong!

One of the most important remarks made by a responding partner about the oral histories collected by the students is an example of what community-based oral historians want to hear:

> [O]ral history interviews contribute to CRVI's efforts. A core goal of CRVI is to increase a sense of ownership among community members, particularly young adults, and oral histories can be a crucial way to contribute to those goals. While engaging with a community, it is vital to always acknowledge the partners' goals and to realize how important each participant is to accomplishing those goals. The students should be proud to know that their work will be essential to promoting the initiative/region and even seeking funding for future work with CRVI and partner communities.

When asked what the students did particularly well during the project, the community partners thought the students "asked cogent questions and were engaged" while doing a "great job collecting the oral histories and communicating them to the group." In short, the partners only reported "positive feedback" about their interaction with the students. This reflects well on the university students as they aptly served as ambassadors. Mutual respect between students and community partners is critical in achieving project goals, but also meaningful in bridging the perceived generational gap. Additionally, such appreciation furthers the trust of community partners and helps establish a strong foundation for future work.

Partner Suggestions

Community partners offered several examples to improve collaboration, including preliminary meetings before interviews, paddling on the Clinch River, and spending more time in the community. Some questions garnered contrasting viewpoints. While one respondent preferred more utilization of phone and email correspondence, explaining, "Visits could squander time and resources better used on production," another countered, "Meeting with like-minded college students here would benefit both groups and probably forge sustained relationships that could help the river and enhance career opportunities." Both make excellent points, as the availability of time and resources is important to all involved. Just like the students, the CRVI partners each have their own schedules to consider when meeting with the students. Perhaps the proposed front-loaded class structure would be appealing to both students and community members, as tangible results would be more immediately available to justify visitation.

A repeated request was for students to be available for the partners' questions while finding creative ways to share the oral history collection. Respondents provided several ideas for disseminating information to the public, including:

- Using QR codes at river access point kiosks
- Developing a book on the collected oral histories
- Embedding the interviews on CRVI's website (which has since been accomplished)[18]

One respondent believed a book would be "beyond the scope of CRVI itself at the moment, given our organizational structure, but we could absolutely provide assistance during that process." This request for help comes with the partners' belief "that a book on oral histories would reach an even broader audience," making this a prime candidate as a future Radford University collaborative project.

CRVI does have a website through its partnership with IEN, but one partner commented that "the internet seems to be one of the primary ways many visitors learn about the area," so this could be a crucial focus in the future. Another partner noted, "We do have books for sale, trails to build and use, projects to plan and implement that would benefit from internet outreach."

Conclusion

Radford University's collaboration with the Clinch River Valley Initiative continued the following two years as additional students and faculty members assisted with CRVI's goals. As noted at the start of this chapter, oral histories can be a critical component to economic diversification with increased resident pride and consequent investment in community, as well as serving tourism efforts. Given the large geographic footprint of the Clinch River, which originates in Tazewell County and extends through Russell and Scott Counties before entering Tennessee, CRVI maintains a long list of project needs. Based on the ongoing feedback from CRVI partners, as faculty members continue to participate in CRVI meetings and deepen relationships with community leaders, Radford students have opportunities to not only obtain more oral histories/river stories, but also to create online story maps to further showcase community assets and consequently increase tourist visits.[19] This project directly responds to the community member's request for help as Kasey Campbell notes above. Burriss and Stacy Penven, another Radford Appalachian studies faculty member, met with colleagues in the Department of Geospatial Science to obtain access to GIS software necessary in the creation of more sophisticated story maps. Additionally, a Geospatial Science major will assist with the story map creation, using this real-world experience as a capstone project. Such interdisciplinary work is vital to universities' holistic community contributions that yield usable products.

Thus, the circle widens, demonstrating the best of town-and-gown collaborations that evolve and ultimately serve the varied needs and interests of the community. With each passing year of Radford University's involvement with CRVI, faculty learn important lessons to apply in subsequent years. In many ways, the instructors must remain humble, realizing they cannot anticipate every challenge and do not have as much control as in a traditional classroom setting. Yet such vulnerability unites them with their students. Indeed, all grow and learn from the community partners together, while knowing their time and energy have been spent to make a positive difference in our world.

Notes

1. http://www.clinchriverva.com/; University of Virginia Institution for Environmental Negotiation, "Executive Summary of Building Local Economies Discussion and Next Steps," https://clinchriverva.files.wordpress.com/2011/07/wiselocaleconsummary2010sep28.pdf.

2. https://www.etsu.edu/cas/cass/projects/

3. Preston Pezzaro, "U.VA. Institute Helps Clinch River Valley Explore Economic Revitalization," *UVA Today,* July 25, 2012, https://news.virginia.edu/content/uva-institute-helps -clinch-river-valley-explore-economic-revitalization (accessed February 11, 2018).

4. Robert Sorrell, "Southwest Virginia's Population Continues to Drop, Weldon Cooper Center Data Shows," *Bristol Herald Courier,* February 16, 2019, https://www.heraldcourier. com/news/southwest-virginia-s-population-continues-to-drop-weldon-cooper-center-data -shows/article_5159426c-c295-5a69-a0b5-6a7824f431df.html (accessed June 11, 2020).

5. Weldon Cooper Center for Public Service, *Regional Profiles* (Charlottesville: The Demographics Research Group, University of Virginia, 2014), https://demographics.coopercenter .org/sites/demographics/files/RegionalProfiles_28July2014_0.pdf.

6. Downtown Revitalization Action Group, "Foster Downtown Revitalization," http:// www.clinchriverva.com/wp-content/uploads/2015/01/Downtown-Revitalization.pdf.

7. Ronald D Eller, *Uneven Ground: Appalachia since 1945* (Lexington: University Press of Kentucky, 2008); Peter Crow, *Do, Die, or Get Along: A Tale of Two Appalachian Towns* (Athens: University of Georgia Press, 2007); Richard Lee Fulgham, *Appalachian Genesis: The Clinch River Valley from Prehistoric Times to the End of the Frontier Era* (Johnson City, TN: Overmountain Press, 2000).

8. Sherna Berger Gluck and Daphne Patai, eds., *Women's Words: The Feminist Practice of Oral History* (New York: Routledge, 1991).

9. Claudia Salazar, "A Third World Woman's Text: Between the Politics of Criticism and Cultural Politics" in *Women's Words: The Feminist Practice of Oral History,* eds. Sherna Berger Gluck and Daphne Patai (New York: Routledge, 1991), 93–106.

10. Salazar, "A Third World Woman's Text," 96.

11. Personal communication, February 22, 2018.

12. Personal communication, October 8, 2017.

13. See https://www.gettingsmart.com/2016/11/past-present-and-future-of-place-based -learning/ and https://senseofplacelearning.org/projects/ for overviews and resources for place-based education.

14. https://otranscribe.com/.

15. Personal communication, October 27, 2017.

16. See https://www.nationalgeographic.org/idea/citizen-science-projects/ and https:// www.citizenscience.gov/#.

17. Personal communication, February 19, 2018.

18. See http://www.clinchriverva.com/clinch-river-communities/oral-history-project/.

19. See https://storymaps.arcgis.com/en/ for information on story maps.

10

GIS Mapping of Legacy Oil and Gas Wells

Matthew M. Kropf and Devin Weis

Introduction

The state of Pennsylvania, and Appalachian Pennsylvania in particular, has played a major role in the development of energy exploration and production in the United States. Coal mining began in the mid-eighteenth century near Pittsburgh and grew into an industrial force by the end of the nineteenth century. On August 27, 1859, the first commercial oil well was drilled in Titusville, Pennsylvania, by Edwin Drake. He introduced innovations in oil drilling that changed how oil was extracted and produced globally. Drake's well was a type of shallow conventional well that was 69.5 feet deep and could produce twelve to twenty barrels of oil a day.[1] The well's design and efficacy led to a growth in the number of oil wells that were drilled throughout the country. Most recently, a new drilling technique, hydraulic fracturing ("fracking"), opened the door to Pennsylvania's current natural gas boom in the Marcellus and Utica shale basins.

Looking back over 160 years of oil and gas exploration, it is difficult to even approximate the number of oil and gas wells that have been drilled across Appalachian Pennsylvania, much less accurately locate them. Well assessments calculated by researchers at Penn State University and Stanford University estimate a range as low as 252,000 (for abandoned wells) and as high as 750,000, respectively.[2] Despite this wide range and the difficulty of locating abandoned wells, accurately identifying these so-called legacy wells is an important task. Many disused wells have not been properly plugged. Abandoned wells are a source of methane leakage, a contributor to climate change. Current fracking operations run a greater risk of explosions, methane leakage, and other industrial accidents in the unlikely event that a new well project unintentionally intersects with an old one. Unplugged wells are also a public safety hazard for Pennsylvania's hikers and hunters. The state's Department of Environmental Protection (DEP) goes so far as to describe the situation as an "ever-growing legacy well liability."[3]

Regulations for managing disused wells have existed for over a century. Disused wells were first required to be plugged in 1878 using wood and sediment. Soon after, regulations were enhanced to require wells to be plugged with sand or rock sediment and wood. Regulations have continued to change with better science and technology, but such changes indicate that a large number of wells, even if plugged, fall below current standards for public health and environmental safety.[4] Under these circumstances, locating lost wells is in the public interest. One collaborative method for identifying legacy wells is by examining historical documents alongside the modern databases kept by Pennsylvania's DEP, a task undertaken by faculty and students at the University of Pittsburgh at Bradford (UPB).

This collaboration required obtaining historical maps and other sources of information regarding the locations of former oil and gas wells. To get these documents, researchers worked with a local oil history museum and began to form relationships with private landowners. The local oil industry in northwest Pennsylvania has a sometimes-distrustful relationship with the DEP. The DEP is seen to take a one-size-fits-all approach to implementing new policy, and new regulations and enforcement are often perceived as cumbersome, if not impossible, for small, conventional producers to come into compliance. This distrust commonly extends to any party, including the research team, seeking to work with historical information that could be perceived to be sensitive or potentially creating liabilities.

In this study, researchers were able to identify a component of newer oil and gas regulations that relates to the identification of orphaned and abandoned wells on properties with active production. When justifying the new regulations in a comment period, the DEP attributed zero cost to comply with the locating of orphaned and abandoned wells. The researchers could make the case to collaborators that the study would produce detailed maps that could help reduce the burden of properly plugging wells. Such maps could also establish the extent of effort required by such an endeavor. However, bridging this distrust will require additional work. The sources of well locations used in this study were from publicly available, albeit not easily obtained, sources. Many maps of historic locations of oil and gas industry reside with private property owners, few of which would be convinced to allow this study to access. The researchers' hope is to build on the results of this study by developing further trust with local landowners to eventually bridge a large gap in the Pennsylvania DEP's abandoned oil and gas database.

Challenges to Locating Wells

When well drilling first started in Pennsylvania, wells and their locations were documented on paper maps, land deeds, and court documents. Having well information spread across different platforms and types of documents makes accountability a difficult task. Wells become unaccounted for due to a number of reasons. The location of the wells may not have been mapped accurately to begin with, land transfers (e.g., sales) may not have properly documented well locations, well location and status maps may not have been kept up to date, or old maps may not have been transferred to a platform in current use, such as ArcGIS or other modern mapping software.

These challenges of locating wells are amplified by the unknown, though undoubtedly large, number of wells in Appalachian Pennsylvania. Accurately updating location data on this scale can take several years. In addition to accurately locating the well, data identifying the well type, and the well status are also important to include in an updated database. Many thousands of wells were drilled, plugged, or abandoned across the state before regulations existed.

Well accountability is a historical problem, with implications for the present generation of wells, which make use of recent technological innovations, including hydraulic fracturing. Commonly known as fracking, hydraulic fracturing is a process that allows for oil and gas extraction from within rock layers. Depending on the geological layering of deposits, wells are drilled anywhere from 5,000 to 9,000 feet deep.[5] The crucial technological shift in modern drilling is the combined use of vertical ("conventional") drilling and horizontal ("unconventional") drilling techniques. This allows for a wider range of production from one drilled location; moving horizontally across a shale seam, fracking exposes a greater cross-section of these resources. The horizontal wells are then equipped with explosives that, when detonated, fractures the geologic layer, causing oil or gas to flow.[6] Pennsylvania has drilled more than 10,000 unconventional natural gas wells.[7]

As the number of unconventional natural gas drilling has grown, so too have public concerns about the risks of abandoned shallow gas wells. Abandoned shallow gas wells and older conventional wells pose potential hazards to environmental and public health. Leaked gases and liquids are harmful to animals, plants, and people.[8] When an orphan or abandoned well is not properly plugged, discharges of oil and brine can also affect the land surface, surface water, and ground water. These risks have been realized in several cases in Appalachian Pennsylvania.

In Washington County, stray gas was encountered in soil adjacent to a business. The origins of migration were an abandoned gas well. DEP issued a contract to plug the well and initially vented the well until plugging work could commence.[9] In Allegheny County, stray gas was noted in a residence. The source of this gas was an abandoned gas well, probably located under the parking lot. The stray gas problem at the subdivision was mitigated by installing a venting system until the abandoned wells under the parking lot could be located.[10]

In Tioga County, a well that was abandoned in 1932 produced a methane gas leak that led to a thirty-foot geyser of gas and water.[11] According to reporting, "As Shell [energy corporation] was drilling and then hydraulically fracturing its nearby well, the activity displaced shallow pockets of natural gas—possibly some of the same pockets the Morris Run Coal company ran into in 1932. The gas disturbed by Shell's drilling moved underground until it found its way to the Butters Well, and then shot up to the surface."[12] In addition to the clear environmental and public health implications of this example, new drilling can also inadvertently cause an old well to go dry due to the new production.

In addition to the immediate local hazards, at an atmospheric scale, wells can contribute to the release of greenhouse gasses into the atmosphere. Methane, a hydrocarbon, emitted from orphaned and abandoned wells is a potent greenhouse gas that is about thirty times more effective at trapping solar heat over a hundred-year period compared to carbon dioxide.[13] The emission studies that have been conducted on wells throughout Pennsylvania indicate that a large amount of greenhouse gasses are being emitted each year. Abandoned wells in Pennsylvania added up to an estimated 50,000 tons of methane per year—equal to about 5 to 8 percent of Pennsylvania's annual greenhouse gas emissions.[14] Nationally, methane emissions from wells are assumed to be the second largest contributor to total U.S. methane emissions.[15]

Reclamation regulations aid in the mitigation of risks in Pennsylvania, yet the cost to plug and reclaim well sites are high to operators and the state. For example, the DEP now requires that a fifty-foot plug of cement be installed at the attainable bottom of each well upon completion of drilling.[16] Pennsylvania has introduced bond requirements for unconventional natural gas well permits to support current and future well reclamation efforts. This bonding requirement establishes funds for potential subsequent reclamation and infrastructure improvements and repairs. However, the vast number of older wells continue to pose potential threats to health and environment. Knowing the location, type, and status of these wells is critical under these circumstances.

To address the challenges, the DEP's Abandoned and Orphan Well Plugging Program was established under the authority of the state's 2009 Oil and Gas Act.[17] This program allows the DEP to plug oil and gas well with no responsible party. According to the act, abandoned wells are those that have not produced within the preceding twelve months or "any well considered dry, not equipped for production within 60 days after drilling, re-drilling or deepening;" orphan wells include those "abandoned prior to April 18, 1985, that [have] not been affected or operated by the present owner or operator and from which the present owner, operator or lessee [have] received no economic benefit [other than royalties]."[18] When a well falls under these designations, the DEP is granted the authority to plug the well. The DEP also has the authority to plug a well when no responsible party can be identified and the well status falls under the definitions of an abandoned well.

Well Accountability / GIS Project

Continuing many years of regulatory updates, agencies like the Pennsylvania DEP are in the process of compiling data pertaining to oil and gas well locations. The Pennsylvania DEP estimates that as many as 300,000 to 760,000 oil and gas wells have been drilled in the state, and that as many as 56,000 of these remain unaccounted for.[19] Mapping software can help begin to create a more accurate picture of oil and gas well locations. ArcGIS (Geographic Information System) is a mapping system that is extremely important in today's technically advanced world. Maps created using this system communicate important geographic knowledge through providing precise detail. Maps and map layers can provide the world with vast amounts of information that help us visualize, analyze, interpret, and understand data in new ways. GIS is a tool that reveals relationships, patterns and trends that can aid in decision-making. Geographic information benefits governments and organizations of all size and almost every industry. GIS plays an important role in not only mapping but also in geospatial modeling and analysis. GIS is also beneficial for society and the environment because it provides a way to examine the planet and assess our impact on it.

This ArcGIS project consisted of digitizing paper maps of the Bradford Quadrangle in McKean County, Pennsylvania, that were created in the 1940s and 1950s. McKean County, home to UPB, is closely tied to the history of drilling in Appalachian Pennsylvania. Oil derricks literally covered the landscape in the late nineteenth century, and across industry booms and busts, they have been maintained by a large oil refinery in the town of Bradford. Today's population is a fraction of its industrial heyday in the early twentieth century, but the economic ties to oil and now gas remain. Of 40,625 county residents, 4.6 percent work in the oil and gas sector, which is well above the state average of 0.5 percent.[20] The area also faces economic challenges that make it difficult for residents to take on expenses relating to abandoned wells on their private land. Per capita income is $25,517 and 16.8 percent live in poverty.[21] The digitalized maps can be used to help understand the locations of the sites as well as visualize the relationships between them. Adding layers with information about well location is helpful in analyzing sites and aiding decision-making processes. The information will aid agencies interested in environmental policies, observation, and future planning.

Faculty and students at UPB first became involved in this specific project in 2017, though research related to locating abandoned and orphaned wells and facilitating sensor measurements, like methane, had been ongoing since 2014.[22] Faculty in this project facilitated access to historical maps and guided the process of utilizing modern digitization tools to facilitate a digital database. The faculty also connected the students with a local geological consulting company to ensure that the new database of well locations would integrate with existing databases used by consultants when creating maps for new oil and gas production activities. The students would take the methods and materials prescribed by faculty and industry experts and apply them toward the digitization of possible abandoned and orphaned well locations.

The first step of the process was scanning the paper maps in order to make them recognizable in the ArcGIS system. The ArcGIS system recognizes these scanned JPEG files and the image then can be uploaded as a data layer. These data layers may not be perfectly accurate. One thing to keep in mind when scanning in an image is distortion. This may affect the accuracy of the image once it is added to a base layer such as a satellite image or a topographical map. The accuracy of the scanned map is only as accurate or as detailed as the original image. Older maps may not have the same information as an up-to-date satellite image. Along the same lines, road systems, terrain alterations, buildings and other various features may not be completely accurate or align perfectly. Once the desired image is scanned, the next step is to georeference the image.

Georeferencing is an important aspect used for displaying a hardcopy map in the ArcGIS. This is a great way to use information found on older paper maps and integrate the data into a project. When using a scanned map, it is helpful to have the coordinate system and projection information used to create it, though not all maps have this information. A crucial step in the georeferencing process is to select a reference map or background. It is important to choose a reliable reference map that is spatially accurate and displays similar features to the map that you are giving a location to. This project used the state outline of Pennsylvania, Pennsylvania counties, and a satellite image as the base map. Layers of data can then be added to this base map. The next step in the process is to digitize the points of interest that are found on the map. These points are classified according to several criteria, which helps to identify and sort wells by type. Once the points are digitized, they can be assigned specific attributes depending on various properties (e.g., longitude and latitude). For example, a site-specific code for McKean County, Pennsylvania, would read 37 (i.e., state) 083 (county)-McKean1 (data point), which creates a standardized means of locating and comparing data sites. Coding also includes abbreviations for different well types, such as abandoned gas (AGAS) or abandoned oil (AOIL). Unlike printed maps, this technology allows for new data points or site attributes to be added to the larger database created.

Project Results and Lessons Learned

This project produced positive results as well as posed many challenges. The digitized Bradford Quadrangle map produced 26,395 wells, which were added to the database through ArcGIS. The well types consisted of 10,168 oil wells, of which, 1,731 were identified as abandoned oil wells and 15 abandoned gas wells. The layer with data from the DEP consisted of 23,677 wells within the Bradford Quadrangle area. The well types consisted of 1,884 gas wells, 15,306 oil wells, 2,411 injection wells, 6 test wells, 2,542 undetermined wells, 10 observation wells, 1,346 combination oil and gas wells, 26 dry holes, 25 multiple bore wells, and 121 storage wells. Accounting for duplication between these two sources, our project identified 50,072 wells.

Combining the two layers provided a large-scale overview of how two layers of data compare to each other. The data helps to identify large areas where data have not been currently collected by the DEP. The data also helps to identify areas that have a high density of oil and gas wells. In order to compare which data points are potentially the same points, the two data sets were compared within 300 feet and 50 feet of each other. The average well pad covers roughly an area of 300 feet. This selected data indicates how many data points are potentially the same. By constricting the distance down to fifty feet, the data provides points that are highly likely to refer to the same well.

The two layers produced 7,706 locations that were within 300 feet. This is the average size of a well pad and provides low probabilities that represent that the wells are the same point. When compared to the total number of wells (26,395), wells have a 29.2 percent chance of being within 300 feet of a digitized well. The two layers also produced 611 wells that were within fifty feet of each other. This represents a high probability that the wells are the same. When compared to the total number of wells (26,395), wells had a 2.3 percent chance of being within fifty feet of a digitized well. The best method to further determine whether the wells are in fact the same is through the process of ground-truthing. This activity involves equipping students with high-accuracy GPS devices and going into the field to search for evidence of well sites. The process of ground-truthing is a very time-consuming and laborious effort, as many of the well locations are located in the middle of forests with former oil lease roads being overgrown, rerouted, or abandoned.

There were several challenges to this project despite these results. First, locating historical maps was met with skepticism and mistrust by private landowners. This challenge was overcome by acknowledging how the incompleteness of the DEP database actually can lead to regulations that are justified by underestimating the cost in time and money the activity of locating former well sites on currently producing properties. Although this understanding was established, the study was confined to historic records in the public domain. If the results of the study can be used by the DEP to update its database or adjust reporting requirements for small producers, further studies with privately held lease maps could follow. Until then, there are at least seven additional quadrangle publications for future students to process. Once obtained, dealing with digitizing of maps created before modern GPS tools presents its own challenges. Specifically, major geographical markers, such as roads and streams, would appear consistently biased in location near the corners and edges of the maps. While the georeferencing process described in this section was used to overcome these errors, industry professionals were necessary consults to arrive at the reason for the error and the refined technique to overcome it.

Conclusion

The number of oil and gas wells that have been drilled across Pennsylvania is hard to approximate. Accounting for older wells in particular continues to pose challenges to researchers, governments, and the communities hosting these potential hazards. To meet this challenge, our project looked to involve state agencies, private corporations, and public organizations in a long-term data collection and data-sharing program that answered the DEP's call for improved accountability for legacy oil and gas wells. By working according to state standards, such as well classifications, and in a common system, such as ArcGIS, we not only provided accurate information to governments and communities in the Bradford Quadrangle but also did so in a way that our data could be vertically integrated with other data collection projects around Pennsylvania. Maintaining or extending these partnerships may yet present future challenges, but the imperative to serve the public interest remains clear. The continuation of oil and gas drilling in Pennsylvania, now in its 161st year, means that many thousand more orphaned and abandoned wells are waiting to be appropriately plugged and correctly documented.

While the DEP database has not been updated to include the well sites identified in this study in its entirety, the database created is being used by geological consultants for new oil and gas operations on the land studied. This approach can result in additional wells being added to the DEP database as the digitized locations are mapped and physically confirmed as part of new oil and gas operations.

In the meantime, the project has continued to attract interest from other collaborators interested in digitizing historical production maps, ground-truthing well locations through new smart phone applications and applying imaging tools like LIDAR and aerial photography toward confirming and discovering oil and gas well locations. Most recently, students in related programs have had the opportunity to ground-truth well locations on campus-owned property and public land as a subawardee in a larger funded research project establishing a smartphone application for the location and identification of orphaned and abandoned wells. The large gap between actual historic oil and gas well locations and the modern DEP database has presented an ongoing opportunity for our students to help bridge the gap between small producers and the regulatory body governing their work. With sustained efforts to thoroughly address this gap in information, informed policy formulation and on-the-ground compliance could be significantly improved. This result would help ensure environmental and health safety of drilling operations in the region while easing the burden of compliance.

Notes

1. Pennsylvania Historical and Museum Commission, "Immerse Yourself in over 150 Years of Petroleum History," *Drake Well Museum,* 2017, www.drakewell.org/what-to-see-and-do/outdoor-exhibits (accessed September 20, 2020).

2. Laura Lagere, "New Estimates of Abandoned PA. Oil and Gas Wells Less Dire, Still Daunting," *Pittsburgh Post-Gazette,* November 28, 2017, https://www.post-gazette.com/business/powersource/2017/11/28/New-estimates-abandoned-wells-less-dire-still-daunting-Pennsylvania-Engelder/stories/201711280008 (accessed September 20, 2020).

3. Pennsylvania Department of Environmental Protection, "DEP Well Plugging Program," https://www.dep.pa.gov/Business/Energy/OilandGasPrograms/OilandGasMgmt/LegacyWells/Pages/Well-Plugging-Program.aspx (accessed September 20, 2020).

4. Pennsylvania Department of Environmental Protection, "History of Well Plugging and Risks Associated with Orphan & Abandoned Wells and Improperly Plugged Wells," 2018, files.dep.state.pa.us/OilGas/BOGM/BOGMPortalFiles/AbandonedOrphanWells/CFA Info Presentation_Part1_ History_Risk.pdf (accessed September 20, 2020).

5. Marcellus Shale Coalition, "Marcellus and Utica Shale Formation Map," https://marcelluscoalition.org/pa-map/ (accessed September 20, 2020).

6. Penn State Public Broadcasting, "Explore Shale," August 2014, exploreshale.org/ (accessed September 20, 2020).

7. Jeremy Webber and Andrew Earle, "Abandoned Unconventional Natural Gas Wells: A Looming Problem for Pennsylvania?" University of Pittsburgh, Graduate School of Public and International Affairs, June 8, 2017, https://www.gspia.pitt.edu/news/abandoned-unconventional-natural-gas-wells-looming-problem-pennsylvania (accessed September 20, 2020).

8. Webber and Earle, "Abandoned Unconventional Natural Gas Wells."

9. Pennsylvania Department of Environmental Protection, "Abandoned and Orphan Oil and Gas Wells and the Well Plugging Program," April 2017, www.elibrary.dep.state.pa.us/dsweb/Get/Document-116427/8000-FS-DEP1670.pdf (accessed September 20, 2020).

10. Pennsylvania Department of Environmental Protection, "Abandoned and Orphan Oil and Gas Wells."

11. Scott Detrow, "Perilous Pathways: Behind the Staggering Number of Abandoned Wells in Pennsylvania," *StateImpact,* October 10, 2012, stateimpact.npr.org/pennsylvania/2012/10/10/perilous-pathways-behind-the-staggering-number-of-abandoned-wells-in-pennsylvania/ (accessed September 20, 2020).

12. Detrow, "Perilous Pathways."

13. Ker Than, Mary Kang, and Robert Jackson, "Stanford Study of Abandoned Oil and Gas Wells Reveals New Ways of Identifying and Fixing the Worst Methane Emitters," *Stanford News,* November 14, 2016, news.stanford.edu/2016/11/14/study-abandoned-oil-gas-wells-reveals-new-ways-fixing-worst-methane-emitters/ (accessed September 20, 2020).

14. Than et al., "Stanford Study."

15. Mary Kang, Cynthia M. Kanno, Matthew C. Reid, Xin Zhang, Denise L. Mauzerall, Michael A. Celia, Yuheng Chen, and Tullis C. Onstott, "Direct Measurements of Methane Emissions from Abandoned Oil and Gas Wells in Pennsylvania," *Proceeding of the National Academy of Science of the United States of America* 111, no. 51 (2014) 18173–18177.

16. The Pennsylvania Code, "Well Drilling Operation and Plugging," The Commonwealth of Pennsylvania, 2018, www.pacode.com/secure/data/025/chapter78/subchapDtoc.html (accessed September 20, 2020).

17. Pennsylvania Department of Environmental Protection, "History of Well Plugging."

18. Pennsylvania Department of Environmental Protection, "History of Well Plugging."

19. Pennsylvania Department of Environmental Protection, "Abandoned and Orphan Oil and Gas Wells."

20. Pennsylvania Department of Labor and Industry, "McKean County Profile," https://www.workstats.dli.pa.gov/Documents/County%20Profiles/McKean%20County.pdf (accessed September 20, 2020).

21. United States Census Bureau, "Quick Facts: McKean County, Pennsylvania," https://www.census.gov/quickfacts/fact/table/mckeancountypennsylvania/BZA115217 (accessed September 20, 2020).

22. Kang et al., "Direct Measurements of Methane Emissions."

Appalachia Abroad

Reflections on long-term engagement and student training in South Wales

Geraint Roberts, William Schumann, and Bruce E. Stewart

Introduction

The Center for Appalachian Studies at Appalachian State University began a biannual study abroad course, Postindustrial Wales, in southern Wales in 2001. Across eight iterations through 2016, the course's central occupation was to observe social change and economic regeneration in former mining areas of the Welsh Valleys, and to draw comparisons between Welsh and Appalachian mining communities. In 2003, the emphasis of Postindustrial Wales shifted from a pedagogy of cultural learning within communities to a community-based research model for student education. The curricula reorganized around student-training partnerships with community organizations in the Dulais and Swansea Valleys to learn how to build capacity for sustainability. This chapter discusses two operating principles that helped to maintain Postindustrial Wales over time: personnel availability and programing flexibility, which are analyzed in the context of a website development project conducted in 2016. In turn, we assess how community-based study abroad can prepare students for future leadership in sustainability, and if these efforts similarly strengthen the capacity of Welsh communities for sustainability.

There are good reasons to look for parallels between Welsh and Appalachian communities to learn and teach about sustainability. International education is generally revealing about commonalities across cultures and borders, including similar problems and opportunities. Postindustrial Wales focused students' attention on regeneration strategies in the towns and villages of the South Wales Valleys ("the Valleys"). Between 2001 and 2016, some areas were slowly transformed into bedroom communities of an urbanizing South Wales coast, while other locales faced socioeconomic challenges more akin to those of rural Welsh constituencies.[1] Globally, rural communities are often the least equipped to deal with the challenges of climate change, poverty, poor health care, low educational attainment, and a host of other critical issues vital for sustainable community development. The United Nations notes that rural communities must "build social capital and resilience" in order to "strengthen the human capacities of rural people" to achieve sustainability.[2] Yet the transition to sustainability remains daunting, particularly in current and former mining regions.[3] Postindustrial Wales addressed these challenges through a comparative approach to economic, environmental, and social sustainability in Wales and Appalachia, and one which highlighted how working together can build compassion, patience, and solidarity to meet present and future societal needs. This chapter, written by two course leaders (Schumann and Stewart) and a course adviser in Wales (Roberts), is an account of our efforts to contribute to sustainable transitions for Welsh and Appalachian communities.

Postindustrial Wales: Evolution of a Community-Based Learning Model

The Center for Appalachian Studies at Appalachian State, under the leadership of Helen Lewis and Patricia Beaver, launched its inaugural four-week field school in Ystradgynlais, Wales, in June 2001. Lewis and Beaver had helped to organize a visit by Welsh miners to Appalachia in the late 1970s; additionally, Lewis researched the Welsh coalfields in 1980 while based in the nearby village of Bryn Amon. These were tumultuous years in both Wales and Appalachia, particularly in mining communities. Strikes and other forms of industrial action characterized each. During the late 1970s and 1980s in the United Kingdom (UK), Prime Minister Margaret Thatcher's attempt to denationalize the coal industry and close mines led mining villages and their supporters to organize a yearlong strike in opposition, but the government ultimately prevailed, leading poverty and economic inactivity—already a problem—to soar in the Valleys. "Postindustrial Wales" was hatched from conversations among participants of the original Wales–Appalachia exchange about "where the Valleys were" at the dawn of the twenty-first century. Generally, things were better, but there were still many questions about the quality of life in and sustainability of post-coal communities.[4] A study abroad course would provide the means for renewing ties, observing socioeconomic change, and building new networks and exchanges through student learning. The 2001 curriculum was rich in community interactions that added insight into the past and present of mining communities. Students met actors involved in the 1984–1985 miners' strike, visited businesses in the former coalfields, and even observed parliamentary election campaigning. The 2001 edition also posed a question to students that remained a constant throughout the course: how do we, as a globally interconnected society, achieve sustainability in postindustrial and/or rural areas?

The question was addressed in different ways after 2001. Between 2003 and 2016, Postindustrial Wales was led or coled by Beaver (2003–2005), Schumann (2003–2016), and Stewart (2011–2016). Between 2003 and 2011, individual students worked with community-based organizations in three village communities to support local capacity-building. For 2013 and 2016, projects focused on supporting one community organization per course. Students have interacted with everyday citizens, nonprofits, sustainable private enterprises, local leaders as well as representatives of the National Assembly for Wales (i.e., the Senedd) and the House of Commons. Across these phases, students have applied networking and skills through projects ranging from survey research to community gardening.

Evaluating Postindustrial Wales

The staying power of Postindustrial Wales was arguably rooted in two factors: *personnel availability* and *programming flexibility*. Personnel availability includes faculty and administrators as well as key international partners. First, the ability of faculty to devote time and thought to study abroad is necessary to deliver more than an interesting itinerary. International learning can (and should) be transformative, but it is not the obvious fact that students spend time in another country that drives this process. Preparation is multileveled and multisited. Study abroad must reinforce and extend the curricular goals of departments and disciplines while enabling places—that is, specific human and environmental histories—to become the fulcrum of the learning experience. Faculty must recognize where their training can overlap with local needs and opportunities. For example, Beaver, a scholar of culture and community, brought attention to industrial labor history through everyday interactions in the Welsh communities where students were based. Students crowded into community development offices, visited retired miners in their homes, attended dances at local welfare halls (i.e., community centers), and, in one instance, met with technicians in the control room of a worker-owned coal mine. Stewart, an historian of nineteenth-century America, deepened understanding of the lived realities of history and widened the comparative perspective of the course. For example, recurring visits to a decommissioned underground mine, an eighteenth-century iron works, and the renowned Museum of Welsh Life were better grounded in pre-and post-departure learning about Welsh and Appalachian industrialization. Schumann, trained in anthropology and political science, highlighted connections between community-based development and public policy. He organized regular student interactions with elected representatives from the Senedd, local development officials, and nongovernmental organizations.

Personnel availability also encapsulates the capacity of global partners and advisers to coimplement an applied learning pedagogy that provides real assets to communities. Study abroad inherently requires an up-to-date awareness about places of international learning. Planning for outcome-based student learning experiences demands another level of local knowledge. Above all else, exchanges should be mutually beneficial. Yet the mere presence of a university cohort does not ensure this. Postindustrial Wales posed a significant time commitment from community organizations to enable student participation. To find mutually supportive opportunities, course leaders relied on a number of informal supporters and advisers in

Wales. The participation of coauthor Roberts, a native of Ystradgynlais and an educator, is instructive about the value of community input in course development. After a chance meeting in 2001, he became a technical and logistical adviser to the program. Over many cups of tea (and the occasional pint), Schumann and Roberts discussed how students could become directly involved in community activities that promoted local regeneration and sustainability. Through Roberts and other networks, the curriculum became more deeply embedded in community culture and better connected to a wider spectrum of Welsh life. One key outcome was a curricular plan for "mini-internships," or student placements with community organizations as individuals or in small groups. Schumann worked through the networks already established by Lewis and Beaver to identify some opportunities, while Roberts identified additional organizations in anticipation of a student cohort of eight to ten. He also identified a residence, a Boy Scout hut within walking distance of Ystradgynlais, that would serve as a low-cost base of learning. The wider stream of contacts supporting Postindustrial Wales enabled the course leaders to adapt, which meant working with different community partners at different levels of intensity over the life of the course. In this way, Roberts remained a constant contributor and provider of guided tours, Welsh language training, and up-to-date information "on the ground." As he recalls:

> Two callow Appalachian State students walked into my office in Penrhos Youth Club in the summer of 2001, in search of contacts with local young people. Those students and I are not so young anymore, but the contacts between "App State" and my local area have continued and, in many ways, deepened. (The Youth Club, however, is under threat of closure due to governmental financial cuts.) I was Chair of Ystradgynlais Town Council at the time, and was therefore able to organize a civic reception for the students and staff. Students were able to meet a broader range of local people than they had perhaps been able to interact with hitherto in Wales. For example, a student who was a volunteer firefighter met a member of the local Fire Brigade; those who were interested in coal mining were able to meet many ex-miners; and so on. Other contacts were made which were followed up during the remaining time of the students' visit, and so a student from an agricultural background was able to tour several farms with a local contractor. Many were invited into local homes.

Roberts and many others formed a network of advisers, associates, and friends that kept student learning in conversation with changes in Welsh communities. The long-term benefits were curricular and financial. Foremost, local knowledge networks were essential to retooling the schedule every two years. In most cases, they deepened opportunities interactions with existing partners, such as attending practices and socializing with the Onllwyn Voice Choir. Strong networks helped establish additional educational relationships in other areas, such as with the Afan Valley–

based South Wales Miners' Museum. Local knowledge was equally instrumental in helping course leaders identify money-saving opportunities in transportation and housing, which made Postindustrial Wales Appalachian State's most affordable summer study abroad option in the United Kingdom for several years.[5]

As implied in this discussion of personnel availability, "programming flexibility," the second key to program durability, was paramount to enabling students to help build community capacity. Given that the course ran about every two years, developing broad, long-term community and institutional networks remained essential to effectively designing a new project focus each time. Postindustrial Wales inevitably changed in response to faculty and student interests, university protocols for study abroad, Welsh government policies and funding, the resources and needs of community partners, and less-direct shifts in economy, politics, and demographics. Above this baseline of structural considerations, the instructors, upon arriving in Wales, sometimes found it necessary to adjust the research design of the course's community-based projects due to on-the-ground circumstances, such as sudden staff changes, previously unrecognized resource needs for delivering certain aspects of projects, or (less frequently) the discovery of new resources and opportunities that would benefit from student involvement.[6] Once in Wales, planned meetings or events sometimes had to be rescheduled or dropped for a variety of reasons. Everyday needs like laundry and shopping, or unexpected ones such as tire and/or windshield repair arose.

Study abroad is intensive, and culture shock is real, so course expectations and goal-setting once in the field were ultimately based on student well-being. The sounds and signs of the Welsh language were new to every student, as were more subtle differences, which cumulatively challenged each student to adapt. In this respect, Welsh-language tutorials were not only educational about culture and history but also assisted students in settling and learning. In turn, managing the educational content of the course helped to support student well-being. Course leaders sometimes packed too much into the agenda. Supporting students' adaptation to Wales meant facilitating personal days-out for students and, as needed, creating pockets of time in the daily schedule when students needed rest. Communication is the fundamental element for being both flexible and successful as educators in this context. Course leaders kept students regularly informed about the schedule of activities and the circumstances of their participation. Before traveling out of our home village, students would assemble at our residence to review maps and be refreshed about the significance of a particular place or activity. Weekly group reflections, whether focused on the status of projects or the state of the group residence, were a built-in opportunity to adapt to student feedback.

The skills and social capital of our Welsh advisers were positive supports for course flexibility. Call of the Wild, an outdoor adventure partner since 2001, allowed students to select the group activities that would highlight the course's leisure agenda. Long-term collaboration with Roberts, an author of books about Welsh castles written for the tourism industry, fostered an awareness of a wider chronology and cultural context for understanding Wales. Postindustrial Wales always examined the history of industrialization, but as Roberts remarked, "I have been keen that South Wales before coal has not been forgotten." By 2005, Roberts led the "castle visit" event that kicked off the course, which became an instant foundation for student discussions and analyses of Welsh communities.

Roberts' historical orientation filled gaps in historical knowledge but also invited reflection about the nature of histories, the presentation of historical narratives, and the effect of history on cultures today. His personable approach to teaching Welsh history early in the trip gave students the confidence to participate in hours of subsequent discussions about Wales and Appalachia in Welsh communities. A case study from the 2016 edition of Postindustrial Wales illustrates the importance of personnel availability and flexible programming in building strong partnerships and empowering students to take on applied leadership roles in study abroad.

Case Study: The Seven Sisters Rugby Project

Programming flexibility is always at a premium when working with community-based organizations in an international context. Between 2003 and 2009, the backbone of one-on-one student placements with community organizations was the Communities First (CF) program. Students interacted with the offices of CF in three villages—Banwen, Ystalyfera, and Ystradgynlais—all within a 10-mile radius of where the Dulais and Swansea Valleys intersect. The CF program began in 2001 as an early policy outcome of Welsh devolution. CF sought to empower former mining and other communities most disaffected by poverty and underinvestment. Offices opened across the Valleys to fund local development initiatives, facilitate local networks to build community capacity, and communicate local needs up the Welsh development bureaucracy.[7] Between five and seven students typically worked through this partnership each course year and additional placements—generally involving nonprofit organizations—were arranged only after these were set. By 2011, budget cuts began to impact CF and other course partners and that program was completely wound down by 2017. Securing student placements across multiple organizations became increasingly difficult, even if Appalachian State's ties to the area were as strong as ever. Many partners simply no longer had the capacity to develop and monitor a student plan-of-work. Equally important to considerations of program change, student evaluations of placements/partnerships over time indicated that not all had worked out as planned. In response to both factors, course leaders and Welsh advisers reevaluated the curriculum for 2009–2010, opting to develop projects that primarily supported a single Welsh community organization per trip. While losing some one-on-one learning opportunities, a one-partner format transition added project depth, reduced logistical complexity, and provided some financial savings. A 2016 partnership with the Seven Sisters Rugby Club is a good example.

Students in Postindustrial Wales were assigned to produce a website on the history of rugby in Seven Sisters, a village nearby our traditional base of operations. The goal of the website project was twofold. First, to create inclusive public education and tourism resources about the village and the cultural significance of rugby. Tourism and outdoor recreation interests had slowly developed in the decades after the collapse of the Welsh coal industry; our course goal for 2016 was to add cultural resources to these efforts. Second, to create to field-based opportunities for students to hone their skills in research, writing, interpersonal communication, leadership, and design. Students would interact with villagers through the rugby club and add scholarly perspectives to these experiences that, combined, would promote the value of local assets. The 2016 project was altogether new, yet years of relationship-building in South Wales eased the transition. Seven Sisters was already familiar to Stewart and Schumann as the office headquarters of our outdoor partner. Dr. Hywel Francis—a participant in the original Welsh exchange with Lewis and Beaver, historian, and former MP—connected the course leaders to the rugby club leadership. Faculty also renewed prior collaborations with staff at Swansea University's Richard Burton Archives and South Wales Miner's Library (also connected to Francis) to organize archival research on the social and economic history of Seven Sisters. Finally, Stewart and Schumann built on experience running a web-based project in Wales in 2013 to develop a timeline of actions and set project benchmarks for 2016.

The idea for a working with the Seven Sisters Rugby Football Club (SSRFC), formed 1897, was then put into action. Course instructors identified visitation and interview opportunities to organize project logistics. Archive staff in Swansea provided consultation about the scope and volume of club records, photographs, and other materials. To familiarize students with Welsh society and rugby's considerable role within it, the instructors developed several online assignments that students completed before departing for Wales.[8] Students watched a series of lectures delivered by the instructors on Welsh history, coal mining in south Wales, Welsh culture, and modern Welsh politics. To place the Welsh experience with community regeneration in a comparative context, students viewed two lectures on the history and impact of coalmining in Appalachia. For background on Welsh rugby, students read and answered questions on six articles and a centenary history of the SSRFC. Students were assigned excerpts from books on ethnographic methods. Once informed of the project's historical and methodological contexts, each student was required to design and share ten questions to ask members and supporters of the SSRFC.

Additional preparations ensued upon arrival. Instructors and students discussed how to utilize primary and secondary sources to analyze the past through the archives. The cohort of ten students was divided into three groups to address three research subtopics: the general history of the SS RFC, club–community engagement over time, and, to emphasize the curricular goal of inclusive community-based research, the rise and impact of women's rugby on Seven Sisters since the 1990s. The instructors also led a workshop on creating websites using freeware. Team- and leadership-building was encouraged. For example, research groups were required to share resources to complete the website project. To promote collaboration, the group was convened prior to the interview session to examine all the questions students developed before arrival. The instructors discussed the "do's and don'ts" of interviewing and tasked students with narrowing the questions down to a master list of that captured the scope of research and limited bias in question design.

Having been prepped on website design, historical methods, and interviewing practices, students began project research. They first visited the Richard Burton Archives for four days to examine the club's minutes, account books, and membership records; potential website images were noted. Two more days at the South Wales Miners' Library complemented this work. Crucially, the research team had permission to bring a scanner into the archives to collect data for later review. The class was welcomed to SSRFC prior to interviewing, including small meetings with club leaders and a year-end awards banquet for the women's and men's teams. These visits helped to give students familiarity with the environ and also revealed additional records for review. By the third week of the course, students arrived at the club scheduled to interview twenty village residents, mostly current and former players, who had volunteered to participate.[9] Students had become somewhat accustomed to the need for flexibility in administering the project by that point. Once in the archives, for example, students discovered specific content areas that would be better suited for the project (e.g., per volume or topic) and adapted their collective plan of work around these resources.

Programming flexibility was in most demand when the class arrived at the club for the interview night. Pubs are a regular feature of sports clubs and welfare halls in the United Kingdom, and SSRFC was no different, but the students' plan was to utilize the club's meeting hall to arrange well-spaced interview tables around the large room. A scheduling oversight, however, meant that another community group was using the meeting hall that night. All interviews had to now take place in two small rooms making up the pub section of the building. Not only filled with pub regulars and interview volunteers, space was made tighter by a buffet table set up to honor our visit. Moreover, the class needed to set up two digital scanners for document collection. Students were asking last-minute questions about consent forms and where to set up. All of this happened at once.

What followed was a somewhat chaotic but ultimately productive and enjoyable evening. Interviews took place within a few feet of each other around small pub tables in the pub's overflow room. Students explained the terms of interview consent over the din of background conversation and laughter. Though trained to interview in one-on-one settings, some sessions spontaneously morphed into de facto focus group discussions with multiple club members squeezed in around one table. Due to the need to access an electrical outlet, one of the scanning stations was set up so close to the bar that a person could just about order and receive a drink without leaving their seat. Club members, instructors, and students combed through neat stacks of old photographs and documents around a pool table. Out of this activity, students managed to record numerous interviews using their smart phones that ran between twenty and forty-five minutes in length.[10] With one week in Wales remaining, students regrouped to organize web page templates featuring original student writing, digitized photographs and records, and audio clips of interviews, all presented in a larger context of Welsh socioeconomic history. Students had taken full responsibility for the project at this point and coordinated across their groups to deliver the project assets back to the community. The Sisters Rugby Project beta website was unveiled to community partners at a going-away celebration on the students' last day in Wales. Later, Appalachian State agreed to sponsor the SSRFC project website on its servers. While providing professional maintenance and IT support, migrating the voluminous content from one location to the other has been slow, due in part to personnel availability.

Outcomes and Legacies

Cocreating resources to build local capacity is a challenge for campus–community partnerships, even when personnel availability and programming flexibility positively converge. There are positives to reflect upon from 2016. First, students finished the course with a greater awareness of and ability to support community-based solutions to the interrelated environmental, economic, and social problems that define the twenty-first century. Drawing from student assessments of the SSRFC project, feedback on the website assignment was overwhelmingly positive. The majority of students believed that the project helped them to enhance their research and analytical skills. "Experience with archival research, something that I had not really done prior to this project, was one of the most pertinent skills that I learned," a student explained. "The archival research . . . allowed me to look over documents with a critical eye and attempt to make connections between them." Several students also remarked that the assignment allowed them to better learn how to "work as a team." As one student wrote, "It was pretty much up to us to make all of the decisions regarding the website, so we really had to work together and communicate well to get it done. We had to be willing to help each other out because some of the archives we looked at may have pertained more to one part of the project rather than another one." Most students also felt that the project increased their confidence in conducting interviews, and—perhaps more importantly—encouraged them to interact with local residents and gain a deeper appreciation of another culture. "It was an amazing experience to sit down and talk face to face about the rugby club in ways that the members did not have a platform to talk on a regular basis," one student recalled. "You could tell that the community truly cares about where they are from and what the sport means to them." The skills inherent to making these observations—the confidence to collaborate with others, and the ability to empathize with other points of view—are basic to sustainable development, but not given. Obviously, there are myriad factors that transform students of sustainability into leader-practitioners of sustainability, but evidence suggests that former students build upon their experience back home in the United States. Several course alumni moved into Appalachia's nonprofit sector, including organizational leadership roles. Others now promote sustainability by training future generations in the classroom. One alumna, in fact, discusses some of her subsequent work in this volume (Terman, Chapter 7). More broadly, Postindustrial Wales sharpened awareness of the importance of community participation and empowerment in any walk of life. Several students have maintained contact with course leaders or community partners in Wales to update them about their work.

The second way of responding to the overriding question that confronts all community-based research—"Are we building capacity?"—requires that we think beyond the class itself as an indicator of sustainability. The seeds of Postindustrial Wales planted by Helen Lewis, Pat Beaver, and their Welsh compatriot Hywel Francis continue to germinate. For example, the library systems of Appalachian State and Swansea University have developed memoranda of understanding for collaboration and recently finalized a formal international partnership agreement that encourages student and faculty exchanges. Tom Hansell, another member of faculty at Appalachian State, devoted years to making his documentary film, *After Coal: Welsh and Appalachian Mining Communities* (2016), which has earned national and international attention.[11] A 2011 course alumni, Trevor McKenzie, returned in 2016 to play Appalachian music at Wales' prestigious Hay Literary Festival, on BBC radio, and for a community fundraiser in the Valleys. In 2018, two long-time course allies in Wales were flown to the United States to contribute to a fortieth anniversary panel on the Center for Appalachian Studies. Equally important, the tragic passing in 2021 of Francis, who facilitated the Welsh–Appalachian exchange for more than 40 years, speaks to the need to maintain and grow those collaborative roots.

Other collaborative paths have emerged as well. An Appalachian/Carpathians conference has been meeting from almost a decade, and East Tennessee State University has recently deepened ties with a study abroad program in Scotland and Northern Ireland.[12] Appalachian studies faculty at Appalachian State are developing new international learning opportunities in Austria and South Africa. In this sense, the capacity for international learning about community development and Appalachia is greater now than it was in 2001. Yet Wales may not be a focal point of these changes. Program leaders failed to recruit a required cohort of eight to ten students to run Postindustrial Wales again in 2018. Turnover in program leadership, time demands (i.e., international and domestic preparations), and competition for study abroad options combined against the course. As of 2022, however, there is renewed interest in the course from stakeholders in Appalachia and in Wales, which may lead to a revised Postindustrial Wales for 2023, which would focus on renewable energy and community resilience.

Conclusion

With the successes and challenges to community-based study abroad in view, are communities in the Dulais and Swansea Valleys better prepared to practice sustainability? Certainly, students' time and labor proved invaluable to many organizations, allowing them to complete projects for which they lacked the internal capacity. The types of help which students offered varied according to their experiences and abilities. Perhaps the most successful projects were those during which students were given responsibility for specific activities built upon their existing knowledge and skills, and allowed them to apply these skills within a Welsh context. Whatever the outcomes of collaboration, one must be cautious in measuring or claiming "capacity gained." Community-based sustainable development is intersectional and processual, so it is difficult to isolate one factor or actor as determinative. This is especially true of the Wales course where visits were biannual and relatively short. A project from 2003 offers a final example of this analysis. Students surveyed public opinion in Ystradgynlais to learn about preferences for community improvements. The local Communities First office used the data in a proposal that was awarded European Union funding to reclaim an abandoned strip mine on the edge of the village for a public health/exercise area. Realistically, the proposal may have been funded with or without the survey data. But it would have certainly failed without already-existing networks of place-making that extended from the local to the supranational. Was the survey a tipping point for success? Probably not. The history of Appalachian State's engagement in South Wales is a study in how small efforts, when guided by the principles of equitable and inclusive regeneration, adds to a collective shift toward community sustainability. The results can be immediate and materially apparent, such as a reclaimed strip mine, or be deferred and diffuse, like a documentary film or a nonprofit career.

This chapter has examined how community-based study abroad, when codesigned by community organizations, provides novel connections to place and disciplinary learning while demanding high levels of personnel availability and programming flexibility. In reflecting on the outcomes and legacies of Postindustrial Wales in his home village, Roberts rightly points out that the most important outcomes of the course may be intangible. To paraphrase: many friendships have been forged, some of which have continued to this day. Wales has learned about Appalachia, the United States, and many other things; students learned more about Wales and, maybe, themselves. People who would never have met under other circumstances were able to interact and grow. Recalling Mark Twain's observation that "travel is fatal to prejudice, bigotry, and narrow-mindedness," Roberts added, "This can be true for travelers, and for those whom they meet."

Notes

1. Paul Milbourne, ed. *Rural Wales in the Twenty-First Century: Society, Economy and Environment* (Cardiff, UK: University of Wales Press, 2012).

2. United Nations, Sustainable Development Knowledge Platform, https://sustainable development.un.org/topics/ruraldevelopment/decisions, accessed May 31, 2017.

3. Anthony Bebbington and Denise Humphreys Bebbington, "Mining, Movements, and Sustainable Development: Concepts for a Framework." *Sustainable Development* 26 (2018): 441–449.

4. This is a complex issue. The Valleys were comparatively better off economically in 2000 than in 1980, and anyone who lived through the earlier era would tell you that the natural environment is greener and cleaner in the present. However, rural and semirural Welsh communities continued to lag behind the rest of the nation. Over the progression of the course, the UK territory encapsulating our Valley partners had with rare exception higher unemployment rates than

Wales and the UK as a whole. For example, see Office for National Statistics (UK), Local Authority Profile, Neath Port Talbot, Unemployment Time Series, https://www.nomisweb.co.uk/reports /lmp/la/1946157394/subreports/ea_time_series/report.aspx? (accessed June 12, 2020).

5. Cost is always of concern when designing a study abroad experience for students. In the case of Postindustrial Wales, students paid a fee that covered all tuition, room, board, and events. This did not include airfare or optional personal spending money.

6. Course leaders were sometimes challenged to provide the methodological training required to deliver on projects. Over time, student cohorts learned principles of questionnaire design, interviewing, surveying, GPS mapping, website design, and archival research to deliver on projects. Some methodological content had to be delivered on a "crash-course" basis; however, quality control was supported by facilitated discussions about research ethics and post-research group reflections.

7. National Assembly for Wales, *Communities First Lessons Learnt* (Cardiff, UK, 2017), https://senedd.wales/laid%20documents/cr-ld11141/cr-ld11141-e.pdf (accessed June 14, 2020).

8. These assignments were posted on Appalachian's open-source Moodle Learning Management System nicknamed "AsULearn."

9. Three of the interviewees were women.

10. The interview recordings were later donated to the archives at Appalachian State University and Swansea University.

11. A screening in Tokyo led a Japanese student to join the MA program in Appalachian Studies at Appalachian State.

12. By coincidence, Appalachian State students attending a community concert in Ystradgynlais, Wales, in 2001, met East Tennessee State students who were performing the concert as part of an international bluegrass performance course.

Conclusion

The contributors and editors[1]

Guiding Principles

Collectively, the preceding chapters highlight the potential of higher education to help build Appalachia's capacity for sustainability. First, we have illustrated how community-based research and learning can bolster local capacity; second, we have analyzed how colleges and universities prepare students to collaborate and lead society toward more sustainable futures. The breadth of our case studies reflects the diversity of challenges that must be addressed to achieve sustainability in Appalachia. Sustainability demands environmental protection and renewal. Sustainability demands equality of economic opportunity and public services. Sustainability demands inclusive democracy and representation. These interconnections are revealed in chapters focused on issues as varied as food security and cultural knowledge, community-based addiction treatment and reintegration, economic diversification, environmental monitoring, coalfield redevelopment, and cultural memory and the arts. Collectively, the chapters indicate the many areas in which sustainable partnerships can be cultivated and capacity can be built. Contributors have homed in on the details of research methods, logistical planning, technical organization, democratic leadership, long-term collaboration, administrative networking, federal partnerships, and multi-institutional/multistate projects. The differences between the cases we have presented suggest that any person, any community organization, and/or any institution can work toward place-based sustainability in Appalachia (or anywhere)—from virtually any starting point. Capacity-building is happening at small colleges and large universities. It is being organized with few financial resources and (in few cases) with substantive monetary support. It is shaped by and shapes Appalachian places, including the specializations of faculty and the needs of communities. Contrary to its detractors, we have argued that Appalachia possesses the human and cultural resources to respond to our shared environmental, economic, and social challenges.[2] Rather than deconstructing neoconservative approaches to "Appalachian development," we have presented evidence of how place-based approaches to sustainability can actually build the capacity of communities to contribute to just futures.[3] At the time of writing, a global pandemic has exposed the urgency of this issue to a much wider audience. Everyday inequalities—such as links between health, environmental pollution, and race—visibly intersect on television, through social media, and in Appalachian communities. We have also seen hope in Appalachia and across the world: civic awareness signals that people from most walks of life are ready for change, and many are prepared to participate.

We have recommended campus–community partnerships as an important conduit for realizing the changes that are needed. This conclusion takes the form of advice from this volume's contributors for successful collaborations. Each contributing author was asked to respond to an anonymous survey, which contained two writing prompts: "What advice would you offer others about lessons learned from your project?" and "Please give an example or examples of problems you encountered and how you addressed them." The responses have been combined, edited, and expanded to offer guidance to readers who are interested in building or expanding on campus-community partnerships in their own places. Appalachia's problems are globally inter-connected, and our region's responses to them illuminate a path for others to respond.

Build Bridges Now toward Sustainability in the Future

If universities and colleges want to build bridges to communities, it is important to develop relationships. Realize that connections are a two-way street, and expertise and resources flow both ways. Academics need to step outside of their comfort zone. They must be willing to try and fail in order to revise and create something worthy of sharing with others. Remember that faculty are not the (sole) experts. The community collectively is the expert—listen and learn, share and grow. An important element in community engagement work is building and maintaining trusting relationships with the community partners. It requires investing significant time and energy in order to create a meaningful and respectful dialogue. The benefits of such work are enormous and can impart lasting lessons to students for their future work in communities.

To do so, both communities and higher education institutions must develop internal capacities to effectively participate in campus–community partnerships. "Community" should expand to include diverse citizens, regional stakeholders, and, ultimately, colleges and universities. Often, there is an implicit bounding of "commu-nity" as outside of institutional or political life. Some of this reflects a recognizable fact: colleges and universities often are ring-fenced places of difference (i.e., separa-tion is material and ideological). Yet students, staff, and faculty are cocreators of Appa-lachian places *on and off campus.* If colleges and universities do not coconstitute Appalachian places, after all, then where do they exist? In turn, the cultural and socio-economic differences that do exist within an expanded Appalachian community can highlight local needs and strategies for social, economic, and environmental justice.

Community includes Appalachian campuses. Faculty and administrators typi-cally enjoy higher income and education levels than the region (or home county) as a whole, but colleges and universities employ staff who are more socioeconomically representative. At the time of writing, they are also frontline workers who bear the greatest burden of reopening campuses amid a pandemic. There will always be opportunities to dissolve social divisions to build for a sustainable future. Capacity building requires widespread community participation, and successful collaborations may involve input from local municipalities, schools, churches, and other community organizations that are not the primary project partners. Establishing a broad survey of campus stakeholders will only support the mutual understanding and exchange of ideas that is required of long-term partnerships.

Over time, one can learn from the successes and failures of previous projects to better estimate what is feasible. It is helpful to design projects in stages, so that they can continue over several semesters and achieve a more lasting impact. Sharing assessment tools with students, such as records of project benchmarks or measures of project outcomes, can help students conceptualize their role(s) in a longer history of collaboration. Ongoing projects have a degree of uncertainty about how they might fit into curriculums and community work year after year. Participants may be unsure if projects will have resources or support to continue. One strategy to address this is through keeping the collaboration in the forefront of community members' minds. Adapting collaborations to remain relevant is necessary to keep communities convinced of a partnership's value. Otherwise, turnover is a challenge that can inhibit long-term engagement and real capacity-building. University students graduate and move on, after all. Staffing changes within partnering organizations might lose or add staff that shifts the scope of work. Faculty and administrative champions of community partnerships may retire or change jobs. Finding stable supporters as well as ways to get new people excited about collaborating can keep projects moving forward, even as relationships within community partnerships shift.

Foster Mutually Beneficial Student Participation in Community Sustainability

It is incumbent on colleges and universities to prepare students to serve as institutional ambassadors, instructing them not only with content knowledge but also interpersonal skills and good etiquette. Both faculty and students need to be open to listening and learning, at times setting aside personal opinions. If done carefully, students can build respect and connections with the community they would not have otherwise experienced. Faculty and students must be flexible and willing to pivot and change quickly when working with community partners. Community-based research does not fit neatly into traditional classroom time. It's not uncommon for students to have otherwise learned by strictly adhering to well-defined measures of "success" (i.e., standardized learning). However, flexibility and adaptability are valuable life skills that are taught very well by community collaborations. Students can benefit from opening their minds to a more abstract set of goals and equipping them with flexibility and adaptability is a great introduction.

Ultimately, students can and should be entrusted with the responsibility to meet the demands of academic training by delivering on collaborations with assets, resources, and visioning for communities and campuses. While the classroom power dynamic is never truly erased in community-based research, it is incumbent upon faculty leaders to enable nonhierarchical student participation. Setting projects that align with students' work schedules should never be a hindrance in a project. In other words, if the scope of community need exceeds the duration of a semester, it is also incumbent upon campus and community leaders to implement parts of a larger plan within the university timeframe. Sustainability requires longer-term engagement, but the orientation of students and their calendar of work are not detriments to pursuing projects that may not finalize during a student's time of participation. It is more important to focus on what is possible, rather than what is not. New cultural settings (i.e., codes and practices) can be challenging to student learning. Students can rise to the occasion in these opportunities, but it is not a given: precourse networking, classroom-based preparation and reflection, clear communication with communities, and administrative support all matter in teaching college student leadership in the field.

Students should not be expected to simply conform to local norms, however. A potential challenge is student needs conflicting with traditions in the host community. One simple example is that some students with dietary restrictions may be unable to eat food offered to them by community members, creating a potentially tense situation. Communicating with the community partner in advance about student needs can avoid awkwardness and the risk of offense. Additionally, working with students at the beginning of the semester to teach them what to expect during visits with community partners can help students feel better prepared in unfamiliar situations.

Adapt to Cultural and Institutional Norms to Advance Realistic Projects

Deep capacity-building work will necessitate an institutional reassessment of faculty expectations. While we argue for greater campus-community collaboration, we also recognize its limits. The boundaries and expectations that define higher education institutions, and the faculty that work within them, are only semipermeable. Colleges and universities maintain and renew accreditation by working within regional and national guidelines and regulations. Departments must reflect and add to research currents within their respective fields. Faculty are required to meet the different expectations of teaching, scholarship, and service on specific campuses to maintain career advancement. The advantages of project funding, when present, can also mean additional operating guidelines and/or reporting requirements. All of these factors and more present opportunities and constraints for faculty participation, particularly as community-based teaching is time intensive.

Fostering interaction among community members and leaders with university students, faculty, and administrators can lead to more resources and support for long-term collaborations along with better communication and understanding of community and university priorities, systems, and structures. One technique for accomplishing this is by identifying a network or "scaffold" of support people who are invested in the success of these engagements. Scaffolding can mitigate the challenges that cany occur between stakeholders at all stages of a project. Faculty participation is crucial in most campus-community partnerships, but college administrators and staff can be equally important allies. A provost, college president, or dean, for example, may leverage resources in the form of: dedicated offices or programs for collaboration; support for community-oriented student activities or clubs; direct or match funding of initiatives, personnel, or material items that facilitate partnerships; or, perhaps more profoundly, a curricular organization that substantively integrates community-based learning into the student experience (i.e., learning needs and community needs overlap) *and* recognizes community engagement as a significant component of faculty development and professional achievement. Faculty can put a plan into action, but administrators and staff can engrain a philosophy of engagement for sustainability into an institution's very structure.

Depending on the context of the project, there are likely other institutional norms to contend with. Governmental priorities and policies are sometimes antithetical to community sustainability, but government bureaucracies, which are expressly depoliticized, are also sources of information and civic interaction. Projects and collaborations that aim for statewide or regional impacts must contend with governmental bureaucracies, which offer funding and other forms of support that may overlap with some of the needs of community organizations. Yet bureaucracies are also sites of hierarchy. The timing and organization of bureaucratic action may be well off the rhythms of organizations and classrooms.

Concepts of "time" may be the ultimate norm to attend to in campus–community partnerships. Faculty may have particular goals or learning outcomes that they are trying to meet; these may not always mesh with community needs or wants. Because the semester is quick moving, difficulties around communications or meeting deadlines can derail a project. Coordinating deadlines and any adjustments to them must happen within the fairly narrow confines of a semester. Additionally, preparing final reports or publications can be a potential source of conflict. Team, group, or partner writing poses difficulties; there is deadline coordination and making sure the distribution/contribution of work is equitable, and then final edits must unify tone and tenor into one voice. The time limit of the semester is a frequently identified constraint, especially for collaborations that require coordinating university and K–12 school schedules. One way to work around this is through breaking projects up into chunks that can realistically be tackled in the course of a semester. Another strategy is through creating "scaffolds" of engagement, with different levels of involvement by different groups of students. This is also useful in that it doesn't overwhelm a community partner with more students than they are equipped to handle. Often, it takes experience to accurately budget both time and capacity, and faculty may have to make changes midsemester.

Develop Structures and Methods That Suit Collaboration

Interpersonal skills and team management, especially across multiple stakeholders, can make or break a project. In some types of projects, the more face-to-face interaction between students and community members, the better. Modern technology might be convenient, but absolutely nothing replaces in-person interaction, which can help to engage students with the course content and generate enthusiasm. Training students in interpersonal communication is essential in this context. Shaking hands. Looking each other in the eyes. Asking questions. Sharing viewpoints. Breathing the same air. Experiencing the same spaces. Simultaneously, individuals might experience stress on personal, professional, or societal levels, including in community-based projects. Participants need the tools to effectively communicate and communities/projects must be safe spaces for communication. People should be able to step back, evaluate a situation, and formulate productive responses to project stress or interpersonal conflict. Being too quick to overact can unnecessarily damage relationships. An "authority figure" may unintentionally stagnate or muzzle voices who do not conform to a single viewpoint.

Good partnerships recognize difference as a strength of collaboration. Every point of view is important, and it is incumbent on faculty to assist students in understanding the trust and vulnerability involved in a community organization partnering with a higher educational institution. When differences of opinion arise, stakeholders should explore the problem until a consensus is reached about a solution. To guide this process, it is useful to have a clear, expressible vision of the collaboration from the outset, which can serve as a reference to project goals, objectives, and benchmarks of progress.

While not a glamorous task, developing a structure for identifying progress in collaborations, such as inventories of collected data or meetings held and their outcomes, can help projects move smoothly. It is one means to collectively mark a completion of a stage of a project and recognize progress toward a longer-term goal or partnership plan. Equipment and other forms of technology may also pose a significant barrier in some projects or communities. Even for experienced researchers, it is not unusual to face a learning curve about what technology is needed or what tools work best in particular situations. Participants need to be trained in how to use equipment and may have uneven skills, particularly if community participation is broadly inclusive (e.g., multigenerational). Funding may also be an issue with equipment, even if a particular technology or tool is ideal for a project or collaboration. Sharing digital content is becoming an increasing priority for community organizations, yet many lack access to staff with the required expertise to collect, manage, edit, and distribute information and content. In one instance, a team working with a cultural arts museum spent six months setting up and populating data into one web software product, which, in the end, proved unworkable for the museum's needs. Considering the rate of technological change, community expectations for specialized services (e.g., website customization) will be costly to maintain. Web-based assets are often popular with community organizations, but it is vital that organizations understand the costs and risks (e.g., malicious breaches of data) when partnering on online projects. Good communication at the planning phases of a web-based asset development project can avoid or minimize these challenges, but any such projects require an up-front strategy for long-term web resource management.

Concluding Thoughts

Our project began with the goal of demonstrating Appalachia's internal capacity for leadership in sustainable community development. Contributors were purposefully asked to reflect on the successes and failures of their work to build community capacity and train students for leadership in sustainability. This volume has presented evidence from small colleges and large universities, from localized projects to multistakeholder regional partnerships, and from relatively new and long-term collaborations to argue that campus–community partnerships—in Appalachia or anywhere else—can build needed capacity for sustainability, which we have argued is grounded in social, economic, and environmental justice. The chapters have featured perspectives from the sciences and technological fields, from the social and behavioral sciences, and from the arts and humanities. Each case can be said to address at least one aspect of sustainability, and all can be argued to add to the capacity of communities to continue on this path. At the most basic level, successful campus–community partnerships have been demonstrated to require: broad and inclusive participation; deep planning and administrative flexibility; regular communication with stakeholders; and trust in students to become coleaders of community-based projects. Relationships matter. It is our hope that this volume, in documenting a small part of sustainability work in Appalachia, can offer ideas for other students, community organizations, faculty, and administrators to collaboratively prepare for more just and sustainable futures.

Notes

1. Rebecca Adkins Fletcher (editor), Patrick Angel, Christopher Barton, Geoffry W. Bell, Dylan Burns, Theresa L. Burriss, Kasey Campbell, Mary Dickerson, Chris Dockery, Karrie Ann Fadroski, Robert Frank, Jared Friesen, Louis Gaunch, Sarah Hall, Jonathan Heck, Barry Hollandsworth, Kathleen Ingoldsby, Sara Johnson, Rosann Kent, Bethany Kier, Cheryl Laws, Rebecca-Eli Long (editor), Johnny Lynch, James Maples, Diana Marvel, Stephanie McSpirit, Angela Myers, Catherine Pauley, Denise A. Piechnik, Ron R. Roach, Geraint Roberts, William Schumann (editor), Shaunna Scott, Bruce E. Stewart, Rachel Terman, Melinda Bollar Wagner, Devin Weis, and John Winnenberg.

2. For a popular yet scholarship-free assessment, see J. D. Vance, *Hillbilly Elegy: A Memoir of a Family and Culture in Crisis* (New York: Harper, 2016).

3. For specific responses to Vance, see Elizabeth Catte, *What You Are Getting Wrong about Appalachia* (Cleveland, OH: Belt, 2018); Anthony Harkins and Meredith McCarroll, *Appalachian Reckoning: A Region Responds to Hillbilly Elegy* (Morgantown: West Virginia University Press, 2019). Important broader critiques include Ron Eller, *Uneven Ground: Appalachia since 1945* (Lexington: University Press of Kentucky, 2013); Shannon Elizabeth Bell, *Fighting King Coal: Challenges to Micromobilization in Central Appalachia* (Boston: MIT Press, 2016); Stephen L. Fisher and Barbara Ellen Smith, eds., *Transforming Places: Lessons from Appalachia* (Champaign: University of Illinois Press, 2012).

Epilogue
Community-based research in Appalachia

Rebecca Adkins Fletcher, Rebecca-Eli Long, and William Schumann

Engaging Appalachia has largely focused on classroom-based cases of collaboration and highlighted the importance and conditions for longer-term partnerships within specific colleges. As editors, we see further value in analyzing the historical context of higher education engagement in Appalachia. Without attempting a full survey of campus–community partnerships, we situate our case studies as part of a long-standing tradition of engaged education in Appalachia. There are many intellectual threads to Appalachian studies; however, we purposefully make linkages between Appalachian studies' history and movements for social justice, seeing this work as an act of civic professionalism.[1]

Arguably, one of higher education's oldest and most enduring campus–community collaborations began in 1855 on the western edge of Appalachia's Cumberland Plateau. Abolitionist Reverend John G. Fee obtained ten acres in Madison County, Kentucky, to build a one-room church and school that would promote education and equality for all Americans. He named his settlement Berea, a Biblical reference to an enlightened city. Fee and his teaching faculty were chased out of Madison County in 1859 by pro-slavery vigilantes but returned in 1865 and began admitting students by 1867. The first class of students included ninety-six African Americans and ninety-one whites, and Berea College was officially incorporated by 1869. In 1891, student tuition fees were eliminated to enable greater public access to education. Multicultural education continued at Berea until the state legislature passed the Day Law in 1904, which outlawed desegregated learning in Kentucky. About the same time, growing demand for enrollment from white Appalachians encouraged Berea president John Frost to refocus its existing mission in order to serve and reflect the Appalachian region. Frost was culpable of essentializing this message, even to the point of ignoring Appalachia's multicultural history, but Berea College can be credited with envisioning an inclusive, place-based learning experience that could support local communities and prepare students to engage positively in civic life. Coupled with its model of self-sufficiency (e.g., a college farm and student work program), celebration of the mountain environment, and support for local and regional economies, Berea College was a prototype for supporting sustainable community development through higher education engagement. Certainly, the college planted some of the first seeds of an engaged Appalachian scholarship.

"Appalachian studies" took shape in the 1960s and 70s as an interdisciplinary field of scholarship. Though diverse in interests, an early scholarly trend was making connections between marginalized Appalachian communities and other marginalized groups. Though not all of Appalachian studies embraces activism, the field is "quite similar to women's and black studies in its 'radical' nature and social movement parentage."[2] Helen Lewis was among its first leaders to promote critically engaged regional learning in Appalachian higher education, beginning with a stint at Clinch Valley Community College in southwestern Virginia. Notably, Lewis's commitment to just and sustainable Appalachian communities led her to lead the Highlander Research and Education Center in New Market, Tennessee, perhaps Appalachia's most important site for Civil Rights organizing. She also continued to write and publish about community-based research and socioeconomic justice. It is beyond the scope of this volume to discuss the breadth of Lewis' work, or the many strands of higher education–community engagements that she has inspired, but a cursory overview reveals the institutionalization of a progressive educational vision.[3]

In southern Appalachia in particular, there is now a network of Appalachian studies programs, curricula, and, in some cases, dedicated centers that form a collaborative infrastructure of higher education in the region.[4] Appalachian studies is also professionally organized through the Appalachian Studies Association (ASA; formed 1977), which is based at Marshall University in West Virginia. Graduate master's programs in Appalachian studies at Appalachian State University, East Tennessee State University, and Shepherd University regularly train students for careers that support sustainability through nonprofit management, environmental education and action, cultural heritage and the arts, and community organizing. The Appalachian Center at the University of Kentucky has been a presence in eastern Kentucky communities with an array of activities—from Appalachian music to forestry—that reflect the expertise of its directors over time. Numerous Appalachian studies programs in southwest Virginia, such as Radford University and Virginia Polytechnic Institute and State University, have addressed a variety of community issues, including economic revitalization, environmental protection, and the opioid crisis. Smaller private colleges, some of which are members of the Appalachian College Association, have led efforts to support the capacity of rural communities to transition to sustainability. For example, Berea College features a multitude of community-centered programs, both academic and civic, that are intended to enrich and sustain public life in Appalachia. Emory and Henry College in Virginia has a notable record of community-based collaboration, including the development of a sliding-scale public health center in rural Washington County.[5] And faculty at Southeast Community College and Technical Institute in Harlan County, Kentucky, have established a long-term, community-based arts program to reflect on social change in the coalfields. Considering that ASA meetings have always featured a mix of academic, nongovernmental, arts, and activist participants, it is not surprising that these and other examples of campus–community collaboration exist where Appalachian studies has been taught.[6] Yet this is only one part of building capacity.

Contrary to the majority of media coverage, Appalachia also possesses the civic capacity to transform Appalachian places for just and sustainable futures. Appalachia has important historical roots in American reform movements, sometimes at the center of change. Booker T. Washington hailed from Appalachia, for example, and labor activist Mother Jones spent considerable time organizing the region's coalfields. Unionization, though diminished, has left an important memory of collective organization and action.[7] Today, there are several organizations that encapsulate the environmental, economic, and sociocultural justice dimensions of sustainability in their work. One of the oldest and greatest is the Highlander Research and Education Center in New Market, Tennessee, founded by Miles Horton, Don West, and Jim Dombrowski in 1932. A hub of multiracial organizing from its outset, Highlander became a site of Civil Rights training in the 1960s, sometimes including Dr. Martin Luther King, Jr., Rosa Parks, and Ralph Abernathy, Jr., among others.[8] Highlander's grassroots empowerment model, based on participatory research and popular education, eventually came into conversation with movements in the Global South.[9] Today, the organization works to connect the issues and communities of the Global South and North, promotes language justice in America's multilingual society, utilizes the arts to mobilize community action, and supports young generations of Appalachian activists to enact a regional transition to sustainability.

East Tennessee's Save Our Cumberland Mountains (SOCM) has likewise followed an expansive and inclusive path to fostering regional sustainability. SOCM was established in 1972 on the heels of a successful civic campaign against state tax exemptions for coal companies. Decades of opposition to mountaintop removal mining, often in perilous circumstances, resulted in a string of successes: revealing multicounty inequities in absentee landownership and taxation rates (i.e., service base); making public lax regulatory enforcement in the coalfields; defeating proposals to bring toxic waste facilities to mountain communities; and, perhaps most significantly, overturning laws allowing coal companies to access minerals under privately owned surface land.[10] SOCM then rededicated itself to responding to *all* of the needs of its membership, and to the needs of *all* Tennesseans, as a necessary extension of its mission to promote socioenvironmental justice in the eastern coalfields. Renamed Statewide Organizing for Community empowerment, SOCM has expanded its mission and diversified its membership, including work to increase voting access, improve and expand affordable housing, sustain natural resources, and lead statewide discussions about a just transition to renewable energy.

Kentuckians for the Commonwealth (KFTC), originally formed in 1981 as the Kentucky Fair Tax Coalition, initially focused on changing the tax-exempt status of coal companies. By the end of the decade, KFTC could claim several victories against "King Coal" and, equally significantly, expanded its membership and scope to address issues across the state; a truly statewide network of local branches was established by

1997.[11] To date, KFTC has cultivated links between environmental sustainability and socioeconomic justice through initiatives as diverse as opposing an incinerator project in a predominantly African American neighborhood in Louisville; creating an annual I Love Mountains lobbying day at the state capitol; campaigning to raise the state minimum wage; organizing to restore the voting rights of felons; getting net metering laws passed in support of renewable energy; creating supports for statewide LGBTQ visibility; training youth in leadership and climate activism; and organizing vertically to participate in national movements. Other larger-scale community-based justice organizations include the Ohio Valley Coalition, the West Virginia Highlands Conservancy, and Appalachian Voices, yet these barely scratch the surface of Appalachia's total civic capacity for sustainability. Add to these hundreds of smaller, often place-specific grassroots organizations across the region. The capabilities and actions of Appalachia's civic base are well-chronicled in Appalachian studies scholarship. Much of this research focuses on analyzing citizen efforts to mobilize against power and injustice.[12]

One single-issue project of the late 1970s and early 1980s, the Appalachian Land Ownership Study, is an instance of when many of the community organizations and higher education institutions described above came together to study land and mineral rights in eighty Appalachian counties across six states. Led by the Highlander Center and Appalachian State University, the mixed-methods project produced knowledge about the scope and context of widespread absentee landownership in Appalachia that still informs regional scholarship today. It also cemented a culture of networking for collective action on many of the region's campuses and in its communities.[13] In fact, a new study group spearheaded by the LIKEN activist network and faculty at the University of Kentucky has formed in recent years to reassess Appalachian land ownership. The project seeks to retain the participatory framework of the original project while introducing new methods and objectives for the twenty-first century.

Lessons from Making Just Connections

Just Connections (JC), a higher education–community partnership formed in 1995, was launched as a region-wide extension of Appalachia's academic and grassroots traditions of community engagement. Whereas the land study demonstrated the power of local-to-regional grassroots collaborations with academics, JC sought to organize this potential to address a wider breadth of issues. JC operated until 2016 with the goal of building the capacity of Appalachian communities through coordinated partnerships involving community organizations, academic faculty, and students. Applied learning in particular would build local capacity for sustainability through the creation of resources and assets, while preparing students for future leadership of healthy communities. The initial partners were a mix of small Appalachian colleges, universities, and community development organizations who shared three interrelated objectives: sustainable development, grassroots democracy, and

Figure 13.1. Flyer from the original Appalachian Land Study project. (Courtesy of the W.L. Eury Appalachian Collection, Special Collections Research Center, Appalachian State University.)

social justice in Appalachian communities. Methodologically, the founders questioned the ability of academic approaches to community research to encourage social justice in Appalachian communities. The editors of *Engaging Appalachia* arranged interviews with four former JC members between May and July 2020 to understand the opportunities and challenges this network faced during its history.

At a meeting in 1995, faculty from Maryville College and Carson-Newman College in East Tennessee, Emory and Henry College and Ferrum College in southwest Virginia, and the University of Kentucky joined in a dialogue about coordinated collaboration with community organizers representing Big Creek People in Action of West Virginia, the Clearfork Valley Institute in Tennessee, and the Grassroots Empowerment Alliance of suburban Atlanta, Georgia. Helen Lewis and Richard Couto (the latter of the University of Richmond) served as consultants. Each organization had experience in supporting communities through community-based research partnerships with colleges and universities. It was an opportunity and challenge to make the whole greater than the sum of its parts.

"Vision and Action" was a guiding principle of decision-making. Projects and partnerships would contribute to the organizational goals of participating community organizations, rather than stem from faculty work. They shared a clear idea of how to raise Appalachia's capacity for sustainability by integrating these individual efforts into a network of community–university partnerships. A central goal was democratizing collaboration to address the inherent potential biases that favor professional expertise over local knowledge. The participants made a self-conscious effort to create equal representation among community-based and higher education stakeholders. Not only in board meetings, this also included considerations about who traveled, who hosted meetings, how grant funding would be shared and distributed, and who would speak for the organization at conferences and other public forums. Faculty would share their training and experience beyond their respective campuses to support the sustainability of communities and community-based organizations. In turn, students would learn methods of community-based engagement and participate in problem solving for project delivery.

Faculty who participated wanted students to be able to see life in rural Appalachia and contribute to research projects and/or applied and service-learning work in communities. The objective was to overlap community and classroom learning in mutually reinforcing ways. Whether classes focused specifically on the region or on broader content, faculty instructors would overlap theory and application through place-based pedagogies. Student field experiences were tied to course readings and drawn out for analysis through writing assignments. Shared learning about grassroots development would grant communities a better understanding of how to do research as well as an orientation of how to apply local knowledge to wider political and economic systems. Collectively, these engagements over time would clarify a strategic vision for initiating further change.

Just Connections had early success with getting funding and support from the Appalachian College Association, the Bonner Scholars Program, the Andrew W. Mellon

Foundation, and the Sociological Initiatives Foundation. Additional partners soon joined JC to create a seven-state network from Georgia to West Virginia. By 2011, JC was chartered as a 501c3 organization. The challenge and opportunity for JC was to not only create this network for building capacity but also to simultaneously create a road-map to grow the breadth and influence of the network itself. JC produced two primary assets for "double capacity building." The first was a Summer Institute. In general, participating organizations shared best practices for community-based development based on previous years' experiences, but the content varied. (In 1997 and 1998, for example, meetings focused on creating service-learning projects.) The summer workshops were funded so that anyone could attend. The JC executive board convened at the same time to raise the accessibility and collaborative productivity of these meetings. Funding also supported learning about participatory action research in the classroom and using technology as a tool for social change. Additional monies were dedicated to support outreach in communities and the academy as well as assisting in the organization of summer conferences.

Just Connections also produced a Toolbox. The Toolbox is part manual and part chronicle of the process and outcomes of community-based research projects conducted across the network. Multiple contributors created the content, which typically included information about methods in participatory research, guides for creating community service projects, reading lists, course syllabi, grant writing information, and project case studies. Collectively, the partnerships reflect a confluence of community need, local capacity, faculty skills (and availability), and higher education resources for outreach. These factors varied in strength across projects or places, yet JC's membership shared a commitment to a deliberative process for setting common goals and actions that could overlap local opportunities (i.e., "needs") with curricular goals, and local knowledge with faculty expertise.

A review of the 2003 edition of the Toolbox is indicative of JC's collaborative philosophy. Several contributors emphasize the importance of a participatory plan of work to guide projects or allow for alterations if and when circumstances change. Projects from the 2003 Toolbox focus on a wide variety of topics, which are shaped by the resources and needs of specific Appalachian places in Georgia, Kentucky, Tennessee, and Virginia. Projects include: recording oral histories; studying affordable housing strategies; empowering women; creating place-based educational resources for youth (e.g., the military service experiences of local community members); surveying customers on behalf of a farmer's market; and documenting culture change and industrialization, the decline of main street economies, and the environmental impacts of absentee land ownership. Many documents touch on the importance of promoting racial and gender inclusion in community-based research projects. Successful projects described in the 2003 Toolbox share the features of long-term collaboration, direct student engagement in communities, and democratic decision-making over projects. One case study describes the process of supporting migrant farm workers in Appalachian Virginia through second language tutoring programs and coordination with area service providers. In this example, students translated documents from nearby health clinics and grocery stores. Crucially, Spanish-speaking migrants collaborated directly with students to refine their translations to meet the norms of the local linguistic communities. While many documents effectively serve as how-to guides for community-higher education collaboration, personal narratives of shared experiences indicate the value of collaboration to local identity, such as an account of how a community—including faculty from the local college—came together to recover from a flood. However, the Toolbox is not presented as a promotional vehicle for colleges or community organizations. Accounts of challenges and, in some instances, project failures are presented as equally instructive to learning and applying community-based research strategies in other communities. For example, various accounts include student complaints that a project were more of a job than a form of applied learning; challenges with conducting interviews and organizing project logistics; a warning about the vulnerability of community organizations underpinning outreach to be overloaded with students or research groups; cases where community demand far outstripped faculty and student availability; reports of clashes between local cultural values and the norms of students; and (perhaps related to the preceding) occasional notes about negative student behavior.

Like many NGOs, JC had to adjust to structural and personnel changes that impacted its ability to continue previous work as-is. Within the academy, some participating faculty had to decide between continuing their engagement or working toward institutional benchmarks for contract extensions, tenure, or promotion. Between 2011 and 2014, considerable effort went toward reinvigorating networks and partnerships to address the underrecognition of community-based faculty service and research. JC's leadership reached out directly to college presidents to sanction professors to give communities time and commitment as a part of their job expectations. There were additional shifts in pedagogy. Robert Donnan, the director of the board at the time, reflected:

> The early commitment to examining Participatory Research strategies to level the playing field faded somewhat in favor of service learning. Colleges were still engaged with communities but were now sending cohorts of students to have an experience, including things like building people's homes. These efforts were appreciated, and service learning should not be dismissed, but the earlier approach gave the community a higher level of control.[14]

Colleges also began entering into service and outreach agreements with national civic engagement organizations, thus refocusing campus resources away from JC. According to one former board member, the shift to a corporatized model of civic engagement may have come at the expense of "deeper experiences of significance and connection that can encourage a shift in human relations and awareness about an economic system that is not working for everybody. It's not that something big doesn't happen with those relations but [it] can't be captured in a number."[15]

Nor were partnerships always seamless. Susan Ambler, a founding member of JC, recalled occasional objections from community organizations about ensuring local control and leadership. Whatever their record of participation or level of involvement, faculty were still viewed as "outsiders" who were "invading their space." And though Just Connections provided spaces for women's leadership and participation, the culturally inclusive coalition of colleges that started in 1995 was short-lived. Travel issues eventually became costly and, as one member put it, "stressful." And while representing several Appalachian states in principle, the projects (much like the 2003 Toolbox described above) tended to focus on the communities of East Tennessee and eastern Kentucky. Administratively, staff limitations kept some programs from being assessed. For example, JC worked to get its Toolbox digitized to promote broadened usage but did not fully develop a means of measuring online traffic or other indicators of public use. Despite committed efforts, conversations about the inequity of resources were frequent and ongoing. People became busy within their own communities or institutions, which ultimately dictated their availability to participate in a regional action network. Most telling, perhaps, is that JC was predominantly made up of white people from highly educated backgrounds (both academia and community groups), a limitation that was never overcome. A 2013 program assessment noted that Toolboxes did not substantively address "the topics and the intersection of class, race, rural & urban, gender, sexuality; as well as identity and intersectionality [which] could really enrich an updated toolkit." Lacking structural or funding incentives to maintain and grow participation and facing the cycle of turnover that is normal to nonprofits, the board of JC made the difficult decision to wind down operations in 2016. Looking back on the experience, former members interviewed for this chapter highlighted areas where the partnerships created social capital and the means for sharing ideas, frustrations, and solutions in a supportive and energizing network of common cause.

That Just Connections began as a coalition of multiracial organizations and institutions also echoes Appalachian studies' early commitment to social justice. That the sole organization made up of a majority of People of Color left this outstanding group within a year speaks to the challenges of reintegrating these streams of action. Just as our nation demands change, so too must Appalachian communities and campuses make connections to cultural sustainability clearer and more actionable.

Beyond Appalachian Studies

An ongoing attempt to make actionable progress toward community sustainability is the Appalachian Teaching Project (ATP), which began just a few years after JC in 1999. Organized through the Center for Appalachian Studies and Services at East Tennessee State University, the ATP was envisioned as a partnership sponsored by the Appalachian Regional Commission (ARC) to answer the question, "How do we build a sustainable future for Appalachian communities?" Since its inception, dozens of Appalachia's colleges and universities and thousands of its students have participated in an annual student-focused conference to highlight community-based research projects based out of classes taught on Appalachian campuses. Several authors in this volume are ATP teaching fellows, and one chapter—by Fletcher, Lynch, and Roach—delves deeper into this story. Two key takeaways are that, through the ATP, the ARC has given institutional recognition and credibility to community-based research and creative projects linked to Appalachia's college classrooms; and second, the ATP offers a model of collaboration and shared learning that, while involving Appalachian studies campuses, effectively defines a wider network of colleges and universities as coparticipants in achieving regional sustainability.

Quite obviously, there are many institutions that do not have direct associations with the Appalachian studies community in Appalachia and yet significantly contribute to the capacity of communities to meet the challenges of our time. Two in southern Appalachia stand out for their connections to the ATP. Faculty at the University of Tennessee in Knoxville developed an ARC-sponsored leadership program that will train and empower dozens of local officials and community leaders to create stronger communities. At Auburn University, the Office of Civic Learning Initiatives in the College of Liberal Arts has enjoyed years of collaboration with Appalachian Alabama's African American communities to preserve history, create educational resources, and recognize their contributions to society. In addition, the disciplinary makeup of ATP participation, such as technical and health fields, is arguably more representative of the wider range of actors and skills needed to address Appalachia's interrelated ecological and socioeconomic injustices.

This discussion suggests two areas to grow Appalachian studies' place-based model of research engagement. First is connecting participation in problem-solving from underrepresented disciplines and from additional educational institutions.[16] There are parallels and divergences to learn from. For example, northern Appalachia's small set of Appalachian studies programs is not representative of all of the collaborations occurring between communities and higher education in this subregion. The University of Pittsburgh at Bradford, which is represented in two chapters of this book (Kropf and Weis; Heck, Kier, Johnson, and Pietcnik), has few connections to Appalachian studies yet engages in multiple community partnerships for regional sustainability. An Environmental Studies club, which is attached to disciplinary and multidisciplinary academic programs on the small campus, brings together students and faculty from several majors. A rotation of faculty mentors and student leaders extends the life and vitality of the organization and introduces students from different majors to a variety of perspectives on the environment (e.g., from nature writing to environmental monitoring). Annual retreats in a nearby state park bring community stakeholders, environmental officials, and sustainable local businesses together with UPB students and faculty for career talks, guided walks, and locally sourced meals. Throughout the year, members of the campus community work together with communities, whether via internships with sustainable farms, technical guidance on energy efficiency, nursing training and outreach, or environmentally related collaborations with civic organizations. Like most campuses with a culture of engagement, other projects and partnerships also define UPB's institutional commitments to sustaining place. Nursing faculty have maintained a multiyear program with county health officials to educate the public about immunizations; another recent classroom-based project has begun to address local food insecurity among elderly, disabled, and LGBTQ populations.

This range of activity is both noteworthy and part of a wider pattern of community-based engagement that, while similar to efforts in southern Appalachia, does not always feature in Appalachian studies scholarship. Additional examples of classroom-based engagement include social work at California University of Pennsylvania, social sciences at Indiana University of Pennsylvania, and technical fields at Alfred State University in Appalachian New York. (The latter two are also affiliated with the ATP.) Across the region, an institutional and faculty culture, rather than a specific organizational structure or history, is what connects higher education to Appalachian places in pursuit of a sustainable future.

A second lesson is that there is also the need to grow the inclusivity of regional sustainability efforts.[17] Appalachian studies has deep roots in social and environmental justice, and Berea College could very well lay claim as Appalachia's original campus–community partnership for sustainability. However, the subsequent histories of "Appalachian studies schools" and Appalachia's historically Black colleges and universities (HBCUs) generally diverged despite long-term, intentional work from organizations like the Appalachian Studies Association to center social justice and inclusion in its operational mission.[18] Future efforts to democratize and sustain Appalachian communities through campus–community partnerships should take into account the role of HBCUs in the history and present of Appalachian community engagement. With the exception of three of the thirteen current Appalachian states—New York, Ohio, and Pennsylvania—segregated education in the Jim Crow era resulted in the founding of several colleges for African Americans across the region. Knoxville College (1865–), Morristown College (1881–1994), Swift Memorial College (1885–1955), and West Virginia State University (1891–) were among them. Appalachia's HBCUs were not substantially represented in the growth of an Appalachian studies scholarly network (and many struggle to survive today). However, HCBUs have always focused explicitly on community service and support, including the campaign for Civil Rights. The opportunities and needs for this work are substantial in 2022.

Current Challenges: COVID-19 and Racial Injustice

Campus–community partnerships must adapt to changing circumstances. Partnerships moving forward will inevitably look different due to the still unfolding impacts of the COVID-19 pandemic. New methods of engagement may be necessary, as it currently appears as though this virus will remain a threat, and we are all reminded that future pandemics are not unlikely. Events such as these require new strategies to build and continue collaboration while adhering to public health guidelines and protecting vulnerable community members. Community practitioners may find themselves having to engage remotely and carefully considering risk, especially as universities become likely places for outbreaks and the structure of academic instruction changes. As disabled academics have argued, continued remote access is important for inclusivity, and virtual platforms offer new affordances for engagement.[19]

In the beginning of the pandemic, rural Appalachia was presented as isolated, a travel destination for those looking to move from urban areas to escape the virus's spread. As some areas saw an uptick of out-of-town visitors, concerns grew not only about the virus but also about health, food, and infrastructure resources that are already stretched thin.[20] As restrictions on travel begin to be lifted, communities that typically rely on tourism attempt to find a balance between economic activity and public safety. The Appalachian Regional Commission has tracked economic development efforts and hosted virtual discussions with community leaders, as we are forced to rethink what sustainable community development might look like under new conditions.

Appalachia's health disparities mark the region at increased risk for COVID-19. For those living with black lung disease, the virus is especially threatening. The Appalachian Citizens' Law Center has worked to make sure that those with black lung disease know the steps they can take to minimize their risk. Community mental and behavioral health programs have been forced to suspend or modify service delivery. Increased anxiety and isolation pose real risks, especially for those in recovery from addiction.[21] While the increase in telehealth appointments provides some relief to rural areas underserved by medical practitioners, lack of high-speed internet connections can prove a major barrier. Further, events such as free clinics have been postponed, making it more challenging for people to get the health care they need.

COVID-19 has brought social inequities to the foreground and magnified disparities among race, class, and region. It has also emphasized the need for building local support networks and mutual aid projects, many of which have long existed in Appalachia. Community organizations quickly mobilized to meet the new challenges and increased demand. Dropping items off on the front porch, once simply a neighborly thing to do, is now a lifeline helping Appalachian residents get masks, groceries, and other supplies.[22] Courtney Rhoades, Black Lung Coordinator at the Appalachian Citizens' Law Center, said that she had noticed an increase in people checking on each other, especially on older neighbors, who might not have access to the internet.[23] The pandemic has especially highlighted weaknesses in the food supply chain. As many people became wary of shopping in large grocery stores, local food economies received a boost. Other people are growing their own food or coming together to seed share or create community gardens and other food resources.

In an article entitled "Your Pandemic-era Sourdough Starters and Victory Gardens Never Went Away in Appalachia," Beth Ward writes, "While many people in the U.S. were experiencing a kind of quarantine-induced nostalgia for these old traditions, some across the Appalachian region were simply shrugging their shoulders, looking out and seeing their fellow Americans perhaps discovering for the first-time practices and folkways that they'd never abandoned."[24] Whether it's baking, gardening, or taking up a new craft, Appalachian cultural heritage has proved a useful tool for navigating life in during a pandemic.

Additionally, Appalachia's history of social justice and community activism also deserves renewed attention, in light of uprisings around the country that challenge systemic racism and police brutality following several high-profile police murders, including that of Breonna Taylor in Louisville, Kentucky. During May and June 2020, many towns across Appalachia participated in public demonstration and calls for changes in policing. This included small towns in rural Appalachia, challenging stereotypes of these places as home to intractable racism. Many of these events were organized by teenagers and young adults, including in Harlan County, Kentucky, where a reporter for Appalshop noted the signs reading "I can't breathe," in reference to George Floyd's final words, having the same demand for liberation used by black lung activists.[25]

These events have also sparked discussion among educators, both around the omission of Black history from curriculums and among the discrimination faced by Black academics, especially in higher education. Groups such as Academics for Black Survival and Wellness, and social media discussions such as #BlackInTheIvory, made more explicit the barriers and trauma many faced by many Black people in the academia.[26] It is important for those involved in higher education to reflect on these efforts and seek to redress them through their teaching, including community-based partnerships.

While some observers might gloss Appalachia as backward and racist, those working in Appalachian studies are often aware of regional histories of resistance, including against racism, such as Berea College's efforts at providing an integrated education or the Highlander Center's involvement in the Civil Rights movement. Yet, as recent events have made painfully clear, the goals of the Civil Rights movement are still not fully realized. As ongoing struggles for social justice attest, we have not reached the oft-touted goal of sustainability. Sustainability is frequently used to discuss regional aspirations by our universities, community partners, and policy makers—both to address the need to mitigate anthropogenic climate change and to transition from an economy based on extractive industries. While both extremely important and pressing issues, forms of sustainability predicated only on the environmental or economic dimensions will fail to address the existing cultural inequities that have only became clearer through the connected issues of racial injustice and the COVID-19 pandemic. We hope our case studies offer a starting point for future, more inclusive engagement on these issues, in Appalachia and beyond.

Notes

1. Herbert Reid and Betsy Taylor, "Appalachia as a Global Region: Toward Critical Regionalism and Civic Professionalism," *Journal of Appalachian Studies* 8, no. 1 (2002): 9–32.

2. Shaunna L. Scott, Phillip J. Obermiller, and Chad Berry, "Making Appalachia: Interdisciplinary Fields and Appalachian Studies," in *Studying Appalachian Studies: Making the Path by*

Walking, eds. Chad Berry, Phillip J. Obermiller, and Shaunna L. Scott (Urbana: University of Illinios Press, 2015), 8–41.

3. For a compendium of her work, see Helen Lewis, *Helen Matthews Lewis: Living Social Justice in Appalachia,* eds. Patricia D. Beaver and Judith Jennings (Lexington: University Press of Kentucky, 2012).

4. For a survey of interdisciplinary teaching in Appalachian studies, see Theresa L. Burriss and Patricia M. Gantt, eds., *Appalachia in the Classroom: Teaching the Region* (Athens, OH: Ohio University Press, 2013).

5. See https://www.svchs.com/locations/meadowview-health-clinic/.

6. For a history of Appalachian studies, see Chad Berry, Phillip J. Obermiller, and Shaunna L. Scott, eds., *Studying Appalachian Studies: We Make the Path by Walking* (Urbana: University of Illinois Press, 2015).

7. For more on these histories, see Booker T. Washington, *Up from Slavery* (New York: Dover Publications, 1995 [1901]); Robert Logan, *The Battle of Blair Mountain: The Story of America's Largest Labor Uprising,* (New York: Basic Books, 2006); Ginney Savage Ayers and Lon Kelly Savage, *Never Justice, Never Peace: Mother Jones and the Miner Rebellion at Paint and Cabin Creeks* (Morgantown: West Virginia University Press, 2018).

8. See Frank Adams, with Miles Horton, *Unearthing the Seeds of Fire: The Idea of Highlander* (New York: Blair Press, 1975).

9. See Miles Horton and Paulo Freire, *We Make the Road by Walking: Conversations on Education and Social Change,* eds. John Gaventa and Barbara Bell (Philadelphia, PA: Temple University Press, 1990).

10. Bill Allen, "Save Our Cumberland Mountains: Growth and Change Within a Grassroots Organization," in *Fighting Back in Appalachia: Traditions of Resistance and Change,* ed. Stephen L. Fisher (Philadelphia, PA: Temple University Press, 1993), 85–100.

11. Joe Szakos, "Practical Lessons in Community Organizing in Appalachia: What We've Learned at Kentuckians for The Commonwealth," in *Fighting Back in Appalachia: Traditions of Resistance and Change,* ed. Stephen L. Fisher (Philadelphia, PA: Temple University Press, 1993), 101–122.

12. Surveys of community-based activism in Appalachia include Stephen L. Fisher and Barbara Ellen Smith, eds., *Transforming Places: Lessons from Appalachia* (Urbana: University of Illinois Press, 2012); Fisher, *Fighting Back.*

13. See Appalachian Land Ownership Task Force, *Who Owns Appalachia? Land Ownership and Its Impact* (Lexington: University Press of Kentucky, 2015); Shaunna Scott, "Discovering What the People Knew: The 1979 Land Ownership Study," *Action Research* 7, no. 2 (2009): 185–205.

14. Interview, June 2020.

15. Interview, June 2020.

16. The Appalachian Studies Association has led initiatives to engage with the sciences, such as its selection of keynote conference speakers, though membership leans heavily toward the arts, humanities, and social sciences.

17. As editors, we begin by acknowledging the need for more inclusivity in this volume. For example, the diversity of scholarly voices in Black Appalachian studies has steadily grown since the publication of Turner and Cabbell's edited volume, *Blacks in Appalachia,* in 1985. Regional communities will benefit from greater efforts toward normality of diverse representation of minority groups and perspectives within collaborations and publications. See: William H. Turner and Edward J. Cabbell, eds. *Blacks in Appalachia* (Lexington, KY: University

Press of Kentucky, 1985); William H. Turner, *The Harlan Renaissance: Stories of Black Life in Appalachian Coal Towns* (Morgantown: West Virginia University Press, 2021); Joe William Trotter, *Coal, Class, and Color Blacks in Southern West Virginia, 1915–32 (Blacks in the New World)* (Urbana: University of Illinois Press, 1990); Joe William Trotter, *African American Workers and the Appalachian Coal Industry* (West Virginia University Press, 2022).

18. The ASA has sought inclusive participation over the years through its Diversity and Inclusion Committee, Black Belt Committee, and the Young Appalachian Leaders and Learners (Y'ALL) network. Since 2011, ASA has also sponsored Camp Happy Appalachee, a networking event for LGBTQ attendees. Most recently, ASA has put its support behind the Black Lives Matter movement. Another notable example is the STAY project, which grew out of the 2008 ASA Conference with the aim of supporting youth with skills and leadership experiences necessary to stay and work in their communities. STAY has been supported by Appalshop Media, High Rocks Educational Corporation, and the Highlander Center. Programming includes a Black Appalachian Young and Rising project and an LGBTQ caucus.

19. See https://www.mapping-access.com/the-remote-access-archive; Zoe Beery, "When the World Shut Down, They Saw it Open," *New York Times,* August 24, 2020, https://www.nytimes.com/2020/08/24/style/disability-accessibility-coronavirus.html (accessed February 1, 2022).

20. Alison Stine, "People Are Fleeing to Appalachia to Escape COVID-19: That Needs to Stop," *100 Days in Appalachia,* March 26, 2020, https://www.100daysinappalachia.com/2020/03/people-are-fleeing-to-appalachia-to-escape-covid-19-that-needs-to-stop/ (accessed August 12, 2020).

21. Fernando Alfonso III, "A 'Pandemic's-worth of Triggers' Are Causing an Increase in Relapses Across the Country," *100 Days in Appalachia,* May 14, 2020, https://www.100daysinappalachia.com/2020/05/a-pandemics-worth-of-triggers-are-causing-an-increase-in-relapses-across-the-country-heres-how-appalachians-are-coping/ (accessed August 12, 2020).

22. Alison Stine, "The Front Porch Network Is a Lifeline in Appalachia," *WV Public Radio,* May 8, 2020, https://www.wvpublic.org/post/front-porch-network-lifeline-appalachia#stream/0 (accessed August 12, 2020).

23. Personal communication, June 4, 2020.

24. Beth Ward, "Your Pandemic-era Sourdough Starters and Victory Gardens Never Went Away in Appalachia," *100 Days in Appalachia,* May 28, 2020, https://www.100daysinappalachia.com/2020/05/your-nostalgic-sourdough-starter-and-victory-garden-never-went-away-in-appalachia/ (accessed August 12, 2020).

25. Sydney Boles (@SydneyBoles), "EKY young people held signs saying, 'I can't breathe,' not for Appalachian coal miners afflicted with black lung, but for Black people here and around the nation . . .," Twitter, June 3, 2020, https://twitter.com/sydneyboles/status/1268151556526014465 (accessed August 12, 2020).

26. For example, see https://www.academics4blacklives.com/.

Contributors

Rebecca Adkins Fletcher is assistant professor in the Department of Appalachian Studies, assistant director of the Center of Excellence for Appalachian Studies and Services, and an associate director of the Center for Cardiovascular Risks Research at East Tennessee State University. She is an Appalachian Regional Commission Appalachian Teaching Project fellow and director of the Governor's School for the Scientific Exploration of Tennessee Heritage. As an anthropologist, she focuses on place-based health, environment, and community engagement. Rebecca has published in *Medical Anthropology Quarterly, Economic Anthropology, Journal of Appalachian Studies, Online Journal of Rural Nursing and Health Care*, and *PeerJ*. She is coeditor of the book *Appalachia Revisited: Regional Perspectives on Place, Tradition, and Progress* (2016) from the University Press of Kentucky. She is also a coeditor of the online magazine, *Appalachian Places: Stories from the Highlands* and serves on the *Journal of Appalachian Studies* Editorial Board.

Patrick N. Angel, PhD, is a native of eastern Kentucky and has been employed by the Office of Surface Mining Reclamation and Enforcement (OSMRE), United States Department of Interior, in London, Kentucky, since the implementation of the Surface Mining Control and Reclamation Act (SMCRA) in 1978. Dr. Angel supervised the inspection and enforcement operations for OSMRE in the coalfields of Kentucky until he was appointed senior forester and soil scientist for the agency in 2005. He is currently promoting reforestation partnerships on active, abandoned, and legacy surface mines through the Appalachian Regional Reforestation Initiative and Green Forests Work. Dr. Angel is a graduate of Stephen F. Austin State University, Nacogdoches, Texas, with a BS and MS in Forestry. He is also a graduate of the University of Kentucky, Lexington, with a PhD in Soil Science. The focus of his studies was the reforestation of surface mines.

Christopher D. Barton, PhD, is director of the University of Kentucky's Appalachian Center and Professor of Forest Hydrology and Watershed Management in the Department of Forestry. As a research hydrologist with the USDA Forest Service, Savannah River (1999–2003), his work focused on hydro-chemical processes associated with restoration and remediation of disturbed and/or contaminated ecosystems. Dr. Barton is currently working in the areas of ecosystem restoration, reforestation, and remediation primarily in stream and wetland habitats and mined lands. In addition, improved methods for preventing water quality degradation from logging and mining activities are currently being examined. Dr. Barton is an associate editor for the

International Journal of Phytoremediation and the *International Journal of Mining, Reclamation and Environment.* Dr. Barton is also currently serving as the co-team leader of the Appalachian Regional Reforestation Initiative's Science Team and founder of the Green Forests Work program. Dr. Barton was recently honored as the American Society of Mining and Reclamation's 2015 Richard and Lela Barnhisel Researcher of the Year Award. For more information, visit www.greenforestswork.org and www.facebook.com/Greenforestswork.

Geoffrey W. Bell, PhD, is associate teaching professor in the Environment, Ecology, and Energy Program (E3P) at the University of North Carolina at Chapel Hill. He teaches courses in Earth systems science and applied ecological issues, including Introduction to the Environmental Sciences, Restoration Ecology, Conservation of Biodiversity in Theory and Practice, Ecosystem Based Management, and Marine Fisheries Ecology. Dr. Bell implements innovative active learning teaching pedagogies in his courses including flipped classroom, online instruction, lecture videos, service learning, and multimedia production. He also offers several experiential education opportunities including a capstone course that travels to eastern Kentucky to conduct reforestation research, a summer school course that travels to Tampa Bay to work with the Florida Department of Environmental Protection on coastal management, and a study abroad program in Australia where students assist with wildlife, forest, wetland, and coral reef conservation. Most recently, he has received a grant to create a workshop for training UNC faculty to fly drones and explore their uses in natural resource management with the goal of creating a drone center at UNC.

Dylan C. Burns is a graduate of Eastern Kentucky University. He earned degrees in Sociology, Political Science, Philosophy, and Paralegal Science while also minoring in Women and Gender Studies. He is currently finishing an MA in Sociology, with aspirations to teach. Dylan loves reading history and hopes to live in the forest with a herd of housecats.

Theresa L. Burriss has a BA from Emory University in Atlanta, an MS from Radford University, and a PhD from the Union Institute and University in Cincinnati. She serves as the chair of Appalachian Studies and director of the Appalachian Regional & Rural Studies Center at Radford University. She teaches undergraduate and graduate multidisciplinary classes on Appalachia. She serves as Appalachian cultural consultant for the Community Health Center of the New River Valley, and is a board member for the nonprofit organizations Appalachian Community Fund, Appalachian Sustainable Development, and MountainTrotter. She serves as Education Committee chair for the Appalachian Studies Association.

Kasey Campbell graduated from Radford University in 2014 with a BS in Sociology and Psychology. During her time as a student and continuing after graduation, she has been involved in several community-based projects in Appalachia as a mentor, presenter, and researcher. She currently resides in the Roanoke Valley area.

Mary Dickerson received her MS degree in Education from Radford University. She is a sixth-grade math and history teacher at Check Elementary School in Floyd County, Virginia. She works with students in a multitude of ways in and out of the classroom and community. While receiving her bachelor's degree in Sociology from Radford University, Mary was a mentor and community liaison in the Roots with Wings Project.

Chris Dockery holds an MFA degree in drawing/painting from Clemson University and a PhD in art education from the University of Georgia. She is a professor of Art and Art Education at the University of North Georgia, where she is program coordinator of the art education degree. She is also the studio coordinator and instructor of the UNG Letterpress, Book Arts and Papermaking studio in the Department of Visual Arts. She served as the Appalachian Teaching fellow for the Georgia Appalachian Studies Center at University of North Georgia from 2012 to 2017, facilitating undergraduate arts based research projects with students from many disciplines to consider issues relevant to Appalachia and build community around the creative making of things. In her academic research, Chris explores alternative approaches to creative education and place-based pedagogy, and in 2018 she founded the Little Village Montessori School in Dahlonega, Georgia, to provide a practicum laboratory for her art education interns looking to explore and experience alternative, experiential play and creativity based learning modalities in children's early education. The school serves children ages three to six in the North Georgia surrounding community. As a visual artist, Chris's work explores notions of domestic ritual, symbolic alchemy, cultural narrative, and personal mythology. She is the owner and proprietor of Hound Dog Democratic Press, an independent letterpress and bookmaking studio and has published two artist books based on her academic research, *Farm School: Recalling Meaning & Memory of the Lynn Bachman Memorial School* (2014) and *Community Playthings: Utopian Experiment* (2016). Chris sees her academic research, her artistic work, her service to the community, and the various fields of knowledge in which she works as a means to the same end. She is a product of her Southern Highland heritage, a native of Murphy, North Carolina, infusing her abiding love for the region and her Appalachian identity in all products of her creative and scholarly search.

Karrie Ann Fadroski is a senior lecturer in Biology at the University of North Georgia, where she has been teaching since 2004. She earned her MS from Auburn University studying the interactions between spiders and carnivorous plants. Most of her research endeavors have involved students investigating local, entomological diversity. Karrie Ann's ecological interests were shaped at an early age working with her family on their Christmas tree plantation and playing in her Polish grandma's immense garden in northern Michigan. She began the SAGAS seedbank as one of the initial projects sponsored by the Georgia Appalachian Studies Center. The seed bank continues to acquire new varieties and has begun sharing them with other local seed repositories. With the help of other faculty, the Historic Vickery House's garden now regularly supplies food to local schools and food bank programs. Karrie Ann has coordinated several scientific outreach programs, in which local ecology, sustainable agriculture, and food democracy are major themes.

Robert Frank became dean of the College of Arts & Sciences on Aug. 1, 2012, and leads the College of Arts & Sciences in its mission to provide a twenty-first century liberal arts education that prepares students for success lives. Before coming to Ohio University, Frank was professor of Psychology and associate dean for Research and Graduate Studies in the McMicken College of Arts and Sciences at the University of Cincinnati. He also served at Cincinnati as interim dean of the Graduate School, associate dean of the Graduate School, and associate vice president for Research and Advanced Studies. Frank received a BA in Psychology and Philosophy from Allegheny College, an MA in Psychology from the University of Cincinnati, and a PhD in Experimental Psychology with an emphasis in Neuroscience from the University of Cincinnati.

Jared Friesen earned a BA in Psychology from Huntington University and a MA in Student Affairs from Ball State University. Jared spent his first career working in student affairs on several college and university campuses and outside of the United States. One of these positions was living in Belize, Central America, and serving as the program director for a semester study abroad program. Following a thirteen-year career in student affairs Jared returned to graduate school to pursue a PhD in Sociology at the University of Kentucky. Jared is currently working on a dissertation exploring the intersections of rural communities and private colleges and universities while working as a visiting instructor of sociology at Manchester University in North Manchester, Indiana.

Louis Gaunch (1969–2021), a married father of three, focused his doctoral research at the University of Charleston in West Virginia on Appalachian leadership. He served in the West Virginia Department of Homeland Security and Emergency Management as an internal review specialist. Louis was also a board member of Pollen8, Inc., the South Charleston, West Virginia, nonprofit described in Chapter 7 and a self-described "unrepentant baseball junkie." After his passing, Louis was awarded an Honorary Doctorate from the University of Charleston in 2021.

Sarah L. Hall grew up on a small beef cattle farm in central Kentucky and has enjoyed life outdoors ever since. She attended Appalachian State University for her undergraduate degree in Environmental Education, and then received a Master of Science in Forestry followed by a PhD in Crop Science, both from the University of Kentucky. Her graduate work focused on restoration of forested systems on surface-mined lands and native grasslands on pasture. Her research interests include restoration of disturbed systems as well as cultural traditions related to agriculture and natural resource management in Appalachia. She is associate professor and chair in the Agriculture and Natural Resources Department at Berea College (Berea, KY).

Jonathan Heck holds a BA in Environmental Studies (2017) with a minor in Biology (2017) from the University of Pittsburgh at Bradford. Jonathan is currently a GIS Technician at New York State's Office of Parks, Recreation, and Historic Preservation in Salamanca, New York, at Allegany State Park. His future plans include continuing his GIS career, as well as pursuing an interest in the environment and studies abroad.

Barry Hollandsworth received his undergraduate and Master's degrees in Education from Radford University. He is the principal of Floyd County High School in Floyd, Virginia. The high school combines students from four county elementary schools, to serve over 800 students in eighth through twelfth grades. Barry has been an educator for thirty years, including positions in special education teaching and twenty years in administration, as Career and Technical Education director and as principal. Barry originated the Roots with Wings Project at Floyd County High School.

Kathleen Ingoldsby, a graduate of Massachusetts College of Art, Hollins University, and the Modern Archives Institute, oversees the archives at the Floyd Story Center at the Old Church Gallery in Floyd, Virginia. A former art teacher in the Boston Public Schools, Kathleen moved to Floyd in 1980 after a career as a professional potter. She's since documented local soapstone, completed an architectural survey of the Town of Floyd, archived historic images for the Floyd County Historical Society, recorded county life in video and audio, and presented at TEDx Floyd: "Patterns in Place, Evidencing Ingenuity."

Sarah Johnson received a BS in Restoration Ecology (Defiance College 2005), MS in Forestry (Penn State University 2007), and PhD in Forest Ecology (Penn State University 2014), and began working with The Nature Conservancy as a conservation GIS analyst and forest ecologist in 2012. As a TNC Pennsylvania staff member, Sarah leads forest health collaborations with area stakeholders and landowners, conducts forest health evaluations and treatments on TNC preserves and partner lands, provides GIS support for the freshwater and terrestrial conservation programs, and participates in several collaborative partnerships and scientific advisory panels.

Rosann Kent is the director of the Appalachian Studies Center, a unit of the College of Education at the University of North Georgia (UNG) in Dahlonega. She speaks and performs for audiences on the use of foodways as a transformative tool for cultural sustainability and community-driven social change. Since 2012, she has served as faculty mentor for the Appalachian Teaching Project, an applied research training program for Appalachian college students to design economic development initiatives for their communities. She, along with two other UNG faculty, developed courses that were situated at the intersection of food, story, and community. In 2017, she won UNG's Best Practice in Service Learning Award for demonstrating exemplary, innovative, integration of academic service learning in courses that met identified community needs. Previous community development experience includes serving on the founding management team for Access to Capital for Entrepreneurs, a microfinance nonprofit serving north Georgia. She received her MS in Reading with an Emphasis in Storytelling from East Tennessee State University. As a traditional storyteller, she enjoys sharing family stories about her Appalachian ancestors.

Bethany Kier holds a BA in Environmental Studies (2017) and a BS in Biology (2017) from the University of Pittsburgh at Bradford. She is an active member of the UPB Environmental Studies Club, Student Government Association Senate, and serves as a student member of Pitt-Bradford's Academic Advisory committee. Bethany has participated in other Appalachian regional projects, such as the Appalachian Teaching Project *Sustainable Community Development: GPS Mapping and Promotion of Community Assets.* Her interests include botany, herbalism, environmental sustainability, and community development.

Matthew M. Kropf (PhD in Engineering Science and Mechanics, Pennsylvania State University) is a biodiesel engineer and associate professor of Natural Sciences & Petroleum Technology at the University of Pittsburgh at Bradford. He also serves as the director of the university's Energy Institute where he facilitates energy education and efficiency training for campus, state government, and private organizations.

Cheryl Laws is a native of South Charleston, West Virginia. A temporary position at Kanawha County Drug Court sparked her interest in helping people recover from substance use disorder. In 2011, at forty-two years old, she returned to college at West Virginia State University where she graduated summa cum laude. She graduated with a Masters of Arts in Appalachian Studies from Appalachian State University in 2016. Cheryl's thesis work served as the basis of a business plan for Pollen8, a nonprofit organization dedicated to holistic recovery from addition and family reintegration. Cheryl is currently the chief operating officer of Pollen8 and resides in South Charleston with her daughter, Sydney. Her son, Nicholas, helped her build one of the social enterprises, Café Appalachia, where he continues to work. Cheryl has two granddaughters she adores and hopes to inspire through her work.

Rebecca-Eli Long is a scholar, activist, and artist who uses lived experiences of disability to imagine a socially just, sustainable future. They hold an MA in Appalachian Studies from Appalachian State University, and they are currently a doctoral student in the Department of Anthropology and Center on Aging and the Life Course at Purdue University. Their research explores the links between disability, violence, and activism, with a commitment to applying disability justice principles in campus and community settings.

Johnny Lynch has served as mayor of the Town of Unicoi, Tennessee, since 2004. Johnny is a US Army veteran, farmer, wildlife artist, wildlife rehabilitator and former professional taxidermist. He and his wife Pat operate a seventy-five-acre farm, which includes the Farmhouse Gallery and Gardens, an event venue and art gallery.

James N. Maples is an assistant professor of sociology at Eastern Kentucky University. Dr. Maples' research focuses upon the economic impact of outdoor recreation and how outdoor resources (such as rock climbing crags) are accessed and utilized by nonlocal residents. He has published research the *Journal of Appalachian Studies*, *Southeastern Geographer*, *Kentucky Recreation and Park Society Quarterly*, *Journal of Gastronomy and Tourism*, and *International Journal of Wilderness*, among others. He is the editor of *The Southern Sociologist* and archivist for the Southern Sociological Society.

Diana Marvel completed her doctorate at Ohio University in 2017 and has since been working as an independent consultant in Montréal, QC and Seattle, Washington.

Stephanie M. McSpirit received her PhD in Sociology (1994) from the State University of New York at Buffalo and has taught sociology at Eastern Kentucky University since 1995. Her teaching areas include statistics, research methods, and environmental sociology, and over the past twenty years she has worked closely with undergraduate students and communities on research projects in eastern Kentucky. Some of these community-based research projects that have involved undergraduate students include community assessment and community recovery after the Martin County coal waste disaster (2000), water quality monitoring, coal waste impoundment risk assessments, museum projects, communities in transition as well as other oral history, tourism and conservation projects in the Appalachian region.

Angela Myers received her BS degree in Technology Education from Virginia Tech. She taught public school for twelve years, ten of those at Floyd County High School, Floyd, Virginia. She taught the Video Production course that harbored the Roots with Wings: Floyd County Place-based Education Oral History Project for four years. Angela transitioned into self-employment for four years but came back to education with Virginia Virtual Academy where she is currently an online high school Career and Technical Education (CTE) teacher. She remains connected to the Roots with Wings Project on a volunteer basis.

Catherine Pauley received her Master of Science in Art Education degree from Radford University in Radford, Virginia. She is an artist, and taught art and humanities in the Floyd County, Virginia, Public Schools for forty years. Catherine is executive vice president of the Old Church Gallery, Ltd., a nonprofit organization, and co-director of The Floyd Story Center, an outreach of the Old Church Gallery. The Floyd Story Center is the community sponsor for the Roots with Wings: Floyd County Place-based Education Oral History Project.

Denise A. Piechnik is an assistant professor of biology at the University of Pittsburgh at Bradford. She earned her BS in Ecology (San Francisco State University, 1995) and her PhD in Ecology (Conservation Biology) (University of California at Davis, 2007). Her postdoctoral research included developing an arthropod monitoring program for the Gettysburg National Military Park (Penn State University, 2007) and evaluating the effect of spatial resolution when using GIS data to place best management practices (Penn State/USDA-ARS Lab, 2009). Her teaching and research interests are in understanding local and regional biodiversity patterns and their mechanisms.

Ron R. Roach is chair and professor of the Department of Appalachian Studies and Director of the Center for Appalachian Studies and Services at East Tennessee State University. Ron's research focuses on the rhetoric of Appalachia as manifested through literature, music, speech, and heritage tourism. Ron coteaches a study abroad program in Scotland and Ireland and has conducted field research in the Carpathian Mountains. His work has appeared in *Journal of Appalachian Studies, Appalachian Journal,* and *Popular Culture Review.*

Geraint Roberts is a native of Ystradgynlais in the Tawe Valley, part of the anthracite coal belt of South Wales. He lives there still. Many of his ancestors worked in the heavy industry that characterized the area over the past couple of centuries but which have virtually disappeared by now. Geraint studied History, Archaeology and Education at the University of Wales. He has worked as a schoolteacher; for a Menter Iaith (a community initiative to promote the Welsh language); as an education officer for a National Park; and as an Adult Education tutor. He has volunteered with many bodies, at local and national levels. He plays traditional music on various instruments, including the Welsh bagpipes. Sometimes he tells stories and plays music for dancing and singing. The history, culture, language, and future of his area and nation are fundamentally important to him—as is being a citizen of a wider world.

William Schumann is professor in the Department of Rural Resilience and Innovation at Appalachian State University and the author or editor of three other books, including *Appalachia Revisited: New Perspectives on Place, Tradition, and Progress* (University Press of Kentucky). He has participated in a range of community-based collaborations in Appalachia, South Africa, and Wales for more than twenty years. Schumann and his students were recognized with the Inspiring Youth Award by the Pennsylvania Wilds program in 2011. Between 2010 and 2018, Schumann was named as an Honorary Teaching Fellow in the Appalachian Regional Commission's Appalachian Teaching Project.

Shaunna L. Scott is an associate professor of Sociology and Director of Appalachian Studies at the University of Kentucky. She is the editor of the *Journal of Appalachian Studies*, a past president of the Appalachian Studies Association (ASA), and a current member of the (ASA) Steering Committee. Along with her colleagues Chad Berry and Phill Obermiller, she coedited the Weatherford Award-winner for best nonfiction work on Appalachia, entitled *Studying Appalachian Studies: Making the Path by Walking*. Her current research and community engagement focuses on a just post-coal transition in Central Appalachia as well as studying tourism impacts, environmental health and justice, and land ownership and use in this region.

Bruce E. Stewart is professor of History at Appalachian State University. He is the author or editor of several books, most recently *Redemption from Tyranny: Herman Husband's American Revolution*.

Rachel Terman is assistant professor of Sociology at Ohio University, an affiliate faculty member of the Women's, Gender, and Sexuality Studies Program, and a core faculty member of the Wealth and Poverty Theme. She is the OU Internship Director for the Shepherd Higher Education Consortium on Poverty internship program. She specializes in the sociology of Appalachia and the rural United States. Before moving to Ohio, she worked with the Pennsylvania Women's Agricultural Network and is a coauthor of *The Rise of Women Farmers and Sustainable Agriculture* (University of Iowa Press, 2016). Terman earned her PhD in Rural Sociology and Women's Studies from Penn State University, her MA in Appalachian Studies from Appalachian State University, and her BA in Psychology and Women's Studies at West Virginia University.

Melinda Bollar Wagner received her PhD in Anthropology from the University of Michigan. She is Professor Emerita of Anthropology and Appalachian Studies at Radford University in Radford, Virginia, and past president of the Appalachian Studies Association. Her research has included work on religion in America and sense of place in Appalachia. Melinda has received awards in recognition of innovative undergraduate teaching, having led groups of students in collaborative projects with communities since 1983.

Devin Weis is a 2018 graduate from the University at the Pittsburg at Bradford, receiving his bachelor's degree in Energy Science and Technology and an associate's degree in Engineering Science. As a capstone project Devin studied the role Pennsylvania's strong history of oil and gas exploration and discoveries throughout the state has created the difficult task of accountability for the location of historic wells. During his capstone project he collected paper maps of McKean County, Pennsylvania, that were created in the 1940s and 1950s and transferred them into Arc GIS mapping software. Digitizing the maps can better help to determine location data, classification of a well, and well status. This process plays an important role in determining the number of wells that have been drilled across the state. Devin is currently state certified in water distribution and working at the St. Mary's Area Water Authority located in St. Mary's Pennsylvania.

John Winnenberg is a veteran community development practitioner and consultant working in the Little Cities of Black Diamonds microregion of southeastern Ohio. A graduate of Bowling Green State University, where he studied journalism and education, his career in community engagement began as cofounder of Residential, Inc. in New Lexington, where he served as executive director for eleven years. At Residential, Inc. he and his colleagues developed a nationally recognized individualized approach to housing and service options for persons with disabilities returning from state institutions during the 1970s and 1980s. In 1988, Winnenberg launched the *Community Life News*, a community newsletter turned magazine that focused on rural communities in southern Perry County. During its twelve years of publication, not only did the publication help create a new sense of place around these once thriving coal mining communities, it also identified assets of nationally significant history and the returning forest that led to the formation of the Little Cities of Black Diamonds/Little Cities of the Forest cultural district in the former the Hocking Valley Coal Fields of Athens, Perry, Morgan, and Hocking Counties in Ohio. In 1990, Winnenberg helped form Sunday Creek Associates, a nonprofit community development organization in this same region. That organization has engaged in community organizing around historic preservation, heritage education, tourism development and youth engagement that includes the Little Cities of Black Diamonds effort.

Index

Place Matters: New Directions in Appalachian Studies

Series Editor: Dwight B. Billings

This series explores the history, social life, and cultures of Appalachia from multidisciplinary, comparative, and global perspectives. Topics include geography, the environment, public policy, political economy, critical regional studies, diversity, social inequality, social movements and activism, migration and immigration, efforts to confront regional stereotypes, literature and the arts, and the ongoing social construction and reimagination of Appalachia. Key goals of the series are to place Appalachian dynamics in the context of global change and to demonstrate that place-based and regional studies still matter.

Appalachia in Regional Context: Place Matters
Edited by Dwight B. Billings and Ann E. Kingsolver

Engaging Appalachia: A Guidebook for Building Capacity and Sustainability
Edited by Rebecca Adkins Fletcher, Rebecca-Eli Long, and William Schumann

Literacy in the Mountains: Community, Newspapers, and Writing in Appalachia
Samantha NeCamp

Appalachia Revisited: New Perspectives on Place, Tradition, and Progress
Edited by William Schumann and Rebecca Adkins Fletcher

The Arthurdale Community School: Education and Reform in Depression Era Appalachia
Sam F. Stack Jr.

Sacred Mountains: A Christian Ethical Approach to Mountaintop Removal
Andrew R. H. Thompson

Rereading Appalachia: Literacy, Place, and Cultural Resistance
Edited by Sara Webb-Sunderhaus and Kim Donehower

Religion and Resistance in Appalachia: Faith and the Fight against Mountaintop Removal Coal Mining
Joseph D. Witt